M000309670

Hugh Mackay has had a 60-year career in social psychology and research. He was a foundation member of the Australian Psychological Society and was elected a Fellow in 1985. In recognition of his pioneering work in social research, he has been awarded honorary doctorates by five Australian universities and elected a Fellow of the Royal Society of New South Wales. In 2015, he was appointed an Officer of the Order of Australia.

He is the author of 21 books, including *What Makes Us Tick*, *The Good Life* and *Australia Reimagined*. He lives in Canberra.

www.hughmackay.com.au

Also by Hugh Mackay

NON-FICTION

Reinventing Australia

Why Don't People Listen?

Generations

Turning Point

Media Mania

Right & Wrong

Advance Australia . . . Where?

What Makes Us Tick

The Good Life

The Art of Belonging

Beyond Belief

Australia Reimagined

FICTION

Little Lies

House Guest

The Spin

Winter Close

Ways of Escape

Infidelity

Selling the Dream

The Question of Love

THE

The joy of discovering

INNER

who we really are

SELF

Hugh Mackay

MACMILLAN
Pan Macmillan Australia

First published 2020 in Macmillan by Pan Macmillan Australia Pty Ltd
1 Market Street, Sydney, New South Wales, Australia, 2000

Reprinted 2020 (twice)

Copyright © Hugh Mackay 2020
The moral right of the author to be identified as the author of this work has been asserted.

All rights reserved. No part of this book may be reproduced
or transmitted by any person or entity (including Google,
Amazon or similar organisations), in any form or by any means,
electronic or mechanical, including photocopying, recording,
scanning or by any information storage and retrieval system,
without prior permission in writing from the publisher.

A catalogue record for this
book is available from the
National Library of Australia

Typeset in 12/18.5 pt Adobe Garamond Pro by Midland Typesetters, Australia
Printed by IVE

We advise that the information contained in this book does not negate
personal responsibility on the part of the reader for their own health
and safety. It is recommended that individually tailored advice is sought
from your healthcare or medical professional. The publishers and their
respective employees, agents and authors, are not liable for injuries or
damage occasioned to any person as a result of reading or following
the information contained in this book.

The author and the publisher have made every effort to contact copyright
holders for material used in this book. Any person or organisation that
may have been overlooked should contact the publisher.

The deepest form of despair is to choose to be another than oneself.
Søren Kierkegaard, *The Sickness Unto Death*

Any life, no matter how long and complex it may be,
is made up of a single moment – the moment in which
a man finds out, once and for all, who he is.
Jorge Luis Borges, 'The Life of Tadeo Isidoro Cruz'

It is a joy to be hidden, and disaster not to be found.
Donald Winnicott, *Playing and Reality*

To Sheila

Contents

Preface

If you're interested in the question 'Who am I?', and you're unsure of the answer but have a sneaking suspicion that the way other people perceive you is not the *real* you, then you are precisely the person I had in mind when writing this book.

The Inner Self represents a significant departure from my work in social research – a return to my core discipline of psychology, but also a turning inwards. As a social researcher, my professional life has naturally been focused on the social dimensions of human attitudes and behaviour. When it came to the question 'Who am I?', I have sidestepped the philosophical puzzle about what we mean when we say 'self' and concentrated on the identity, or image, we display to others and they project onto us.

That's why I have previously suggested that if you want to understand your identity, you should look into the faces of the people you live among – your partner, family, friends, neighbours, colleagues – and I have downplayed the idea of an authentic inner self that might exist independently of our socially constructed identity.

But that was only ever half the story. While we all have a socially constructed 'personal identity', we *also* have a deeper, more private sense of self. That idea of an inner self has been the subject of endless philosophical and theological speculation for millennia and, more recently, an enthralling subject for psychologists to study. And, for reasons we'll explore together, that's the self we often try to hide from.

You might have noticed the quote from the nineteenth-century Danish philosopher Søren Kierkegaard at the front of the book: 'The deepest form of despair is to choose to be another than oneself.' The idea that we could choose to be someone other than ourselves might seem strange, but the more I explored our favourite hiding places, the more I was persuaded by the wisdom of Kierkegaard (along with many other sages, ancient and modern): to pretend to be someone we're not is indeed likely to be a source of despair, even though we might not easily recognise its cause.

In case 'despair' sounds a bit grim, I should assure you that the tone of the book is constructive and hopeful. It is intended to help you *avoid* the despair that comes from pretending to be someone you're not. The reward is a freer, richer, undiminished life.

ONE

What is this thing called 'the self'?

How can I get in touch with this real self,
underlying all my surface behaviour?
How can I become myself?

Carl Rogers, *On Becoming a Person*

When she was about to turn 60, British actor Emma Thompson told *Time* magazine she had reached a point where 'all the roles that society has so successfully forced upon you – from daughter to wife to mother to professional person – could be questioned. You could take these things away from your face, one after the other, and go, "Who actually am I?" Which I've always thought was a terribly boring question, and I now find fascinating.'

Turning 60 can certainly do it. So can turning 40 or 50 – or even 80.

Trauma, pain and suffering can do it: a divorce, a life-threatening illness, a brutal retrenchment, a serious accident, a bereavement. Catastrophes like pandemics can do it: the social isolation, widespread unemployment and other disruptions caused by COVID-19 led many of us to re-think our priorities. Pleasant upheavals can do it, too, like falling in love or the birth of a baby.

Private, personal epiphanies can also occur at apparently un-exceptional moments, delivering insights that seem perfectly obvious once they've landed in your psyche. You're lying awake at night, wondering why your life isn't turning out the way you had imagined it would, and asking yourself: Isn't there supposed to be more to it than this? And then you think: Isn't there more to *me* than this? And you decide it's time to find out what's missing.

Or you're chatting on the phone and you become aware that there's no response: the line has gone dead and for the last little while – how long? – you've been talking to no one. In that instant of feeling a bit foolish and a bit irritated, you wonder whether this is a metaphor for your life: too much talking into the void; not enough real connection. And then you wonder whether a bit more talking – and listening – to yourself, a bit more introspection, might actually be quite helpful.

Or perhaps you've just stepped out of the shower, refreshed and glowing, and you have a sudden sense of liberation; a sudden clarity about the kind of person you really are. And then, towelling yourself, you wonder whether if you were truer to that person, you might also be more authentic in your relationships with other people.

Sometimes, we glimpse such possibilities from a gloomier place. Perhaps you've been feeling a bit frustrated with some aspect of your life, lethargic without being able to explain why, vaguely out of sorts, or simply exhausted by the demands being made on you. A sense of futility; being adrift from your moorings; losing your bearings . . . such hollow feelings lead some of us to decide to set more goals to get us 'focused', perhaps composing daily lists of things to do or writing lofty statements about 'where I want to be in five years'.

Here's a better suggestion: *look inside.*

The ancient Greeks weren't kidding when they promoted 'Know thyself' as the foundation of a complete and fulfilling life, even inscribing those words in the forecourt of the famous Temple of Apollo at Delphi. It was a concept taken up with great zeal by Socrates who, according to Plato, taught that 'the unexamined life is not worth living'. Although it was a bit rich (to say nothing of elitist) for a man in Socrates's privileged position to suggest that unexamined lives are *not worth living* – since not everyone has the capacity or the opportunity for self-examination – the idea behind his proposition is valid: the more we understand ourselves, the better equipped we are to lead a meaningful, purposeful life; the sort of life capable of generating that highly desirable mental state we call 'self-respect'.

To respect the self, we must first be in touch with the self we truly are. Otherwise, we might fall victim to that rather fatuous substitute, self-esteem, which is more about thinking we're terrific (despite inevitable evidence to the contrary) rather than experiencing the quiet confidence of knowing we are being true to ourselves. Yet, like many philosophers, psychologists and mystics who have pondered the human condition, the British Buddhist teacher and author Stephen Batchelor believes we spend a great deal of our time actively avoiding the truth about who we really are:

How often do we find ourselves happily indulging in some trivial pursuit, even though a deeper awareness is whispering to us of its futility? How often do we observe ourselves engaged in serious conversation while another part of us silently acknowledges our words to be a vain attempt to uphold a comfortable illusion that we do not really believe in?

To live in ignorance of who we really are is to live a kind of half-life, and who wants that? A journey of self-reflection, self-examination and self-discovery will not only benefit (and perhaps even transform) us; it will also bring a new sense of integrity to our encounters with people whose lives we touch – in the family, in the neighbourhood, at work, or wherever our influence is felt. Self-knowledge is not the key to a perfect life, but it is a necessary condition for an authentic and fulfilling one.

The journey is not likely to be easy: it might involve peeping into some dark corners, unearthing some hidden motives, and facing some unpleasant facts about our own frailties and inadequacies (along with some *pleasant* surprises, too, we may hope). If it's any consolation, writing this book has been at least as challenging as reading it will be. I've had to face some deep questions about my own inadequacies.

How, for example, did two marriages come to an end when I had always thought of myself, and still think of myself, as a 'one-gal guy'? Could I have handled those separations and divorces more compassionately, more sensitively, more generously? (Indeed I could – so why didn't I?) Why have some friendships blossomed and others, that once seemed equally promising, withered? Have I let my work interfere with my family life? (Yes – so how did I allow my priorities to get out of sync with my values?) Am I as smart as I have sometimes pretended to be? (Of course not, and no one ever fell for it anyway – so why did I bother pretending?)

A few other questions I've faced that you might also face: Why have I so often fallen short of my own standards – as a parent, as a partner, as a friend? Could I have been more attentive to the needs of strangers? What is the most worthwhile thing I could do with the remaining years of my life? Now I'm in my 80s, that particular question has more potency than it once did, but there are many other possible triggers for such questions, at any stage of life.

Let's go back to that state of ennui – confusion, frustration, lack of motivation, lack of direction – that so often signals a disconnect between the life we are leading and the life we dream of; between the image we are projecting and the inner voice we are ignoring. American psychiatrist Robert A. Berezin says that each of us has 'a resonance that our deepest self is not encompassed by our ordinary sense of self'. And that, he says, generates understandable confusion about our nature: 'Every person feels the presence of their hidden Authentic Being one way or another.'

To test that idea, ask yourself this: Do I have a different, deeper, more enduring sense of my true self than the versions of myself I present to the world in my various roles – partner, friend, colleague, son or daughter, brother or sister, father or mother, neighbour, customer, service provider, citizen? Does it make sense to think of there being a 'real me' that is performing these various roles but is not fully expressed in any of them; a self that seems capable of observing and even judging my own performance; a self that is more than my actions, more than my various roles in life, more than my history, more than the dreams I dream, whether asleep or awake?

Try thinking of the self as a seed, and the face we present to the world as the husk – the visible, external part of us that shields the seed from the view of others and protects it from predators. The husk/persona, being self-protective, is naturally tougher, more defensive, more competitive, less tolerant, more prejudiced, less forgiving than our inner seed/self. The husk is a perfect hiding place for the seed, but it would be a tragic mistake to become so focused on the husk that we forgot to nurture the seed within it.

In *Dostoevsky: Language, Faith and Fiction*, Rowan Williams points to the loss of authenticity in modern life and the high price we pay for losing touch with our own 'depth' as central themes in Fyodor Dostoevsky's writing. Here's a typical quote from *The Brothers Karamazov*: 'Above all, do not lie to yourself. A man who lies to himself and listens to his own lie comes to a point where he does not discern any truth either in himself or anywhere around him, and thus loses respect for himself and others. And having no respect, he ceases to love.'

In his Quarterly Essay *Net Loss*, renowned Australian art critic Sebastian Smee quotes from a passage in Anton Chekov's story 'The Lady with the Dog': 'He judged of others by himself, not believing in what he saw, and always believing that every man had his real, most interesting life under the cover of secrecy and under the cover of night.' Smee notes that there is a large body of literature – by authors including Virginia Woolf, Marcel Proust, James Joyce, Robert Musil, Albert Camus, Christina Stead and Alice Munro – devoted to 'this troubling distinction between a true core and a sham exterior'. In *Conversations with Friends,* Irish novelist Sally Rooney has her 21-year-old narrator say, quite unequivocally: 'I wasn't the person I pretended to be.'

And here's how J.D. Salinger, the author of *The Catcher in the Rye* (with its central theme of 'phoniness'), described the process of getting in touch with his 'real self' before he could begin to write: 'Just taking off my own disguises takes an hour or more.'

The short story of a marriage

Georgia and Michael were both in their early 30s and madly in love when they decided to marry. They would have said – often did say – they were completely transparent with each other. 'No secrets' was one of their proud mantras. They were comfortable with confessions about each other's past relationships and made a point of sharing whatever came into their heads. They agreed that neither of them had ever been this frank with anyone else.

After two years of living together, Georgia began to wonder whether transparency was all it was cracked up to be. There were things Michael was telling her, mainly about his work, that she felt she would rather not know, and even some of his outspoken reactions to things – such as meals with Georgia's parents or the behaviour of their next-door neighbours' children – were beginning to grate. Occasionally she caught herself saying rather sharply: 'Keep your opinions to yourself,' the very words she thought she would never hear herself utter in response to anything Michael said.

There were also times when she found herself harbouring dark and unwelcome thoughts about Michael – about the integrity of his work as a money-market dealer at a major bank, about his capacity for the kind of love that would endure beyond the highly charged romantic phase, about the strength of his commitment to moderate his drinking. Though they had been in total agreement about having children (one day), she had even begun to doubt his fitness for parenthood: If we had a baby, I'd find myself looking after two children, she was coming to think.

She was alarmed by the discovery that some things – her anxieties, her doubts, some of her most tentative dreams – were easier to express to one of her close friends, Maggie, than to discuss with Michael himself. Maggie had a sympathetic ear, and was always brisk and businesslike in her responses. She herself had recently ditched the man she had been living with for five years on the grounds that, having often described Maggie as a closed book, he had made no attempt to read that book when, as Maggie put it, she left it lying open for him, 'including the dirty bits'.

'He obviously preferred the closed book,' she told Georgia. 'He liked the look of the cover but he didn't really want to know what was inside – who I really was. I think he feared he wouldn't like what he read in that book. And he was probably right. I'd had enough of pretending to be happy, anyway.'

When Georgia tried to imagine what might happen if she actually confronted Michael with her doubts – if she were as honest and transparent as they had always said they were going to be – she found she couldn't picture herself doing it. Gradually it occurred to her that the transparency itself was something of a delusion: she realised that she was often saying things to please, or appease, Michael; things she knew he wanted to hear. She wondered if he was the same:

pretending to be someone she would like rather than revealing his inner self to her.

As these doubts grew, Georgia became increasingly conscious of the many pretences that had been there from the beginning. She didn't really like some of the bands they had gone to hear, but couldn't bring herself to say so in case that altered Michael's opinion of her. Michael's rather uncouth language sometimes bothered her, but she had never felt able to mention it. She couldn't stand Michael's best friend, who she thought was a sleaze, but couldn't bring herself to say that, either, and was relieved when the friend, who worked with Michael, was trans-ferred interstate.

Finally, Georgia confessed to Maggie that she actually felt frightened of what would happen if she was more honest with Michael, even if she didn't articulate some of her deeper doubts about him.

Michael, meanwhile, was confessing to his friend that the fun seemed to have gone out of his relationship with Georgia. 'I try to be honest with her, but there's a bit of stuff going on at work that she gets all moralistic about, and so I've stopped discussing that. There's a bit more drinking than I let on about, too. Her standards are very high, even about this transparency thing, as if we're supposed to share every tiny little thing. I sometimes feel like a bug pinned to a microscope slide.'

They hung on for another year. Then, one night, Michael came home drunk and told Georgia he thought she was a royal pain in the arse. She packed a bag and went to stay with Maggie, and that was that. No children; no mortgage; the logistics of the split were easy. The emotional fallout was more complicated. Michael blamed his drinking and tried to convince Georgia that he was ready to reform, though he wasn't sure he was, and he was also aware of the growing list of other things he felt he couldn't be straight with her about. He wondered whether an unbridgeable chasm had opened between them. Meanwhile, his friend was urging him to move to Melbourne and make a fresh start.

Georgia's main response to the split – apart from sadness and some embarrassment over the brevity of their relationship – was relief at no longer having to pretend to be someone she wasn't.

'I was twisting myself out of shape to seem like the kind of person I thought he wanted,' she said to Maggie, noting the irony of the fact that this was the very thing she and Michael had promised each other would never happen.

'Beware the promise of transparency,' Maggie replied. 'If you have to keep bragging about it, it probably isn't happening. And plenty of people would rather not know everything there is to be known about their partner. My mother always liked to keep my dad guessing. It worked for them.'

Existentialists and essentialists

Not everyone is comfortable with the idea of an essential self. There's a very long history in philosophy of a contest between the idea of the self as an inner reality or 'essence' and the idea, repopularised last century by the existentialists (Jean-Paul Sartre the most famous of them), that the concept of 'self' is a mere illusion; that, in the words of the Spanish philosopher José Ortega y Gasset, 'man has no nature, only a history'. As their label implies, the existentialists believed that the fact of our *existence* – what actually happened to us; the things we did – was the sum total of who we were. To them, all the internal, psychological stuff was meaningless.

B.F. Skinner, one of the mid-twentieth century's most influential American psychologists, agreed with them. Skinner's 'behaviourist' school of psychology insisted that concepts like 'mind' and 'will' are of far less interest than close analysis of *what we actually do*. He dismissed as mere 'mentalism' any attempt to incorporate inner psychological phenomena into explanations of human behaviour. (Pretty weird, you might think, for a person described as a psychologist, but Skinner's approach was partly a reaction to the elaborate and occasionally fanciful storytelling of the Freudian psychoanalysts on the other side of the Atlantic, with their heavy emphasis on the role of the unconscious mind.)

The existentialists and behaviourists came into fashion at a bleak time in human history – during and after World War II – when there was a widespread culture of despair, reflected in the titles of some of Sartre's most popular works, like *Being and Nothingness* and *Nausea*, in the novels of Albert Camus (*The Outsider*), the satirical plays of Bertolt Brecht (*The Resistible Rise of Arturo Ui*), and a spate of deeply pessimistic British novels (George Orwell's *1984*, William Golding's *The Lord of the Flies*, Anthony Burgess's *A Clockwork Orange*, as well as the popular postwar spy novels of John le Carré and Len Deighton). As presaged by Franz Kafka (*The Trial*), meaninglessness was a big theme. If there were an essential human nature, it would be, for such writers, too horrible to contemplate.

All this was in sharp contrast to the idealists/essentialists who, from the Greek philosopher Plato onwards, had permeated Western thought with the idea that there is indeed an essential human nature – an ideal of humanity towards which we may all strive; an inner, authentic self that is more than the mere sum of our actions.

While the existentialists and behaviourists might insist that the idea of 'intention' is irrelevant and illusory, isn't it true that, for many of us, the choices we make are often the result of quite painful inner turmoil as we weigh up the possible consequences of this or that course of action?

And even when we do act, we often experience lingering tension and uncertainty as we face the disappointment of finding that our actions have fallen short of our intentions, that we haven't been as effective as we wanted to be, or that we have done something that twists us out of shape (like Georgia in her marriage to Michael) because our actions are in such obvious conflict with our inner sense of 'self'.

Existentialists and essentialists offer very different ways of approaching the concept of the self – though, of course, they both contribute to our understanding of what it means to be a person. If you believe that, *in addition to* the 'existential you' that others infer from your behaviour, there's an 'essential you', a 'real you', an 'inner you', then read on.

When it comes to the questions at the heart of this book – how and why we hide from ourselves – the idea of hiding from our *existence* makes little sense. It's true that some people do try to hide from their history by rewriting it but, mostly, it is something about our *essence* that we try to hide from.

Before we explore what that 'something' might be, there's an important distinction to be made between this idea of an authentic or essential self, and the idea of 'personal identity' – which is what many people are thinking of when they set out on the quest to find themselves.

Our 'personal identity' is socially constructed

Identity is all about individual differences. As the word itself suggests, this is how we *identify* each other; how we distinguish one person from another. In our essence, we have some remarkably similar qualities, based on our common humanity, but we define our identity by drawing comparisons and contrasts between ourselves and others, emphasising our uniqueness – in appearance, speech, actions, beliefs, opinions, means of self-expression and so on. If I were permanently alone, I could still have a clear sense of my authentic being – my inner self – but the need for an identity would evaporate.

The Australian social analyst Richard Eckersley has a creative way of describing our socially constructed personal identity based on the scientific understanding of atoms as being more like a fuzzy cloud of electrical charges than solid particles with electrons whizzing around the nucleus. By analogy, Eckersley wonders whether we might make better sense of the idea of personal identity 'if we were to see the self not as a separate physical entity, but as a fuzzy cloud of relational forces and fields. This would be a self of many relationships . . . some close and intense; some more distant and diffuse'.

You won't discover your identity by looking into a mirror or gazing at your metaphorical navel. Your identity relies on your social context: your partner or other people who love you; your family; your children (if any); your colleagues; your friends; your teammates; your neighbours . . . the people who are more or less cheerfully prepared to spend time in your company and accept you as part of their group. Examine your roles and responsibilities; review your personal history; assess your impact on the world you live in: those are the dimensions of your personal identity.

Just as the whole idea of 'national identity' is meaningless without the context of other nations (the French need the Belgians, Germans, Spanish, Italians and British to make sense of what 'French' means), so an individual person needs other individuals as reference points for defining their own identity.

Identity is often a performance. I adapt to my circumstances and the demands of the position I'm in; I cultivate a certain persona; I project a certain image. These things are all part of my identity, though they might be a long way from my essence. American country and western singer Dolly Parton put it succinctly: 'I don't mind if people call me a dumb blonde. I know I'm not dumb, and I know I'm not blonde.'

Japanese culture has formalised this distinction between public and private faces: the word *honne* refers to our private thoughts and feelings, our authentic self; *tatemae* refers to the face we put on in public in order to be acceptable to our society. (The Chinese, similarly, refer to 'inside face' and 'outside face', and the Iranian concepts of *zaher* and *batin* identify the two separate and distinct levels of the self: the inner private core and the social or public self.) Given Japan's high population density, the smooth running of Japanese society is heavily dependent on people showing great courtesy and respect towards each other. Sometimes the demands of *tatemae* lead to the outright telling of lies in order to hide inner feelings that might provoke conflict if exposed.

Westerners might describe this sort of behaviour as 'putting on an act' or even as a form of hypocrisy, but the Japanese adhere to the courtesy conventions of their society as a way of preventing the social disintegration that might follow if a more individualistic, competitive ethos took hold. None of this is to deny or repress the self: knowledge of the authentic inner core – *honne* – is as important to mental health and personal integrity in that culture as in any other.

Lucy's coping strategy

When I was in my early teens, my parents split up and an extended period of instability followed for me and my brother Brad. In her search for a new life for herself, our mother moved restlessly from place to place, never quite finding what she was looking for, never quite able to settle. As a result, Brad and I attended six different schools in the space of four years.

After some ugly experiences of being mocked and bullied for my 'strangeness' at the first of those new schools – mainly caused by my accent, which the other girls thought was posh and pretentious – I quickly learnt to fit in. It was quite easy to speak more roughly when that seemed to be called for, and then to revert to a softer style – maybe more genteel – or to become more detached, or more sophisticated or more gauche . . . whatever seemed to be required in each new setting. I dressed differently, too, as we moved from place to place, to conform with the standards of each new group. At one school, I even dyed my hair pink. (Mum loved that, by the way, wannabe hippie that she was.)

It wasn't that I craved acceptance from this or that group, exactly, even though I realise that's probably what it looked like to my mum. It was more that I was discovering how to merge relatively seamlessly into each social setting. It was a bit like trying to become invisible, in some ways. I guess I just wanted to avoid attracting the wrong kind of attention.

Even at the time, I thought of it as wearing a series of different masks, and I was quite proud of myself for becoming so good at it. I knew I was just playing a part, and I often used to wonder just how many other girls were only playing a part, too. That was what you did to make yourself acceptable to your peer group. Occasionally, I'd have a bit of a heart-to-heart with one of the girls, and they often seemed quite differ- ent – generally nicer – than they were when they were with their friends. It was kind of weird. Looking back, I can honestly say that I never lost sight of who I really was deep inside. I always knew that wasn't the real me doing all those things. But it was painful to pretend.

There was another side to this game I was playing – my relationship with my parents. I began to develop different personas with them, too. I'm not sure whether that was a self-protective strategy to minimise the emotional damage caused by their horrible split, followed by their acrimonious divorce, or whether I was simply trying to please both my parents, but in very different ways. It sounds pathetic, but I suppose I must have thought that one way of helping to keep the peace was to try to be the kind of daughter each of them wanted when I was with them. The truth is, they each wanted very different daughters – Mum wanted me to be a free spirit like her; Dad wanted me to be a hard-working, conservative, 'successful' person like him. Later, I came to realise that their different expectations of me – and their completely different ways of relating to me – were just another symptom of the gulf between them.

I sometimes wonder what would have happened if they'd stayed together. I assume I wouldn't have had to become two different versions of myself, each trying to please them in different ways. It was just like it was at school: all along, I had this clear sense that there was

16

a really, really private Lucy – the 'inner Lucy' – that couldn't be changed by all these disguises I was wearing. The real me became invisible to my parents. I guess neither of them ever got to know who I really was at that stage of my life. That's sad, on reflection. Sad for them, and sad for me, too. I would much rather have felt confident to be myself. But it just didn't seem possible. I became terribly defensive around them.

I had a few failed romances in my twenties, but when I met Jack, there was this enormous feeling of gratitude – here, at last, was a person to whom I could reveal my true self. I could even be frank with him about my struggle to keep my true self hidden all those years for fear that it would be diminished or damaged by exposure to my friends' ridicule or my parents' disappointment.

Looking back, I'd say my brother Brad handled it all very differently. His coping strategy was completely different from mine. He kept changing and adapting to fit in with different social groups, just like I did, but he seemed entirely comfortable with the process. It was as if each new identity seemed authentic to him and he never seemed troubled by the need to hide his true self. In fact, I once tried to discuss this whole 'inner Lucy' thing with him and he didn't seem to know what I was talking about. Maybe it's because he was a couple of years younger, but he seemed to take it all in his stride, as if he didn't really need to try at all. He was like a chameleon, whereas I was more like a magician, pulling off trick after trick. We never discuss it now – he's still as gung-ho as ever. I'm not sure Brad knows what anguish is. Not yet, anyway. He's still happy to adapt to whoever he's hanging out with. But they don't seem like disguises – maybe he's just a more easy-going person than I am. He's certainly more popular than I'll ever be.

≈

Brad sounds like a person who is content to go with the flow of an emerging, evolving sense of personal identity that is entirely determined by its context. Lucy, by contrast, accepted the social demands of identity formation but, even at a young age, had a sense of her own essence as being quite different from, and even untouched by, those changing identities.

The desire to distinguish ourselves from others is itself complicated by the parallel desire to define ourselves, at least partly, by the groups we belong to, since our sense of individual identity is heavily conditioned by our conformity to the attitudes and behaviour of those groups. National identity, corporate identity, ethnic identity, 'identity politics' . . . tribal identities of all kinds contribute to the way we perceive and understand each other, because we are, inescapably, social animals. The concept of the essential self doesn't argue against that idea – it simply acknowledges that we are not *only* social beings; we are also unique individuals with our own inner life.

Our most complete understanding of ourselves will draw on both external and internal sources and there is inevitable overlap between them: my social identity is not totally generated from without, and 'the real me' is not totally generated from within. We are constantly writing each other's stories as well as our own.

Getting in touch with 'the real me'

How might we tune into the secret harmonies of our inner life? How might we gauge the significance of the differences between the public 'identity' and the private 'self'?

Some people seek the support of a counsellor/therapist to guide them through the process of coming to terms with that distinction;

some embrace spiritual practices ranging from chanting and yoga to liturgical rituals; some prefer silent and solitary introspection; some use hallucinogenic drugs to stimulate mystical experiences that heighten awareness of the self; some engage with the formal practice of meditation. Some do all those things.

Meditation is the best-known form of contemplative practice, and neuroscience offers encouraging evidence of its benefits in assisting the process of self-examination, including heightened clarity of mind and greater serenity.

A particular type of meditation called 'loving-kindness meditation' has proved effective in stimulating our potential for love and compassion – which, as we are about to see, is the resource we all need to draw on if our species is to thrive. The work of American researcher Barbara Fredrickson and her colleagues at North Carolina and Michigan universities has shown that this ancient Buddhist technique for transforming anger into compassion by inducing positive feelings towards others can also develop an improved sense of purpose and life satisfaction.

Whatever pathway you choose, a good starting point is to reflect deeply on those moments when you have felt some awkwardness or embarrassment arising from the realisation that you were pretending to be someone who was not really you, or accepting another person's flattering view of you that you knew to be wide of the mark. Recall those moments as if you were watching a movie of yourself, and then think about how you'd like to edit that movie so you'd feel more comfortable watching it.

You might also reflect on the way other people *generally* seem to regard you – how they relate to you; what they expect of you;

what they assume about you – and ask yourself whether there are any significant gaps between their perceptions of you and your own sense of the kind of person you really are.

For example, do you often find yourself saying one thing and doing another (as I do)? There are many reasons why that can happen: you might be simply trying to be polite; you might have seriously intended to do what you said you'd do, but then lost heart; you might have realised, even while you were saying it, that you had no intention of following through with action. Underlying all those explanations is the possibility that your true self, your essence, was resisting doing what you had said you would do.

Do you ever hear yourself saying this: 'I really want to simplify my life, but it keeps getting more complicated'? So, which is the real you – the one who says you want to simplify, or the one who keeps adding complexity?

What about this: 'People think I'm such a dynamo, but that's not how I would like to be seen. I actually want to slow down – take things a bit easier – be more serene – so why do I keep running faster?' (Good question, and we'll take it up in chapter three.)

Or this: 'I can tell you the kind of life I'd like to lead, but you mightn't believe me if you looked at how I actually live.' Or even this: 'I get really uncomfortable when people compliment me on my appearance because I know things are not so beautiful deep inside.'

Have you ever secretly worried about the fact that people think more warmly and charitably of you than they might if they knew what was really going on inside your head? Have you ever felt 'lucky to have got away with it' in a situation where you had pretended to be more humble, or more sensitive, or more concerned about others' wellbeing than you really felt; where your 'nice' persona was really only a mask for something more complex, and possibly darker?

Such things might well be hints that the gap between your out-there identity and your in-here sense of self is too wide for comfort, and that you need to take some action to narrow that gap in the interests of your own mental health. They might be warnings that you are jeopardising your integrity by going along with other people's perceptions of you. They might also be signs of the need to do some work on yourself: even so-called character defects can be repaired.

Lucy again

You want to know how I knew there was a different me – a real me – inside, when I was going through all that stuff with the constant changes of school and my parents being so ... difficult? I had awful stomach aches.

At first, I went to the school sick bay, but there was never anything actually wrong with me. The nurse thought it was something to do with my periods, but I knew it wasn't that. It was a totally different kind of pain. Eventually I figured out that this was my gut sending me a message from my brain: You're not being true to yourself, Lucy!

Well, I knew that, but I couldn't see any alternative. I was behaving in the only way I could think of to avoid merciless bullying and all the rest. I thought that was the only way to survive, and I still think it was. And with the conflict between Mum and Dad, what was I supposed to do? Sit them down and give them a lecture on being more reasonable? No way.

The truth is, those stomach pains were curiously reassuring. They were like a secret I carried around with me. As if my stomach and I knew the real truth about me. I lost a lot of weight as a result, but I knew what was happening and I think I would have known if it was getting to the dangerous stage. Some girls called me 'ana', as in anorexic, but that was never true.

Once I left school and started uni, I was determined to be more like the person I knew I really was. And it was easier – there were lots of different kinds of people, and not such pressure to be part of the cool crowd. You couldn't even tell who the cool crowd were. There were little cliques who kept to themselves – mostly from private schools – but I had no trouble meeting people I felt comfortable with. I still have to bend a bit to fit in, but I think I'm a nicer person now. I'm not on the defensive all the time. What a relief! I guess I'm still working out who I am, but at least I know I'm not pretending anymore – or not much, anyway.

~

Creativity: a pathway to self-awareness

Confront yourself. That was the headline of a recent advertisement for the Art Fund's National Art Pass that offers access to over 240 museums, galleries and historic places throughout the UK. Through observing works of art, the campaign implied, something of yourself would be revealed as well: you might catch a glimpse of your own soul by fixing your gaze on an artwork. A subsequent ad in the series bore the headline *Unplug yourself,* which was a neat way of suggesting there's an authentic inner you that doesn't need to be 'amplified' or distorted by a socially determined identity.

There's endless debate about the value of the arts for those who consume them, and the evidence is very variable, according to which art form you're talking about. But we've all seen documentaries showing how listening to old songs can bring people with dementia out of the fog as they reconnect with both the music *and* the words, even when the power of speech seemed to have deserted them. Literature has the capacity to change lives. Poetry can move us to tears of recognition and regret. Exposure to any of the arts can help clarify our private sense of self:

That's not like me.

I'd walk out if anyone treated me like that.

I found that play too close to the bone to be enjoyable.

I can lose myself in this music – or perhaps I mean I can find myself in it.

I wonder why I am so completely unmoved by this when everyone else seems to be so into it.

Sometimes we come away from such encounters merely distracted or entertained; sometimes moved; and, yes, sometimes 'confronted' or even 'unplugged'.

But nothing beats actually *doing* something creative or performative: singing, dancing, writing, drawing, painting, photography . . . creative self-expression can act like a shortcut to self-awareness. Curiously, we can even be confronted by works of art we ourselves produce. People often look at something they've drawn, painted or written and exclaim: 'Where did *that* come from?' And many writers say things like: 'I write in order to find out what I really think.'

Writing poetry is a radically different process from reading poetry written by others – and likely to be even more self-revelatory.

Performing music has positive effects on our cognitive development and brain plasticity, even as we age. Choral singing, in particular, has been shown to have cognitive, social and emotional benefits: many people report finding themselves through losing themselves in the music, as well as developing warm feelings of trust towards their fellow choristers.

The creative process has the power to unlock aspects of the self that might otherwise remain hidden. And, at its best, creative work speaks to us all about what it means to be human. (How else to explain the enduring appeal of Shakespeare?)

The deepest wisdom on the subject of 'knowing yourself' always stresses our interdependence and interconnectedness. Our sense of self is uniquely our own, but it is brought to life and given its richest meaning only when it is expressed in social interactions: most of us have voices that sound best when blended with a choir.

Carl Rogers acknowledged that when a client is engaged in the process of 'being and becoming himself', he will inevitably discover that he is 'soundly and realistically social'. Although we are naturally fascinated by the differences between us, it turns out that, in our very essence, we have something in common with everyone else.

At the core of the self is our capacity for love

The proposition that our capacity for love is the essence of what it means to be human is not some flight of poetical fancy, but simply the acknowledgement of an evolutionary imperative. We humans are social beings whose primary duty to our species (right up there with reproduction) is to create and maintain harmonious, cooperative and sustainable communities. The survival of our species depends on it. We don't simply need each other; we need each other to thrive.

For complex evolutionary reasons (well explained by Richard Wrangham in *The Goodness Paradox*), we are also an aggressive and potentially violent species, but our capacity for social harmony, and our proven ability to sustain communal life over the millennia, represents the strongest possible argument in favour of love as the *essential* characteristic of humans.

'Love' is one of those words we press into service to express a wide range of very different meanings. We blithely say 'I love my dog', 'I love chocolate', 'I love my partner', 'I love my children', 'I love my job', 'I love that book . . . that song . . . that sunset', 'I love my friends', yet no one assumes we mean the same thing in each of those cases. The English language is remarkably deficient when it comes to expressing the varieties of love, but in the context of human relationships, we can easily distinguish between 'the four loves' (borrowed from the title of C.S. Lewis's book on the subject): familial love – the bonds between members of an extended family or other tightly knit social group; affection between friends; erotic/romantic love; and charity, sometimes referred to as compassion or loving-kindness.

Those four different kinds of love all enrich our lives, but the last category – charity/compassion – is the one to focus on when we're thinking about the greatest contribution we can make to a healthy, well-functioning society. We typically think of love as an emotion, but in the case of compassionate love, it's more accurate to think of it as a discipline – a commitment to a particular way of life in which patience, kindness, tolerance and respect become our characteristic responses to *everyone* we encounter. Being kind and respectful towards those we like and those we agree with is neither virtuous nor praiseworthy: love's greatest challenge is to show compassion towards people for whom we feel no affection or affinity at all. Such unconditional love best expresses our humanity. Though we sometimes try to hide from its demands on us, we all share the capacity – the potential – for that kind of love, whether we're rich or poor, short or tall, cognitively smart or not, religious believers or atheists, male or female, or anything in between. It's a species thing, not a personal thing.

Try this metaphor.

Think of the self – *your* self – as being like a personal solar system. The planets are the qualities that comprise your unique character: your genetic traits, your values, your private dreams, doubts and fears, your worldview. Each of those 'planets' has its distinct orbit, its distinct density, its distinct gravity. At the centre of the system is the sun, the source of all light and life, without which those planets would be worthless bits of rock, orbit-less, incoherent, hurtling meaninglessly into the void. (It's only a metaphor, as deficient as any other: what shall we say, for instance, about the fact that some of our personal 'planets' vanish and new ones appear as we mature and develop? But let's stick with the metaphor for a moment: we're coming to the most important bit.)

In our personal solar system, love, in all its variety, is like the sun at the centre – animating us, energising us, inspiring us, ennobling us and giving our soul its warmth. But this metaphorical sun, like a literal sun, is not only the source of light; it also casts deep, dark shadows, sometimes of shocking malevolence. Doesn't our folklore tell us there's a fine line between love and hate? Our actions spring from such mixed motives, it's often hard to separate the noble from the murky, the light from the dark. Every surge of faith or hope casts its shadow of doubt.

Across the universe, there are countless billions of solar systems, each of them unique, but each with a bright sun at its centre. Across the world, there are billions of unique individuals, but each has a bright sun of love at its centre – the most powerful symbol of our common humanity. In this respect, our essential self corresponds to everyone else's essential self, regardless of the myriad differences between us. Whether we acknowledge it or not, we all need this same centre in our lives if we are to flourish as fully developed humans who enjoy the ultimate psychological freedom – the freedom to love.

If that sounds a bit too idealistic, or perhaps even totally unrealistic, then we must acknowledge that having the *capacity* for that transformative kind of love does not always translate into the daily practice of it. The power of the sun at our centre can make us feel uncomfortable, which is why we're sometimes grateful for the shadows it casts – though Plato, as usual, had something useful to say about this: 'We can easily forgive a child who is afraid of the dark; the real tragedy of life is when men are afraid of the light.'

The range of our reactions to the bright light of love explains many of the world's problems: some of us are so daunted by the prospect of living lovingly ('Why should I? I can't stand those people!') that we retreat into the shadows of self-absorption: bitterness, envy, anger, ruthless rivalry, hate, or a callous indifference to the needs of others. In fact, if you accept this metaphorical depiction of the self, the so-called 'problem of evil' evaporates. There is no mystery about the presence of evil in the world: where there is light, there is darkness, and the brighter the light, the deeper the shadows it casts. Where there is love, there is hate; where there is hate, there is a person hiding from love, which is why hate – along with other hiding-from-love states like jealousy, revenge and pride – is such a dismal, self-destructive emotion.

The intensity of love's demands explains why even the most charitable of us need a break from the intensity of 'being good'. Night must follow day, after all, and there is such a thing as compassion fatigue!

Yet love shines relentlessly on: even when we might prefer to stay on the dark side of our personal planets, we may find ourselves being unexpectedly rotated into the light and doing something wonderful. Love's work is often the hardest work of all, but let's not forget that love is also the source of the warmth we all need to comfort and sustain us.

To live lovingly – compassionately – is not to be weak, soppy, acquiescent or a martyr to every unreasonable claim on us. Being kind-hearted is not the same as being soft in the head. Being loving does not mean always trying to please other people, and it's certainly not about accepting responsibility for anyone else's happiness. It's simply a particular way of being in the world.

Being loving does not, for instance, mean that you should indulge a child's every whim, or give people everything they ask for. It doesn't mean you should stay in a relationship that has run its course, but it does mean that your exit should be as kind, sensitive, gracious and respectful as possible. It doesn't mean you should put up with offensive behaviour from your neighbours, but it does mean your complaints should be made respectfully and with the aim of preserving social harmony.

Like all the other varieties of love, compassionate love sometimes needs to be tough. Compassion can coexist with strict discipline, strong leadership, uncompromising convictions and major disagreements over politics, religion, urban planning, clean energy, neighbourhood noise, or anything else. But it also respects other people's boundaries: 'I'm doing this because I'm determined to be loving, even if you don't want me to be'; 'I'm coming to visit you because I need to see you, even though you've said you don't want visitors' – such remarks raise serious questions about our understanding of compassionate love.

The idea that we are at our best – our most *human* – when we are motivated by love is hardly new or revolutionary. Though it can be perverted by fundamentalism and bigotry, or by institutional corruption, the central mission of the world's great religions has always been to nurture our capacity for love and to encourage commitment to a life of compassion and service to others. Every non-religious spiritual or mystical tradition – and most secular philosophy – points to the same idea.

Here's how a selection of people from utterly different traditions have expressed the centrality of love to a meaningful and fulfilling life:

Plato: 'Love is the joy of the good, the wonder of the wise, the amazement of the gods.'

Buddha: 'In the end, only three things matter: how much you loved, how gently you lived, and how gracefully you let go of things not meant for you.'

St Paul: 'And now faith, hope and love abide, these three; and the greatest of these is love.'

Marcus Aurelius: 'Know the joy of life by piling good deed on good deed until no rift or cranny appears between them.'

Carl Jung: 'As far as we can discern, the sole purpose of human existence is to kindle a light in the darkness of mere being.'

Albert Einstein: 'Nothing truly valuable arises from ambition, or from a mere sense of duty; it stems rather from love and devotion towards [humanity] and towards objective things.'

Bertrand Russell: 'The good life is inspired by love and guided by knowledge.'

Philip Larkin: 'What will survive of us is love.'

Iris Murdoch: 'Love is the extremely difficult realisation that something other than oneself is real.'

The latest research into the effects of psychedelic drugs points in the same direction. In *How to Change Your Mind*, American author Michael Pollan reported on recent experimental research into the effects on human consciousness of psilocybin – the active ingredient in hallucinogenic drugs such as LSD. In that research, conducted under carefully controlled conditions, drug-induced mystical experiences have typically generated a heightened and often transformative awareness of love as the driving force of life, usually accompanied by a diminished fear of death and a strong sense of the oneness of humanity.

This is the ultimate paradox of selfhood: when we get to the core of who we are, we find that, just like everyone else, our essence is love – and what can love be about except connection and community? Perhaps, when we are hiding from ourselves, regardless of the hiding place we choose, the challenge to live more lovingly is part of what we're hiding from.

Coda: As for an individual, so for a nation

It's not only individuals who are sometimes coy about facing up to the truth about themselves: entire nations do it, too. They hide from some raw and dark material about their past, for example, in the myths and legends that cast them in a more favourable light than some unflinching historians might think is justified. They sing their own praises in stirring anthems that help them forget the shameful scandals, injustices, inhumanities, land grabs, massacres and cruelties they or their forebears might have inflicted on indigenous people, refugees, enemies in battle, or on some of their own hapless citizens.

Just as individuals need to tone down the demands of compassion in order to remain comfortable in their hiding places, a nation hiding from the truth about itself will dial back its compassion and become tougher and less humane in its social policies. Rampant nationalism, militarism, materialism, triumphalism, racism and other forms of bigotry can be very attractive places in which to hide from the dark side of any nation's character and history.

In Australia, we're as good as anyone else at hiding. We don't like to face the truth about our forebears' genocidal impulses in dealing with First Peoples. We don't like to admit that some of our soldiers have behaved as badly in war as soldiers in any army might do in the heat and squalor of battle. We don't like to think about the prolonged mental torture we have inflicted on asylum seekers in our offshore detention centres or on refugees condemned to the insecurity of temporary protection visas.

We hide from our failure to achieve true gender equality by mouthing platitudes about it. We're in denial about what's happening to our society under the influence of taxation and schools-funding policies that are increasing (and perhaps institutionalising) the distance between the top and bottom of our socioeconomic heap. We like to brag about 'punching above our weight' in sport, but we're reluctant to admit that that's precisely what we're doing when it comes to carbon dioxide emissions.

We use 'the fair go' and 'mateship' to conceal our inequities and injustices, while trying to pretend that this is an egalitarian society. ('If you have a go, you'll get a go', an egregious piece of political blather, is in danger of taking root as a contemporary expression of 'the fair go', 2 million unemployed and underemployed Australians notwithstanding.)

One of our favourite hiding places is the idea of 'the lucky country', borrowed from the title of Donald Horne's 1964 book. How ironic! Horne's book was actually a scathing critique of Australian society. He described us as 'a lucky country run by mainly second-rate people who share its luck'. Horne saw us as a classic case of success being achieved more by good luck than good management, since he regarded Australia's political and business leaders as decidedly lacking in vision and imagination. 'According to the rules,' he wrote, 'Australia has not deserved its luck.' So what did we do with Horne's bleak assessment of us? We turned it into a compliment, as if luck were a virtue to be celebrated.

Australia is not alone in any of this. Most nations tweak their national story to their own advantage. 'Land of hope and glory!' 'The land of the free and the home of the brave!' 'The True North, strong and free!' (In Australia, we even stand and sing 'Our home is girt by sea' as if that's a matter of national pride.)

We could hardly expect nations to parade their dirty laundry in national anthems and slogans – and, after all, every nation on earth obviously takes pride in its unique cultural heritage and its moments of glory and triumph. But when we allow ourselves to hide behind blind nationalism, we are as removed from reality as individuals who deny their own shadows.

'My country, right or wrong . . .' was only part of the famous remark made by US senator (and former German revolutionary) Carl Christian Schurz. The rest of the quote was the really significant part: '. . . if right, to be kept right; and if wrong, to be set right.'

There's a message there for all of us – not just about our country, but about the process of personal self-examination as well. Admitting and confronting our dark side (especially our failure to do love's demanding work), as well as nurturing our virtues, is essential to personal integrity. And we also need to 'set right' the things that are isolating us from our inner life.

TWO

Why we hide from ourselves

*If you have nothing to hide, you have
nothing to fear.*

That slogan, generally attributed to Joseph Goebbels, Adolf Hitler's arch-propagandist, and satirically echoed by George Orwell in *1984*, is now being redeployed, with a straight face, in an attempt to justify governments' increasingly sophisticated surveillance of their citizens. (Here's how a defence company recently promoted its new surveillance system at a trade fair in China: 'If someone exists, there will be traces. If there are connections, there will be information.')

Well, of course, we do have something to hide – at least from governments and commercial tech giants who monitor the teeming torrents of our data surging through cyberspace: namely, our private sense of self. Chair of the UN Taskforce on 'Privacy and Personality' and former NSW Privacy Commissioner, Elizabeth Coombs, once remarked that 'the freedom to choose what I reveal about myself and what I keep private is one of our core freedoms'.

Winston Smith, the central character in *1984*, observed that 'if you want to keep a secret you must also hide it from yourself'. That's advice many of us are all too willing to take when it comes to the inner core of our being. We are not only reluctant to share our 'private face' with our partner, family or close friends; we are even reluctant to confront it ourselves.

The extensive literature on the subject of denial and repression suggests that hiding from ourselves is not only a common practice; it is regarded by some people as a completely sane and rational response to the suspicion that there's a 'real me' they'd prefer not to confront, let alone expose to anyone else.

Why such a defensive attitude to the concept of self? Why are we so willing to admit to wearing our various masks, yet so reluctant to take them off? Why is it apparently so easy to block our access to our own soul, especially when we're so ready to judge the state of other people's; to deafen our ears to our own inner voice; to ignore the threat to our mental and emotional health from living with underlying tension between who we are and who we appear to be? Why is pretending so attractive? And why is it apparently so easy to pull off?

Underlying all our reasons for hiding from ourselves is our reluctance to face the question: *What will be required of me if I get to the core of who I am?* Whatever hiding-place we choose, part of our motivation is likely to be our anxiety about whether we have what it takes to rise to the great human challenge to live more lovingly.

To be habitually loving, as a daily discipline, can seem a daunting prospect. To adopt compassion as a way of life takes courage. To live according to the dictates of the purest essence of self *is* a challenge. No wonder we sometimes feel like hiding, especially when there are so many comfortable hiding places on offer (like the twenty we will explore in chapter three).

Love brings out the best in us, but we don't always *want* the best to be brought out in us because that standard might seem too high and its demands too great. Love promotes goodness, but we don't always *want* to be good. Love encourages us to live noble rather than merely moral lives, but we'd sometimes prefer to settle for the lazy old defence of unloving behaviour: 'I did nothing ethically or legally wrong.' Love nurtures a generosity of spirit, but the temptation to be mean-spirited is sometimes irresistible, especially when we're feeling outraged. Love calls on us to forgive, even though revenge often seems justified and more natural. Love equips us to tolerate and try to understand those who are so different from us that it would be easier to retreat to a position of judgement, prejudice or hostility.

Above all, and very inconveniently, love demands that we sometimes sacrifice our own 'needs' (often first-world code for 'wants and preferences') in favour of the more compelling needs of others. That is a particular challenge as we come to terms with the threat posed to our species' very survival by climate change. Increasingly, we will be asked to make personal sacrifices in the interests of the common good, on a global scale: our diet, our non-essential travel (especially air travel), our reliance on fossil fuel-based energy, our profligate consumerism (especially involving disposable plastics) will all need to be curbed as we face the very real prospect of the planet becoming uninhabitable unless urgent action is taken by *all* govern-ments, *all* corporations and *all* individuals. Never has 'the oneness of humanity', in an ecological sense, been more apparent than now; never has the slogan 'Live simply, so others may simply live' been more relevant.

There are many perfectly reasonable-sounding explanations of why we resist the inward journey of self-examination, but all of them are likely to be tinged by our reluctance to ask ourselves that single, searching question: *What will be required of me if I get to the core of who I am?*

We fear the emotional demands of the process

In his classic collection of papers and essays *On Becoming a Person*, Carl Rogers writes that 'to remove a mask you thought was part of your real self can be a deeply disturbing experience'. In a chapter called 'What it means to become a person', Rogers includes a client's own account of such a struggle, which begins like this:

> As I look at it now, I was peeling off layer after layer of defences
> . . . I didn't know what was at the bottom and I was very much
> afraid to find out, but I *had* to keep on trying. At first I felt
> there was nothing within me – just a great emptiness where
> I needed and wanted a solid core.

That client finally achieved a breakthrough in her search for the core of herself. She had described feeling as if she were holding back the waters of a great dam, fearful of being 'destroyed in the torrent of feelings represented by the water'. Finally, she let go, describing that as succumbing to 'utter self pity, then hate, then love.' Her account continued:

> After this experience, I felt as if I had leaped a brink and was safely on the other side, though still tottering a bit on the edge. I don't know what I was searching for or where I was going, but I felt then as I have always felt whenever I have really lived, that I was moving forward.

Rogers told that client's story, rich with metaphor, to illustrate the 'compelling necessity' that drives people to stop hiding from themselves. Nevertheless, many of us manage to resist that 'compelling necessity', letting our fear of the process discourage us from undertaking the journey. What if it *is* a disturbing experience coming to terms with the person I really am? What if I can't handle the intensity of the process?

How should we confront such fears?

First, we need to acknowledge that people who are close to us might already be more aware of our 'secrets' than we realise, since we sometimes reveal our true feelings in quite unconscious ways.

Second, wouldn't you rather know who you really are, so that you can face the world more confidently? Wouldn't you rather confront the things you don't like about yourself, or that don't ring true for you, and do some work on them? The alternative is to live in a permanently defensive state of mind.

Third, and most importantly, if we persist in a state of frightened ignorance of the truth about ourselves, we are likely to suffer negative health consequences. Anxiety is a very unhealthy state to be in, and sustained tension between the masks we wear and the authentic self that lies beneath those masks is a potent source of damaging anxiety.

If we are to become fully functioning human beings, able to confront and respond to the truth about our ourselves, we will need to overcome our fear of the process of self-examination. Yes, it does require courage. It requires patience. It requires emotional stamina. And our fears might be justified: the inward journey might well be painful, but isn't it the universal human experience that painful experiences often produce the most beneficial outcomes? There's a reason why folk wisdom has always told us that we grow through pain.

Fear of the *process* of self-discovery is closely related to the fear of what we might find if we dig too deeply. 'I'd prefer not to know' is a classic expression of this fear. Yet we are not always hiding from the unknown: some of us know precisely what we're hiding from, and that's why we're hiding. 'I can't retire from work because then I'd have to figure out who I really am'; 'I can't give up the grog – I prefer to see things through a pleasant haze'; 'I know there's some unresolved guilt there – why stir it up?'

It goes without saying that we won't like everything we discover about ourselves. We're imperfect humans, after all; a blend of noble and base urges; an ever-shifting mixture of the rational and non-rational; smart and stupid in our various ways; capable of searing honesty and murky deceitfulness – including our remarkable capacity for self-deception.

You may be familiar with these lines from T.S. Eliot's terminally bleak poem, 'The Hollow Men':

> Between the idea
> And the reality
> Between the motion
> And the act
> Falls the shadow.

'The Hollow Men' was written in 1925, and Eliot may have been using the shadow as a metaphor for the darkness that descended on Europe in the wake of World War I. (His own mood was further darkened by the misery of a collapsed marriage.) But perhaps he was also referring to the shadow within us all. Carl Jung believed that a full realisation of our sense of self involves coming to terms with our own 'shadow', by which he simply meant the negative aspects of our personality: 'the sum of all the unpleasant aspects we like to hide'.

The dark side of human nature can pervert our idealism and diminish our capacity for putting our best intentions into effect. It was imaginatively portrayed in Robert Louis Stevenson's 1886 novel *Dr Jekyll and Mr Hyde* – a title that has passed into the language as a symbol of our two-sided nature. Yet learning to live with the whole truth about ourselves is essential to the achievement of mental health and psychological freedom. The alternative is to live under a permanent cloud of fear about what might be going on in the far reaches of our psyche.

We don't want to rock the boat

If things are going along alright, we're having an okay sort of life, our relationships seem to be working, why risk disruption to any of that by digging too deeply into the self?

That seems like a reasonable question. After all, if I explore my authentic inner being too deeply, I might become more transparent to others as well, and then run the risk of destroying their illusions about me. What if all this transparency were to threaten the peace and harmony of a family, a friendship circle, a workplace or some other social setting by causing me to reveal something about myself that might shock or disturb other people?

Self-discovery is not the same thing as self-disclosure. Most of us go through life concealing aspects of our authentic inner self from people with whom we have only superficial, transient or formal relationships – colleagues at work, perhaps, or neighbours we're not particularly close to, or members of the extended family we rarely see, or strangers on a train. But when it comes to significant, emotionally intimate relationships, too great a gap between identity and self can become a source of great tension and distress. In any relationship that really matters to us, concealment of significant aspects of our true self from the other person is like a ticking time bomb – as dangerous to the integrity of the relationship as hiding from ourselves is to our integrity as individuals.

Katerina maintains a facade of piety

I have kept going to church long after I stopped believing in most of the doctrines. I've given up on all the literal stuff, like virgin birth and bodily resurrection and people going to heaven or hell. I have totally lost faith in the idea of a personal God, or even a Creator, but I still cling to the idea of God as the spirit of love in the world. That's my secret way of coping with all the religious language: I just focus on my own interpretation.

I had an uncle who used to say, 'You just park all the hard stuff in the deep freeze.' I guess that's what I'm doing.

But I never miss a service. I say and sing all kinds of things I simply don't believe and couldn't possibly say outside of a church service. I still take my place on various rosters for jobs around the church, like greeting people at the door and doing Bible readings. I dread the day someone might ask me whether I really believe all the things I read with such apparent sincerity.

But, you know, this is my closest community of friends. And I still basically think of myself as Christian, even if I can no longer tick all the boxes. Maybe I never could. I sometimes wonder whether I just went along with it right from the start because that's what was expected of me.

Anyway, I love the music, and hearing some of the familiar Bible passages is like taking a warm bath.

My husband is as deeply involved as I am, but I think he's more sincere, more committed than me, and I've never confessed my doubts to him. I realise that sounds terrible, but there it is. I don't want to disappoint him, not after maintaining a facade for so many years – and I was sincere in the very beginning. One of our grown-up children is still attached to the church; the others drifted off in their teenage years and won't have a bar of it now. But they all think of me as a devout woman, and they respect that. (If only they knew!)

Am I just going through the motions? It feels like more than that. I really want to maintain those connections and I do really respect other people's faith – I envy it, in fact, even though I seem to have lost my own version. And I accept that a big part of who I am is my attachment to the church. Even though I can't take the institutional church seriously, there

I am – a rusted-on regular! There's something a bit inauthentic going on, to say the least, and I do feel uneasy about that.

But what should I do? Who should I talk to? I feel as if the whole house of cards would collapse if I admitted the truth, even though I occasionally throw out little hints. People just think I'm a bit of a cynic by nature, but that's not true either.

Perhaps my friends – even my husband – might be sympathetic if I explained to them that I was going to stop attending church. But it's not worth the risk. And, to be perfectly frank, I'm not sure who I would really be if I no longer identified myself as a churchgoer. Filling in forms and stuff like that – what would I put? Atheist? That doesn't sound like me at all. Agnostic? That sounds a bit feeble, too.

I suppose I'm a bit afraid of what might happen to me – to my sense of who I am and what I stand for, I mean – if I gave it all away. Being more authentic might upset me, as well as a lot of other people.

Many people have experiences like Katerina's in all sorts of contexts unrelated to religious belief. Family gatherings can be a rich source of genteel hypocrisy, as people hold their tongues rather than risk creating a scene. The temptation can be almost irresistible to disagree about politics, or to bring up some ancient enmities dating back to childhood, or to say what you *really* think about your sister's child-rearing practices, or your mother's tendency to give unsolicited advice, or your father's retelling of jokes that were barely funny the first time.

While restraint can be admirable, it sometimes involves concealment of our true feelings, and how bad would it be if we occasionally decided to strike a small blow for authenticity? What harm would be done by saying – with appropriate respect for others' views, and in a courteous manner – what we *really* think about a political, social or cultural issue, knowing that it is contrary to the conventional wisdom of whatever group we happen to be with? How disastrous would it be for my family, friends or colleagues to discover that I am not quite the person they thought I was; that I no longer hold opinions I once did; that I am capable of loving people I don't always happen to agree with; that I think it would be healthier if we all stopped pretending to agree with each other on every issue just to keep the peace?

Is it healthy to conceal our authentic core values of kindness and compassion, say, rather than admit to them in particular social situations where we fear the risk of being branded as weak? How should we respond when the conversation swirling around us has taken on a tougher, more prejudiced or more intolerant tone than is consistent with our own convictions on the matter under discussion – treatment of people seeking asylum, perhaps, or tax evasion, or a more respectful response to the Uluru Statement, or the funding of public education, or the need for action on climate change? How authentic are our convictions if they can too easily be parked out of sight? Aren't we diminishing our own sense of self if we keep a contradictory mask firmly in place?

In many marriages and other intimate relationships, people learn to hold their tongues in the interests of avoiding conflict. When this involves the trivialities of everyday life, or bowing to the other person's taste or preferences on matters of no real importance, no harm is done. But when people like Georgia (whom we met in chapter one) twist themselves out of shape in order to avoid confrontation or the possibility of disharmony, great harm can be done both to the individual concerned and to the relationship. Ask yourself: Would I rather go on with a relationship based on my own or my partner's concealment of our authentic self, or would I prefer to know that there are serious differences between us, even if open discussion of those differences might prove challenging to the relationship?

Robert Berezin describes love as 'the feeling of resonance between two Authentic Beings'. If the beings themselves are not authentic, how authentic can the resonance be? Or the love?

The fear that people might like us less if they knew what we were really like must be weighed against the emotional price we pay for concealment. And if we fear that they might not like something about us *that we ourselves don't like*, isn't that a message about the need for us to do some work on ourselves – especially if we fear being exposed as less compassionate than we pretend to be?

People who have entered into a committed relationship might feel entitled to ask 'what's going on?' when one partner turns out to have been concealing their true feelings, or their true nature, from the other. 'Why didn't you tell me that's what you really wanted?' 'Why didn't you tell me you were living a lie?' 'Why didn't you tell me your heart wasn't really in it?' Such questions reveal the depth of our desire to be given access to the authentic being of a partner, a close friend, a son or daughter, or anyone in whom we have made a significant emotional investment. Those questions also imply confidence that our love and devotion to another person could withstand exposure to a deeper understanding of their true nature.

Boats might well be rocked by revelations about our authentic self. Applecarts might well be upset. Social harmonies might well be put at risk. Some people *might* like us less if they knew us better. But if we were to go through life avoiding legitimate conflict and confrontation in the interests of keeping the peace, what kind of peace would we be keeping?

We fear the prospect of change

Who wouldn't prefer to let sleeping dogs lie? Who doesn't enjoy the comfort of established habits? Even if life has its occasional challenges and tensions, isn't it easier just to go with the flow?

One of the most curious aspects of human attitudes and behaviour is that, while we actually thrive on change and we need disruptions and surprises to maintain brain plasticity and keep ourselves alert and fully alive, we constantly bemoan the impact of those changes on our lives. Of course, too much disruption can become distressing and destabilising, which is why we're constantly being told that today's accelerating rate of social, cultural and technological change is a threat to our peace of mind and a major contributor to our epidemics of anxiety and depression. It's also why we are warned against making too many changes in too short a period: for instance, if you change jobs, move house and experience a relationship breakdown all at once, you'll probably increase the risk of negative health consequences (though many radical life changes can also have *positive* consequences for us).

The fear of change is easy to understand. Change is like a doorway into the unknown: if we walk through that doorway, what will happen next? What will become of us? Even when our experience has taught us that things rarely turn out as badly as we fear they

47

might, and that change often leads to positive outcomes – or, at the very least, to the realisation that we are able to cope with changes we had previously resisted – we still put the defences up every time the threat of change looms.

There's a natural inertia about us: we tend to go on doing whatever we've been doing – buying the same brand, going to the same holiday destination, voting for the same political party – without needing to give the matter much thought. 'Old habits die hard' captures the idea very well: old habits die *so* hard that we will even go on doing things we know are bad for us – smoking, drinking too much, staying in a relationship that has become toxic, lying around on the couch instead of exercising, spending too much time gazing at our smartphone – because, well, we've got into the habit.

The journey of self-discovery is a classic case of a threat to our habit-bound complacency. To decide that I am going to embrace 'the real me' – to move towards becoming more authentic – would be to declare my willingness to entertain the idea of change, and that calls for some courage.

And yet we know we *can* change because we constantly *do* change. We all modify our behaviour in the run of daily life – not because we wish to change, but in response to social pressure to conform to a particular group, a change in our circumstances like a new job or a rise or fall in income, changes in our physical environment like moving house or decluttering, or turbulent experiences like falling in love, bereavement, relationship breakdown, serious illness, retrenchment . . . or rowdy neighbours moving in next door.

Some people willingly undergo profound life changes – religious conversion, career switches, political radicalisation – to relieve their sense of despair, or to give their life a meaning and purpose that seemed to be lacking. Many people have transformed their view of themselves and their place in the world, and achieved greater peace of mind, through the sustained practice of meditation. And some, quietly and privately, simply decide to 'turn over a new leaf'.

Fear of change is usually about the prospect of losing control. If I can continue to behave habitually, traversing only the same familiar ground, rather like running on a treadmill, then I may well feel that I have things under control. Yet the truth is otherwise. Repetitive behaviour, never lifting your gaze to new horizons, never contemplating alternatives, never having to manage a new situation, is the very opposite of control: it's more like enslavement.

~

Priya's light-bulb moment: 'You can't steer a boat that isn't moving.'

I remember the day I decided I had to do something about my life. I had been working in the same medical practice for ten years. I was right on top of it, I had achieved all the things I had hoped to achieve and, as far as initiatives were concerned – refurbishment of the rooms, streamlining the IT systems, training the support staff to the standard I wanted – every item on my 'to do' list seemed to have been ticked. I was just cruising, which was pleasant enough, and I knew I was offering the best patient care I was capable of, but I felt increasingly restless, as if I wasn't being true to . . . my sense of vocation, I guess. Or maybe just to myself.

Even though I had things well under control professionally, I had this weird feeling that I was actually losing control of my own life. It was a very comfortable existence in lots of ways – even though general practice has its share of challenges, I can tell you – but I knew I had more to offer. I was a bit bewildered, to be frank, because being a GP was the only thing I had ever wanted to be.

So I talked to a senior medical colleague – a woman who had mentored me throughout my career. I tried to explain my dilemma. I was honest about the restlessness I was feeling and this strange contradiction between feeling totally in control, in the sense that I was on top of the job, while having this uneasy feeling that my life was slipping away from me.

She heard me out and then she said something that has stayed with me: 'You can't steer a boat that isn't moving.' At first I thought that was a bit glib, like most analogies, but then I realised it really did explain how I was feeling. I had lost momentum. I did need to get moving again.

I went through a six-month period of reviewing everything, while my family and friends kept telling me I was mad to contemplate doing anything else. My mentor was wonderfully patient, and together we came to the point where I decided to make the switch to emergency medicine. It was like the proverbial light bulb switching on – of course! I think the seed had been sown in my third year at med school when I was really inspired by my exposure to an accident and emergency department, but I had stuck to my grand plan to become a GP.

Oh, I experienced plenty of panic before it was all settled. But I found a registrar's post at a good hospital and got into the four-year training program and I've never looked back.

Never looked back? What am I saying? Of course I've looked back – for the first few months, I think I looked back every day, wondering why

I had abandoned such a well-ordered existence. Emergency medicine runs on adrenaline, and I wasn't sure I had the necessary resources.

But now I love it. I've discovered that I thrive on pressure. And the paradox has been reversed. In the emergency department, you never feel in control, because you're constantly reacting. Yet I feel as if I have more control over my own life than I used to because I'm being who I really want to be. I know this is the right pathway for a person like me. Anyway, there's no time around here to pretend to be anything but who you are.

Priya's upheaval was triggered by her need for greater vocational fulfilment. And yet, underlying that professional restlessness was something else: she needed to feel that she was doing something that was more in accord with her authentic being. Most of us will probably not face disruptions as dramatic as hers, but the inward journey can seem daunting because we know that discovering who we really are might require us to act differently, to work differently, to love differently, to live differently.

Facing the truth about ourselves brings all the benefits that usually flow from being more honest, including an enhanced sense of personal integrity and self-respect. Greater authenticity in the self will also flow into our personal relationships. As Rogers puts it: 'Relationships with others lose their artificial quality, become deeper, more satisfying, and draw more of the realness of the other person into the relationship.'

Priya again

I think I had become pretty uptight with the staff I was working with in the practice. I won't go so far as to say I was a cranky bitch, but I will admit that I was quite tough on them. I often felt irritated by minor things that went wrong – often through nobody's fault – without realising where my irritability was coming from. And, of course, it was coming from my unresolved issues about my own life.

The last few months, once I was clear about the change I was about to make, I became more relaxed with the staff – a couple of them were prepared to tell me to my face that I had become a bit hard to get along with, but now that I seemed more relaxed, they wished I wasn't leaving!

I guess it came down to transparency. I hadn't been honest with myself about what was wrong, so I wasn't being straight with them either.

If we lack self-knowledge, we cannot speak from a place of integrity and fidelity, so it's hardly surprising that other people would find it hard to work out what we are trying to say. They might well perceive us as inconsistent, unpredictable, evasive and 'hard to get to know'. Conversely, when we stop hiding from ourselves and become more authentic, others are likely to perceive us as being more trustworthy, transparent, approachable . . . and compassionate.

And yet, we keep hiding.

THREE

Our top 20 hiding places

(in alphabetical order)

This chapter shines a light into our favourite hiding places. Some of them (like nostalgia, or busyness, or the pursuit of happiness) might strike you as pretty harmless and 'normal'. Some (like ambition, or perfectionism, or work) are so seductive, so comfortable and so strongly reinforced by other people's approval of us, we scarcely realise we're hiding at all. Others (like fatalism or materialism) might be more deliberately chosen as ways of distracting ourselves from our inner life.

The thing they all have in common is that, once we are ensconced in them, they inhibit the desire for self-examination. Spending too long in hiding increases the risk that we will live a half-life of inauthenticity, never reaching our full potential, and wondering why we feel permanently unsatisfied. Since hiding is really a form of self-imposed captivity, it's like giving up our psychological freedom, including the freedom to live lovingly.

The good news is that, once we become aware of our reasons for hiding and begin to see the harm we are doing to ourselves and our relationships, we can plan our escape.

Addiction

*When habits become addictive, they distract
us from our inner life.*

For a brief but dramatic period in my professional life, I worked
with a man – I'll call him Keith – who had been forced to abandon a
promising academic career because of his addiction to sex. So over-
whelming was his urge, he assessed almost every woman he met as a
potential sexual conquest. His liaisons were shamelessly exploitative,
and there was never any question of monogamy – though four or five
women did persuade him to marry them. His preferred strategy for
removing a live-in partner from his life, once she'd passed her 'use-by
date', was simply to move another woman in and let nature take
its course. (At his funeral, two women approached me separately,
each keen to tell me that she had been 'the one he really loved', each
claiming her secret was never to have had sex with him.)

In his first academic post, Keith set out to seduce the female
students in his class in alphabetical order, his approach being

simplicity itself: your grades will be linked to your sexual compliance. One of the women in his class turned out to be the daughter of the head of the department. When her turn came, she rebuffed Keith's proposition, reported it to her father, and Keith was summarily dismissed.

In the short time I worked with him, I found Keith stimulating, razor-sharp and capable of genuinely original thought. Professionally, he was an inspiring, almost charismatic, figure. But his sex life was too complex for anyone to comprehend.

Keith ultimately returned to academia but that stint was also short-lived. Several years after his death, I met a woman who had been one of his students at that second institution and clearly nothing had changed: she told me Keith had made it clear to her (and presumably to other women in the class) that her grades would depend on her willingness to have sex with him. She declined his invitation, but he was dismissed from that job before her non-compliance could be reflected in her grades.

There were other signs of his addictive tendencies. Years after we worked together, he admitted to me that he had been addicted to alcohol while he was in that job. 'Didn't you realise I was regularly slipping out for a drink?' he asked me, and I had to admit that I hadn't noticed. He once visited me for a weekend, bringing with him a sack of turnips: 'I'm only eating turnips these days,' he said, declining all other offers of food. Later, perhaps sensing his looming demise, he drew up a 'bucket list' that included trying cocaine, and he became addicted to that, too.

The saddest thing about Keith was his glaringly obvious lack of self-knowledge. Though a person of unquestionably high intelligence,

and acute in many of his assessments of others, he remained reso-
lutely incurious about himself, buried deep in his addictions.

What drove those addictions? Sometimes I assumed it was his
desperate need for stimulation of all his senses (though that didn't
explain the turnips). At other times I thought he simply needed
constant distraction. He freely admitted to his short attention span
and to his fear of boredom: lunch breaks at work were always filled
with chess games in the office or visits to the local squash courts.
Now, on reflection, I suspect his perpetual surrender to addiction
was an effective strategy for avoiding the moment of truth when he
might have had to ask: 'Who am I?'

In one respect, Keith reminded me of the character Valmont in *Les
Liaisons dangereuses.* He was not, I think, as manipulative as Valmont:
his yearning for his own sexual gratification was, as far as I could tell,
the only motivation driving his addiction to sex. Yet I could imagine
Keith saying, like Valmont, 'It's beyond my control.' His addictions
really did seem to control him: they certainly left him no time, energy
or inclination to embark on a journey of self-discovery.

Addiction happens when any form of behaviour evolves into a such
a repetitive, compulsive habit that we come to feel as if the feeding
of the habit is essential to our survival, or at least to our sanity. (Ironically, addiction can itself sometimes be seen as a form of insanity.)
In some cases, particularly where substance abuse is involved, addictions may be associated with brain chemistry. Even in the case of
habitual use of IT devices, there may be brain effects associated with
the release of serotonin – sometimes dubbed the 'pleasure hormone' –
that reward our use and encourage addiction.

We are not always conscious of our habits morphing into addiction: 'After a day at work, I need a couple of drinks before I can face cooking dinner for the family' may become 'I need a couple of drinks before I can face anything at all', and then a couple of drinks becomes a couple more. A friend recently told me that his smartphone had drawn his attention to the fact that he was using the device for more than two hours a day. He was shocked not only by that piece of information, but also by having it pointed out to him by the device itself.

Quite apart from all the well-documented negative health consequences associated with addictive consumption of alcohol, that addiction offers a remarkably effective hiding place from the self. *In vino veritas* – 'in wine lies the truth' – has often been used as a justification for excessive alcohol consumption, as if to say: 'I am more truly myself when I've got a few drinks on board; I'm more honest and open; I'm more frank about my innermost thoughts.' If that were true, addicts would awake after a night of heavy drinking with an enhanced clarity of mind, and a sharper sense of their life's meaning and purpose. In fact, amnesia is a more common reaction: 'People tell me I fell over when I was leaving your party – did that really happen?' 'I suspect I might have said some things I shouldn't have last night – if that's the case, I apologise to anyone I might have offended.'

Among non-addicts, moderate alcohol consumption is widely regarded as an effective social lubricant and a harmless tongue-loosener. Even then, it's not uncommon for someone to say, 'I think that's the wine talking,' as if to *distance* themselves from a remark they have just made, rather than welcoming the realisation that they have said something they might not have said without the encouragement of alcohol.

Many self-confessed alcoholics (and especially reformed alcoholics) will say that the addiction is (or was) totally beyond their control; that it's a question of metabolism; that they only feel truly comfortable when they are inebriated, partly because they feel absolved of personal responsibility for their words and actions: 'Don't blame me – I was drunk at the time.'

Even mild consumption of alcohol can create a pleasant sense of euphoria – the famous 'mellow' feeling – and heavier consumption can, of course, induce oblivion, which is sometimes the purpose of the exercise. (Oblivion: how's that for a hiding place?) Just as Keith's addiction to sex smothered questions about *why* he was addicted, so 'problem' drinking relieves us of the need to examine the root of the problem.

Alcohol might never quench the addict's thirst, but it certainly quenches any desire to look deeply inwards: who, after all, would want to claim that their 'authentic being' is characterised by intoxication?

The hazards of addictive smartphone use are well known, ranging from traffic accidents caused by drivers being unable to resist checking their texts, to the potentially negative brain effects among young users. But, as with any addiction, the primary psychological effect is not only to reduce our desire for face-to-face interaction with each other as we become increasingly comfortable inside our personal bubble of ritualised addiction, but also to silence the inner voice of self-examination by keeping us permanently distracted: there's always *something* happening on that little screen.

In his Quarterly Essay *Net Loss*, Sebastian Smee makes a strong argument for the proposition that our addiction to online technology is robbing us of our inner life – that it's becoming a hiding place from the self – and yet, even knowing this, Smee himself confesses to a pattern of use that amounts to an addiction:

> Every day I spend hours and hours on my phone. I have Instagram, Facebook and Twitter accounts. I have three email addresses. I watch soccer highlights, comedy clips, how-to advice and random music videos on YouTube. I download podcasts, which I listen to while driving, and I'm addicted to Waze and Google maps. I do all this, and much more besides, without much thought, just a little lingering anxiety.

Smee claims that his pattern of behaviour has become 'completely normal' – implying that this form of addiction is now socially acceptable – and he confesses that even when he is charging his smartphone, 'it pulses away in my mind, like the throat of a toad, full of blind, amphibian appetite'. Though he uses the word 'addiction' and makes clear that much of his internet surfing is haphazard (another Ibrahimović goal, a shark attack off La Perouse, a Trump tweet), it's unstoppable. Even when he acknowledges that he is revealing information about himself to unknown others, he is less bothered by this than he feels he should be, because the urge to stay online is so powerful.

'Completely normal', as Smee claims? If so, then this addiction may turn out to be among the most damaging of all our addictions in its impact on our inner sense of self. The sheer amount of time now being routinely expended on casual online activity robs us of much of the time we might otherwise spend in useful self-reflection – not to mention face-to-face social interaction.

Dennis's smartphone amputation

It began as a sort of joke. My wife, Sasha, had been threatening to hide my smartphone and had even mentioned it at dinner one night, when I was laying down the law to our two kids about how they shouldn't bring their phones to the table. From now on, I told them, their bedrooms were to be a phone-free zone. I was deadly serious – I'd been reading the research and it was obvious our kids were spending far too much time staring at their phones and tablets. I'd sometimes go into the older one's bedroom to check that she was asleep, and I'd see that tell-tale blue light being shoved back under her pillow.

So I had my little rave and Sasha said: 'Does that go for you, too? Or do I have to hide your phone to get you away from it?'

The kids loved that, of course. Much hooting and hollering. 'Yeah, Mum, hide it! Hide it!'

In bed that night, I ventured the opinion that maybe it was a bit unfair lumping me in with the kids. The big problem, I tried to explain, was with the effect of screens on young, vulnerable brains.

Sasha didn't miss a beat: 'What about the effect of screens on old and vulnerable relationships?'

I put my phone down – I admit I had been scrolling through messages while we were talking – and looked into Sasha's face. There were actual tears rolling down her cheeks. I had no idea we had such a problem over the phone.

'Okay,' I said, 'from now on, no phone in the bedroom for me either. That's a promise.'

I kept that promise, though it was tough, and the way I managed it didn't please Sasha. I simply stayed up later, going through messages and emails, tweets and news sites, and feeling like a complete jerk. For the first time, the term 'addict' came into my head. Was that me?

That went on for a week and then, one Friday morning after we'd had a phone-free breakfast and the kids had left for school, I went to my study where I had the phone on its charger and . . . it wasn't there. I called out to Sasha, but she was already running late for work and, as she gave me a fleeting kiss goodbye, she said: 'It will turn up.'

I knew the kids wouldn't have touched it – that was one rule they did obey – and I suspected Sasha was the guilty party. But I, too, was running late for work and had to leave without it.

What a strange day that was! On my walk to the station I noticed all sorts of things I normally didn't see: people walking their dogs with a leash in one hand and a phone in the other; young people with buds in their ears looking completely disconnected from their surroundings. I waved to a few neighbours, which was unusual, and – this will sound a bit feeble – I noticed that the trees in the little park near the station were turning to autumn colours. I also didn't trip once, walk into any lampposts, or have to apologise to anyone for almost bumping into them.

On the train to the city, my carriage was full of people hunched over their phones. They looked really strange – like a bunch of aliens – and I realised I was usually one of them . . . there, but not there. I glanced at the young woman beside me, contemplating a greeting, but she was both budded and glued. So I simply looked out the window. It was rather lovely, actually. Quite interesting. It felt sort of . . . old-fashioned. Just looking. Just watching. Just reflecting a bit. I thought a lot about Sasha. Sasha and those tears.

The day passed as it usually did – I spent most of my time at my desk, staring at my computer screen and hardly even acknowledging my colleagues until we had our ritual Friday afternoon drink. Even there, I noticed that several of the group were scrolling through their phones, occasionally looking up to acknowledge something someone had said. Someone actually commented on the fact that I didn't have my phone in my hand, as though it was permanently attached to me. I managed to laugh it off.

The trip home was similarly revealing: total silence in the carriage, and virtually everyone gazing at their phone. I missed mine – I had actually considered getting a cheap pre-paid on the way home to tide me over, but decided that would be pretty pointless given that I didn't have my SIM card. I found myself imagining what it must be like for a smoker to give up smoking; for a start, they'd have this spare hand, just like I did. I felt a bit twitchy, to be honest.

Sasha and the kids were in full pre-weekend mode when I got home and Sasha had an expectant look on her face.

'What?' I said.

'Did you cope without your phone? Was it hard? Was it really hard?'

She was smiling – a bit like the smile on the face of a tiger.

We had our phone-free dinner and I got the kids to bring their phones and chargers to my study. Day one of the new regimen!

When they were asleep, tucked up in their newly phoneless rooms, I said to Sasha, 'Okay, where is it?' But she only raised her eyebrows and smiled that enigmatic smile.

I tried to join in the spirit of it, but I was actually getting pretty irritated by this stage. 'Come on, Sash, joke's over. You made your point.'

'Not quite over, Dennis. I'll make a deal with you. If you promise not to say one word about your phone over the weekend – and not to borrow the kids' or mine – I'll give it back to you on Monday morning. If not, I'll keep it for the whole week.'

'You're treating me like a child.'

'Say that again.'

'I said, you're treating me like a child.'

'Say it one more time.'

I finally got it, but I didn't like it.

We watched a bit of TV, went to bed, Sasha read for a while with me lying beside her, struggling to control my withdrawal symptoms. Then we talked late into the night.

The weekend was a painful revelation. I realised, for a start, that Sasha hardly ever uses her phone at home. We still have a landline and she makes and receives most of her calls on that. She never picks up her phone just to fill in time. It pings when she gets a text message, and that's about it. I've told her she could have email on her smartphone and she looks at me as if I must be insane.

We went to watch the kids play sport and, this time, I really watched. I didn't miss any of the things I knew I wasn't supposed to miss. Sash and I talked a lot more than usual, and I even spoke to some of the other parents, most of whom were not clutching their phone. Maybe I had been the odd man out – I wasn't sure.

We went for a couple of long walks and we had people over for drinks on the Sunday afternoon. I checked my emails on my computer only once, for an hour, in preparation for Monday morning.

In bed on Sunday night, I said to Sasha, 'Well?'

She said, 'Well?'

I said, 'Do I qualify for the return of my phone?'

There were more tears and a lot of deep, loving talk about how wonderful it had been to have me so closely in touch with her again. I had felt that too, but I felt something else as well: I felt more like my old self, for better or worse, and less like that jerk who was half living in the digital world. Sasha said she felt as if I had been using the phone to hide from her. That hurt, because I knew there was some truth in it. We had been having a rather tough time – a series of misunderstandings, basically – and I guess I was trying to avoid addressing the problem, because I knew it was me. I don't know about using the phone to hide from her, but I do think I had got into the habit of using the phone as a sort of anaesthetic – I could always escape from any tension, or avoid any conflict, by getting lost in that little screen.

The next morning, Sasha handed me my phone as I was getting ready for work. She wasn't smiling.

'It's up to you from now on. I've done my best.'

I kept the phone in my pocket until I got to the office. I checked a few things on the way home and then went to my study, plugged it in and left it there until morning. I can't say this is easy, but I can say I'm going to stick to the new way. I like myself better as a husband and as a father. We're all talking more. I listen more attentively. I think about things differently, if that makes sense – I think I'm more reflective. I'm not always looking for the next chance to retreat into that bloody phone.

And seeing the effect on Sasha is amazing.

❧

Australia has the highest per capita rate of gambling losses in the world, so we're no strangers to the problem of addiction there, too. And it's a safe bet that when any activity carries a warning in its promotion to 'act responsibly', we are in addiction-risk territory.

Like alcohol and smartphones, gambling is embedded in our culture – from our saturation coverage of poker machines (apart from Monaco, Australia has the highest ratio of poker machines to population in the world) to Melbourne Cup office sweeps and two-up on Anzac Day – which means our culture *encourages* gambling. (If you doubt it, take a look inside your local newsagency.) Which means, in turn, that we live with the ever-present risk of an acceptable social pastime morphing into a habit and then into an addiction and then, whether consciously or not, into a hiding place from the self.

Compulsive gambling, like all addictions, distracts us from anything beyond the gamble: the addictive behaviour itself diminishes our capacity to enquire into the cause of the addiction.

A gambler empties his children's bank accounts

It began harmlessly enough – that's what they all say, isn't it? I'd always routinely bought scratchies from the newsagent – just like buying the paper or a litre of milk every day. Never gave it much thought (and never won anything either, by the way). And if I was looking for something to give people as a little thank-you gift, it would always be a scratchie.

Then I heard about someone who had won big-time, and I decided to get a bit more serious. It wasn't as if we were in any financial strife, but my partner, Bev, had been retrenched and she'd had some trouble finding another job, so it made us realise we were a bit vulnerable, what with our hefty mortgage and everything. And the kids always seemed to need new shoes, or excursion money, or something. So a windfall would've been nice.

So, anyway, I decided to get more scientific. I started by spending $100 each week in one full-on purchase – sometimes I'd buy five twenties, sometimes ten tens, and sometimes a hundred ones. Buying a fistful of scratchies like that really felt like I was a certainty to win *something* – like, surely you up your chances if you buy big like that?

Turns out it doesn't work like that. A mate explained it by saying if you toss a coin, it's a 50–50 chance of heads every single toss, even if you've already landed 10 tails in a row. Anyway, for whatever reason, I didn't win a red cent, and Bev started noticing I was spending a bit more money each week. I didn't tell her what I was spending it on – I just promised to be more careful.

I could see I was being stupid, and scratchies were a really childish way to part with that amount of money every week. So I switched to pokies, still aiming to spend about the same amount as I'd been wasting on the scratchies. I have to admit it was more fun – more exciting – and I did actually start to win a few dollars. So I thought, this is looking good.

You can tell this story isn't going to end well, can't you? I feel like such an idiot, but I couldn't see it at the time. I really did get sucked into it. The machines are cute little buggers and, as I say, every now and then I'd win a few bucks and that would egg me on. I'd notice there were regulars up at the pub, just like me, and one of them said to me one day: 'You realise you can never win, don't you? Not in the long term. We're all mugs.' He wasn't smiling.

Anyway, it got worse and worse, and I still hadn't told Bev what I was doing, but she did occasionally tell me I was going through too much money. She thought I was drinking it away or shouting too many rounds.

It became a habit, I guess. No, that's too soft. It was more like an obsession than a habit – I really couldn't imagine giving it up, and I often had this really strong feeling that I was due for a really, really massive win. Sometimes, I'd actually run to the machines because I was so convinced this was going to be the big one. It was as if I had become another person, with the pokies at the centre of that person's world.

A couple of times, I borrowed money from mates, just so Bev wouldn't notice how much I was going through. Anyhow, long story short, I finally realised that if I was going to improve my odds, I'd need to spend a bit more, and I simply didn't have the ready cash to do that. So I started pawning things I could do without – things that Bev wouldn't notice had gone missing – golf clubs, a spare laptop, stuff like that. I told my brother I was strapped for cash, and he came through with a couple of thousand.

I was struggling to get my hands on enough cash to keep it all together. At one point, I actually asked Bev whether she thought we could manage with one car – I had been thinking that if I could sell mine, I'd be properly cashed up for a while. Bev thought I must be out of my mind – we don't live near public transport and we obviously need two cars. But I was getting desperate.

Then I thought of my kids' bank accounts. Bev and I were both signatories to the accounts, and we'd steadily put money away for the kids over the previous fifteen years or so, and there was a bit of a nest egg there. On this one day when I was absolutely convinced my time had come, I went to the bank, drew out almost all the cash from those two accounts and went off to the pub with a smile on my face. I didn't even feel guilty – in fact, I was totally convinced I'd be putting it all back the next day, plus a bit extra from my big win.

It didn't happen.

What did happen was that I finally realised I'd hit rock bottom and I'd have to confess to Bev what I'd been up to, and what I'd done with the kids' money. I can't describe the look on her face when I told her. She wasn't angry, really; she just sort of crumpled, as if I was the biggest disappointment of her life.

Which I was. I could see that.

Once I told her the whole rotten story, Bev gave me a choice: get treatment for my addiction, or pack up and leave. I'd never thought of it as an addiction – I suppose I had tried to convince myself that it was just a bit of harmless fun. But when she put it like that . . . well, there was no way I was going to leave, so I really had no choice at all.

It's been a long road, and I still haven't paid back all the money into those accounts, but I'll get there. I'm sure I will. My brother occasionally reminds me of that outstanding loan – I think he smells a rat. The worst thing is that I'm not sure Bev will ever really trust me again.

Why did I do it? How did I let it get out of hand like that? The counsellor is helping me to understand all that but, basically, it was a kind of escape. I wasn't facing up to my responsibilities at home or at work, so I became that other person who lived for the big win that would change everything. I became someone else.

Sex, smartphones, alcohol, gambling . . . these might be the most obvious contemporary faces of addiction but, of course, we can become addicted to almost anything: video games (an addiction now being classified internationally as a mental disorder), sugary soft drinks, running, work, travel, religious practices, worry, cars, shoes, handbags, shopping, praise, power, seats on corporate boards, food, fitness, fame . . . the list goes on, and it includes many activities that seem both harmless and respectable in themselves. The sign we might have become addicted is when those activities consume so much of our attention and desire that they eclipse any interest we might have in the state of our inner life.

Ambition

*In our surrender to self-serving ambition, we hide
from the truth about our inadequacies.*

It's hard to criticise ambition. We think of it as being like the rocket
fuel that propels us to run faster, climb higher, go further; the thing
that drives us to test the limits of our abilities; the motivation that
often distinguishes 'successful' people – more power, more wealth,
more status, more fame – from the rest of us.

Of course, we recognise that not everyone who 'makes it' has been
driven by a powerful urge to succeed – some success is a by-product
of ingenuity, skill, devotion to a task, persistence, luck or perhaps an
eccentric capacity to see things the rest of us can't, rather than the
result of any determination to achieve some lofty ambition.

And we certainly acknowledge that many people lead deeply
satisfying lives and enrich the lives of others without behaving like
a heat-seeking missile programmed for personal glory. Indeed, some
of the loveliest and most inspiring people we encounter seem not to

have been motivated by 'success' at all, nor to have aimed for any particular goal, but to have responded to an inner 'calling' that was more about the journey than the destination. (The Chinese philosopher Lao Tzu was not an ambitious, goal-oriented guy: 'A good traveller has no fixed plans, and is not intent on arriving.')

Nevertheless, when we say someone *lacks* ambition, we generally intend that as a criticism. We mean to imply that she could have 'made more of herself' or 'done more with her life'. And when we say people have 'real ambition', aren't we praising their focus, their sense of purpose, their drive, their determination to achieve?

We often talk about ambition as if it's a natural human trait – as if everyone wants to improve their situation; everyone secretly wants to aim for the top; everyone wants to acquire the elevated status associated with success; everyone wants to be promoted. 'Every French soldier has a field marshal's baton in his knapsack,' Napoleon Bonaparte claimed (in which case, there would have been a lot of frustrated French soldiers).

But how 'natural' is ambition? I know many people – as I'm sure you do – who would prefer to go on doing what they are doing because they enjoy it and believe it's a worthwhile thing to be doing, rather than yield to the pressure to be more ambitious and then find themselves doing a job they don't much enjoy. Promotion can easily result in a situation where you are no longer doing the very thing at which you excelled and which led to your promotion. Here are two examples.

Larry was an ambitious advertising copywriter who craved the position of creative director – corner office, car, expense account and all – and was eventually rewarded with the top job. He soon found his creative spark had been extinguished by the burden of administration, and by the constant frustration of feeling he could do a better job than some of the people he was supervising.

Ruth was a social worker who had acquired an enviable reputation for empathy with her clients, and for the number of families she had pulled back from the brink of emotional or financial disaster. However the work was very demanding and poorly paid, so she decided to accept the offer of a promotion to a senior role in the organisation. At first, she relished the higher pay and the easing of the emotional burden on her, but after six months she realised she was no longer a social worker and had lost any sense of connection with the casework that was the organisation's core function. She asked for her old job back and was immediately grateful for her revived sense of purpose. Looking back, she realised that what she needed was a break, not a promotion. Her ambition was to engage with the casework, not to run the organisation.

What will we say of all those schoolteachers who eschew offers of promotion because they love nothing more than being in the classroom with their pupils, nurturing their abilities and watching them flourish? You could say that they lack ambition, or you could say they are highly ambitious, but for their pupils, not for themselves . . . and that brings us to the heart of the matter.

There are many types of ambition, not all of them praiseworthy, and not all of them easy to distinguish from simple, old-fashioned greed: greed for power, greed for recognition, greed for wealth or status or fame. The person who wants to become the factory boss simply for the sake of reaching the top is driven by a very different kind of ambition than the person who can see how things could be done more efficiently, or more productively, or in ways that would benefit more people, and wants a crack at the top job in order to implement some of those ideas.

We often hear of politicians who 'always wanted to be prime minister' – indeed, former senator Amanda Vanstone once said that she'd never known any prime minister who *didn't* aspire to that office from a very early age, implying that a person would need that kind of ambition to keep them driving for the top in a notoriously grubby and competitive trade.

But to what end?

I am writing this on the day Australia learnt of the death of former Labor prime minister and ACTU president Bob Hawke. On all sides of politics, Hawke was being hailed as Australia's greatest Labor prime minister and credited – in partnership with Paul Keating, the most visionary and articulate treasurer in modern Australian political history – with having transformed the economy and many aspects of Australian society: dramatically lifting high school retention rates, urging greater gender equality, floating the dollar, deregulating the banks, removing tariffs, achieving broad consensus between the labour movement and the business community in the famous 'wages accord', and so on. Hawke was immensely popular, and immensely ambitious – but for what? There is no doubt that he was driven by a passionate – even ruthless – personal ambition to succeed and, ultimately, to become prime minister. But, equally, he and Keating were both reformers, and thus were ambitious to implement their ideas. In government, Hawke's aim, like Keating's, was to *achieve* something, rather than merely to *be* something.

As in the case of the factory manager, isn't there a huge contrast between the ego-driven ambition to be prime minister for the sake of being prime minister – the classic 'vanity project' – and the ambition to lead a government that is committed to social reforms, perhaps by eradicating poverty and homelessness, transitioning a country to a clean-energy future or restoring the integrity of public education? In the first case, the mere achievement of the office represents the satisfaction of that (perhaps lifelong) ambition: *I've made it to the top – job done.* In the second case, elevation to the top job would be seen as an opportunity to satisfy all those (perhaps lifelong) ambitions to make the world a better place.

Ambition is a moral minefield. Where it is self-indulgent, it is bound to implode, in the end, for lack of a higher purpose. Where it is directed towards the betterment of society, the risk of self-destruction is less serious, though the potential for power to corrupt always lurks, even among those who initially seek it only as an instrument for doing good.

It's hard to disagree with the suggestion of Plato that ambition for power *for its own sake* should be the very thing that disqualifies people from being granted power, because the power seeker – the person who is constantly plotting their pathway to the top and dreaming of accruing power for its own sake – is the very person most likely to be corrupted by the experience of holding power.

If your ambition is to lead, you might like to ponder another piece of ancient wisdom from Chinese philosopher Lao Tzu: 'A leader is best when people barely know he exists. When his work is done, his aim fulfilled, they will say: we did it ourselves.' (Try telling that to the PR flacks charged with raising the profile and burnishing the image of our political and corporate leaders.)

Seeking high office as a means of gaining the respect of others is a sign of deficient self-respect. Ambition to hold a particular position in order to attract admiration from others is usually an attempt to conceal our frailties and inadequacies not only from those others, but also from ourselves. Any ambition that is ultimately about self-aggrandisement and the inflation of self-esteem is a distraction from self-knowledge and is therefore a hiding place.

Ambition whose purpose is to satisfy the needs of an unfulfilled ego does no one any favours. The person who achieves their yearned-for 'high office' will remain unfulfilled, because that ego-need is too deep to be satisfied by extrinsic honours, rewards, position or praise. And those who agree to elevate such a person to a position that appears to satisfy their ambition are bound to be bitterly disappointed, because their inherent failings and inadequacies will gradually become apparent. 'Feet of clay' indeed: we all have them and pretending we don't is a crazy and ultimately self-defeating form of deception. One of the qualities that endeared Bob Hawke to the Australian people was his willingness – unusual among political leaders – to admit his personal failings.

We humans are full of frailty and we get along better with ourselves and each other when we acknowledge that. Indeed, the encounter with the self is, inevitably, partly an encounter with frailty. When our ambition is an attempt to mask that frailty, or to pretend it isn't there (like those who try to appear invincible, refuse to admit fault or acknowledge failure, or find it impossible to apologise for errors), we are likely to fall prey to pomposity, self-importance and the sense of entitlement. All those things act like barriers between us and others (especially those we regard as inferior) and they are also hiding places from the self because they allow us to deny our true character as social beings, built to be cooperators, communitarians and egalitarians. Nothing makes us more competitive – and less compassionate – than naked, self-serving ambition, and few human qualities are less attractive: 'Watch out for her; she's got her eye on your job.' 'Don't invite him on to the board, he'll only want to be chairman.' 'She's not here to play, she's only here to win.'

There's nothing inherently wrong with ambition. But whenever we feel its surge within us, we would do well to ask ourselves: Am I ambitious for myself, or for the people who will be affected by the realisation of this ambition? Is this ambition just another hiding place, distracting me from an encounter with the loving essence of my being, or is it an expression of that essence?

Anxiety

*If we surrender to our anxieties, self-absorption will
block the path to self-examination.*

Why are we here? What does it all mean? What will happen when
we die?

The existential angst embedded in such questions doesn't
surface very often, partly because, as the British Buddhist writer
Stephen Batchelor puts it, 'anxiety is not simply a moment within
the stream of life, rather it is a fundamental way in which we feel
ourselves to exist'. The German philosopher Martin Heidegger
wrote of anxiety that 'its breath quivers perpetually through
man's being'.

Nowhere to hide from that, you might think. And yet, although
facing our existential anxieties is an important step towards understanding who we are, we are very good at pushing them aside and
diminishing their significance by crowding our minds with lesser
worries. Batchelor remarks that even birth, life and death 'enter

our everyday conversation unacknowledged, mingling inconspicuously with the neighbours, the news and the weather'.

Quite apart from the anxiety that 'quivers perpetually', most of us are plagued by more specific doubts and insecurities, haunted by the inherent fragility and uncertainty of life itself, and forced to confront the looming threat to the very survival of our species on a diseased planet. If you add in the stressors of everyday life, and the anxiety-inducing effects of accelerating social, economic and technological changes, there are more than enough worries to keep us awake at night if we let them.

Anxiety can appear as a vague feeling of restlessness: *I'm worried about something, but I'm not sure what.* Or it can be focused on very specific, immediate concerns: *Will I lose my job? Will I pass this exam? How can we make ends meet this month?* Sometimes it produces recognisable symptoms, like sleep disturbances, weight gain or loss, or palpitations. Sometimes it's associated with feelings of stress – indeed, for many people, stress and anxiety seem inseparable.

Given that anxiety is an integral part of the human condition, what's it doing on a list of hiding places? Most of us find anxiety unpleasant but manageable, and we don't try to hide in it. Some of us experience it as a heavy burden to be borne throughout life, and then only with therapeutic support. But some of us actually embrace it as a kind of war wound, and that's when it gets dangerous. Because anxiety is such a self-absorbed state, it allows us to hide from the deepest truth about ourselves – namely, our capacity (indeed our moral duty as members of a social species) to show compassion to others.

When we are gripped by anxiety, we are less likely to respond to – or even notice – other people's needs. Anxiety can work like a cocoon in which we attend only to our own concerns and, in the process, increase the risk of social isolation, which is why anxiety is such a hazardous hiding place.

The epidemic of anxiety in Western societies is associated with some radical changes in our way of life that have been pushing us in the direction of greater social fragmentation – things like our high rate of relationship breakdown, our shrinking households (every fourth Australian household now contains just one person), more high-density housing (fuelling an antisocial obsession with privacy and security), increasing mobility (in countries like Australia and the US, we move house, on average, once every six years), and our heavy reliance on IT at the expense of personal encounters.

More social fragmentation inevitably increases the risk of social isolation, and social isolation can be both a cause and an effect of anxiety. Because we are a species built for cooperative, communal living, we are naturally made anxious when our sense of connectedness is strained or broken. According to American epidemiologist Kassandra Alcaraz, social isolation is also associated with increased hypertension and inflammation, cognitive decline and deterioration in the immune system. No wonder many health professionals are echoing the alert issued by American psychologist Julianne Holt-Lunstad that social isolation now looms as a bigger public health threat than obesity.

Anxiety disorders – as opposed to the grumbling ever-present variety – have become so prevalent, it's tempting to accept them as a normal feature of modern life. In *First, We Make the Beast Beautiful*, Sarah Wilson documented her own struggle with crippling anxiety and showed how seductive the pressures of contemporary urban exist-ence can be. She produced a long list of stressors that increased her anxiety – such as 'working on the fly from laptops', weaving in and out of traffic, eating on the run, keeping up with technology updates, doing online grocery shopping on her lunch break – and then made an astonishing confession. Knowing that such things heightened her anxiety, she nevertheless reported that she was 'arrogantly attached to many of the factors that make me anxious – the speed, the multi-tasking, the constant change'. The very things that induced anxiety became her habits of daily life, which suggested she had allowed anxiety itself to become a habit.

It's too simplistic to try to separate 'clinical' anxiety – anxiety as a disorder requiring professional treatment – from the *habit* of anxiety, but the normalisation of anxiety in contemporary society bears a striking resemblance to the way we normalise many of our addictions. Once we get into the habit of anxiety – even ritualising it – it's easy to lose sight of the fact that we are on a pathway to self-absorption, with the attendant risk of social isolation.

Some anxiety sufferers think that being emotionally contained is the way to conceal their habit. In *Happy Never After*, Jill Stark describes how her anxiety had such a socially and emotionally inhib-iting effect that she was unable to display sympathy even towards friends who had suffered bereavement. 'In a culture that's distinctly uncomfortable with pain,' she writes, 'this was a safe position.' Others believe that keeping to themselves is the best way to deal with anxiety, as if contact with other people induces it.

In fact, the reverse is true. Interacting with other people and responding to their needs is an effective antidote to anxiety, simply because it takes the focus away from the self, breaks the cycle of self-absorption/social isolation, and allows compassion to flow.

Amy becomes an honorary aunt

I guess I have always been an anxious person. Even when I was a child, my mother used to describe me as her little worry-wart and it was true – I was always imagining the worst. As I grew older, I learnt the word 'catastrophise' and that described me perfectly. I worried constantly about what might happen, and if anything even slightly unusual occurred – like if someone was late for an appointment – I would always assume something dreadful had happened.

It affected my love-life, naturally. I think men just found the worrying too heavy-duty. I became known in my group as 'Anxious Amy'; it was said affectionately, but it made me realise that my anxiety was a bit of a barrier between me and everyone else. It wasn't as if I'd inherited this from my own mum – she was so laid-back that this used to worry me, too, as if she wasn't being careful enough, or considerate enough of my feelings. I sometimes wondered if she was being deliberately reckless just to try to jolt me out of it.

I tried counselling at one stage. It was quite helpful and the therapist suggested that part of the problem was that I'd got into the habit of being anxious and it was acting like a self-protective shell. At first I thought that was a weird idea – what was I supposed to be protecting myself from? – but then I began to see how it could be true. I realised my anxiety was making me pretty self-absorbed. She encouraged me to take up meditation, but that only seemed to make it worse.

Anyway, I did eventually move in with somebody, but it was short-lived. I thought he would be good for me – he was rather laid-back, like Mum – but it actually got me down. And my constant worrying got him down. Plus, things like me never being satisfied with the first room we were given in a hotel if we went away somewhere. I was always worried about some aspect of it, and I always needed to be on the lowest possible floor and near a fire escape. Flying was impossible for me – I was just too anxious to get on a plane. If you have to learn the brace position before the journey starts, that's a journey I don't want to go on.

I knew I was a bit hopeless, even though some of the things I was anxious about were perfectly rational, I thought – like climate change, or whether I'd remembered to lock the front door when we went out. I often made him go back to check. But in the end, he couldn't hack it. We agreed to go our separate ways, and the last thing he said to me really floored me. He told me I was too selfish to live with anyone. Too selfish! Maybe that's how an anxious person appears to other people.

It was a relief to be back on my own, to be frank, and I stayed in the house we had been renting. I'm still there, still renting. I'd be too anxious to commit to a mortgage as you never know what might happen down the track – I might lose my job, interest rates might go up again. But once I was on my own, I felt more settled. I mean, my anxiety doesn't worry me.

Anyway, a funny thing has happened. When I had a partner, we were both so busy, I hardly paid any attention to the family next door, except to notice they were Asian. But soon after my partner left, the husband was killed in some type of industrial accident and the wife, Yi-an, was left with three kids under the age of ten. I discovered they were from Taiwan and after we started talking to each other a bit, I realised Yi-an was in a really difficult situation. She had no other family in Australia and her English wasn't that good. She had a part-time job, and she received some sort of insurance pension from the company where her husband had worked, but money was obviously very tight.

Gradually, we grew closer, and I started helping her out with the kids – minding them on weekends so she could go to the hairdresser or do a bit of shopping. I encouraged her to start going to the English conversation class at the local library on Tuesday nights, so that became a regular babysitting night for me. And I go next door some evenings just to help her with dinner and bedtime – I can see what a struggle it is for her. I had never wanted kids myself, but I've become really attached to those three little boys.

The thing is, I never feel anxious when I'm over there helping out. Even when I've taken the kids out to the park or to a movie – to give their mother some respite – I'm so focused on the responsibility, I guess my own worries melt away. And I also realise other people have got a lot more to worry about than I have.

The real test was a few weeks ago when Yi-an had to go to hospital for three days and I took time off work and moved in next door to look after the boys. That was pretty challenging, but there was so much to do, I think I must have forgotten to feel anxious! It was all rather chaotic, and the youngest is a bit of a terror, but I felt a real sense of . . . I think you'd almost say peace, especially when I got them all off to sleep at night.

I think 'Anxious Amy' might be fading, though she's not gone entirely. The boys have started calling me Ant Army – it began as Aunt Amy until the eldest one tweaked it, and Ant Army caught on. I rather like it. The connection with that family has given me a real sense of being needed. I haven't felt that before. I've also never laughed as much as I do when I'm with those boys.

~

Nothing brings us out of hiding like the knowledge that someone else needs us. In *First, We Make the Beast Beautiful*, Sarah Wilson acknowledged that at times in her life when the focus shifted from her own concerns to, in one case, the welfare of her unborn baby and, in another, an elderly woman who needed Sarah's help, her anxiety was either relieved or simply became irrelevant.

Compassion is the balm we need not only to relieve others' distress, but to relieve our own anxiety as well. That is the wonderful paradox of compassion: its focus is on the needs of others, but it brings therapeutic benefits to the one who is exercising it. (Remember that compassion in this sense is not an emotional state, but a mental discipline that commits us to treating other people kindly and respectfully, regardless of how we might *feel* about them.)

There are many examples of people who become so attached to a disorder or an illness that they embrace it as part of who they are and cling to it as to a friend or, at least, a reliable companion. In the same way, some of us cling to the habit of anxiety as a way of avoiding a confrontation with the self. And yet, as both Amy and Sarah have shown us, when we allow our natural compassion to flow freely, our anxieties recede.

Consciously developing the habit of compassion will release us from the trap of self-absorption. That won't only bring us closer to those who need our support; it will also put us more closely in touch with our own authentic self. When we allow anxiety to become a hiding place, the thing we're most likely to be hiding from is our own capacity for love and kindness.

Arrogance

Cocooned by cockiness, we hide from our fear
of our own inauthenticity.

You know the type: hyper-inflated self-esteem; so certain of the rightness of their opinions that they question the intelligence, if not the sanity, of dissenters; supremely confident in the superiority of their view of the world and their place in it.

They often exude a rather cranky, irritated, short-tempered air, as if they can hardly be bothered to put up with the incompetence or the foolishness of the rest of us. They refer dismissively to those they regard as being beneath their own level of refinement or sophistication as 'bogans' or 'riffraff'. Their use of such pejorative labels fuels the pleasing sense of their own superiority which, in turn, encourages them to spread their scorn more widely, perhaps even to include unintelligent, culturally deprived or otherwise disadvantaged and marginalised people.

The ugly sense of superiority that festers in an arrogant person seeps into the psyche like an infection, creating feelings of self-importance and entitlement to whatever they want – whether grabbing a convenient but illegal parking spot, or pushing their way to the front of a queue, or needing to win every argument.

Arrogance is an attitude of disdain for others that sometimes borders on contempt. If you're a driver, you'll have observed it in the smug saunter of a person using a pedestrian crossing at a slower-than-normal walking pace, as if to say: 'I'm a protected species – you can just wait.' If you're a supermarket shopper, you'll have encountered it at the '12 items or less' express checkout, when someone with a basket bulging with groceries rolls up to be served, shooting a contemptuous 'so what?' glance at the irritated shoppers behind them in the queue. If you're a student, you might have seen it in the person who goes to the library, grabs a book recommended for an assignment, and hides it somewhere else on the shelves so no one else doing the same assignment will be able to find it.

Sometimes, arrogance is associated with status, wealth or power – and, to be fair, it must be hard to retain a healthy humility if your job means you are treated with too much deference: the phenomenon of the god-doctor, the god-professor or the god-therapist is not unknown among people who are used to dispensing wisdom and being looked up to as the keepers of arcane knowledge. If other people treat you as if you *are* superior, resisting the temptation to agree with them requires some strength of character, especially if you are routinely identified on public occasions as a VIP or even a VVIP. (I heard of one VIP who had been sent free tickets to a concert but then wrote a letter of complaint because she was not greeted by someone 'official' on her arrival at the venue.)

Arrogance is about the refusal to accept that, in our essence, we share a common humanity; that we are all indivisibly interconnected;

that we are indeed born equal; that many of our apparent strengths and weaknesses – our accomplishments and triumphs, our shortcomings and failures – are at least partly the result of genetic accidents or other forms of luck. The only appropriate response to the plight of people mired in poverty, disadvantage or marginalisation – 'There but for the grace of God go I' – is a response that calls on the kind of empathy inaccessible to the person hiding under a cloak of arrogance.

So, you may ask, is this all about an excess of self-confidence, and isn't self-confidence, up to a point, a good thing? In fact, arrogance, or cockiness, can safely be interpreted as signalling a *lack* of confidence. Arrogant people are declaring by their arrogance that they have not yet embarked on the all-important journey of self-examination – or, if they have, they haven't got far along the way.

How can we be so sure of that? Simple. Anyone who has had any significant confrontation with the self has discovered why humility is often described as 'the queen of virtues': once we encounter our authentic being, shadows and all, we also encounter our essential humanity. And that is a meeting which could never lead to arrogance. It may well induce a new determination to live a more compassionate life. It may generate a new appreciation of the capacity we have for goodness (while also alerting us to our capacity for badness). It may well stiffen our resolve to do something worthwhile with our life. But it could never, *never* lead us to conclude that we are superior to others. Arrogance can never be justified by that kind of comparison: it can only be embraced blindly, in wilful ignorance of what it means to be human.

*

The recent fashion for ramping up everyone's self-esteem may turn out to have been an influential factor in encouraging a culture of arrogance. Low self-esteem is obviously a problem that needs attention and, in some extreme cases, professional therapy. But the idea that we are all supposed to experience high levels of self-esteem has driven the obsession with self-confidence, praise and rewards in children from their earliest years.

The damage done by the 'gold stars for breathing; prizes for showing up' culture is incalculable. It feeds children the idea that we should do things to get a reward rather than because the thing is intrinsically worth doing. It creates the expectation of praise and recognition, whether deserved or not. And it has bred a generation of parents preoccupied with their children's self-esteem as if this were an index of their own success as parents.

The sad truth is that an overemphasis on self-esteem is likely to contribute to feelings of disappointment and confusion as children grow through adolescence and into adulthood. Eventually, they must make the painful discovery that not everything they do will be praised, that not everyone will share their exalted view of their own magnificence, and that it is simply an unrealistic goal to 'make every post a winner'.

Social psychologist Roy Baumeister, formerly of Florida State University and now at the University of Queensland, is one of the leaders of the positive psychology movement. For many years, Baumeister's research pursued the hypothesis that self-esteem might be 'a powerful key to mental health and successful behaviour'. But, as his research proceeded, he came to the realisation that it is self-control, not self-esteem, that offers us the key to a satisfying life.

He now describes self-control as the 'moral muscle' we need to restrain our impulses towards self-indulgence. In the same vein, Martin Seligman's research has found that self-discipline, not self-esteem, is a reliable predictor of success in secondary school.

If there is too much focus on self-esteem, an excess of self-absorption is the likely result. And self-absorption, in turn, diminishes our awareness of our dependence on a community to nurture and sustain us. That encourages individualism which, in turn, increases the risk of arrogance. In other words, an unhealthy emphasis on self-esteem is likely to slow the process of coming to terms with who we really are.

Narcissism – that sometimes pathological, socially isolating condition that leads people to fall in love with their own reflection, as in the Greek myth of Narcissus – is easy to confuse with arrogance, since narcissists regard other people as mere ciphers whose only legitimate role is to supply uncritical admiration. The narcissistic personality is an extreme example of the paradox of arrogance: on the one hand, arrogant people seem to be so preoccupied with themselves – their own ambition, their own 'wins', their own status, the nurturing of their own vanity – that you might imagine all that focus on the self would generate some level of self-awareness. Yet their deep insecurity doesn't permit self-examination, lest their frailties be exposed. (I should add that there's a bit of the narcissist in all of us – a modicum of self-love is consistent with a healthy self-respect, but when it breaks out into a full-blown pathology, it becomes a dangerously seductive hiding place from the self.)

If you believe that you belong to a superior subspecies of human, you'll naturally develop a worldview that supports your elitism:

you will come to see other people in terms of their worthiness or unworthiness to be ranked equally with you, or even to be taken as seriously as you believe you are entitled to be taken. 'They are a lower form of life, simple as that.' 'She's from the shallow end of the gene pool.' 'It's ridiculous that their vote carries as much weight as mine' . . . such expressions of arrogance are typical of the ways this hiding place is reinforced.

Reflecting on the culture of corporate Australia, Rod Sims, the chair of the Australian Competition and Consumer Commission, told the *Australian Financial Review* in January 2019 that 'there's an element of arrogance . . . that they are in a privileged position and they can do as they like in an almost unfettered way'.

To employ the vernacular, arrogant people are 'up themselves', and while that might be an effective hiding place, it's a notoriously poor vantage point from which to view the state of your soul.

You think you're *entitled* to your good fortune? That's merely your resistance to the idea that we are all, to some extent, shaped by the luck of the draw – genetic and otherwise. You think there are always 'winners and losers' in any society, and nothing can be done about it? That's merely a defence against compassion for the less fortunate. You think the top of the heap is where you naturally belong? Beware of the resentments festering among those beneath you.

You *could* go through life clinging to the cloak of arrogance, but you might be in for a shock: the increasing vehemence of your prejudices against other, 'lesser' beings might one day strike you as being a symptom of something wrong with you rather than them (see 'Projection', later in this chapter). You may also eventually experience the deep discomfort and confusion, sometimes amounting to psychological pain, that comes from realising that, as Robert Berezin put it, 'our deepest self is not encompassed by our ordinary sense of self'. If Berezin is right that 'every person feels the presence of their hidden Authentic Being one way or another', then even our arrogance will ultimately be challenged by some deep and searching questions about who we *really* are.

Kim is accused of 'natural arrogance'

I cringe now when I think of how I used to be – well, how I have been for most of my life, to be honest. My partner and I both had a pretty privileged upbringing – the right schools, a top university, secure and well-paid jobs right from the start – and we had parents who supported us every inch of the way, including financially. You could say we were a pretty successful couple, in conventional terms.

Yet both of us ran into the same kind of trouble at work. At various times, we were both called in for 'counselling' about our behaviour towards other members of staff, especially juniors or people in support positions – IT staff, interns, drivers, cleaners, people at that sort of level. Looking back, we were pretty arrogant. *Bloody* arrogant, I suppose. But we weren't admitting that to ourselves, nor to each other, nor to anyone else.

In fact, quite the reverse. We had a great laugh over how hopeless those HR counsellors were. All that touchy-feely stuff – that wasn't for us. I remember thinking the woman who counselled me was a real bogan, and so I simply wrote her off. I wasn't going to take advice, let alone correction, from someone who obviously wasn't as smart as me and who didn't even appear to understand some of the language I was using – she kept asking me to explain what I meant. At one point,

I remember, she said I had something of a reputation for 'not suffer-ing fools gladly'. I took that as a compliment, which didn't go down particularly well. But in fact it was a matter of pride with my partner and me that we wouldn't suffer fools gladly. Why should we? Life's too short, right?

We regarded ourselves as total realists, total pragmatists, utilitar-ians, totally unsentimental. Our friends were the same. We all furiously reinforced each other's prejudices. We all thought we were terrific. Like a sort of golden circle. In many ways, we *were* terrific, but we were inflating each other's egos like balloons, so you can imagine where that was heading.

There were tensions within my family. Neither of my brothers thought we were as terrific as we did. And one of our daughters pulled us up one day for saying something she thought was unkind about a woman in a shop who had done something really stupid. Our own daughter! We explained to her that it's not unkind to describe someone as really stupid if they *do* something really stupid.

When that same daughter went into secondary school, she found religion, much to our disgust – that was the risk, I guess, of sending her to a Catholic school. She became very pious for a while – she even reckoned she was going to become a nun – and it was hard to figure out how to handle it without putting her down. She got over it, but I think that was when we began to realise that she was possibly a nicer person than we were.

Then I had a couple of setbacks. A promotion at work I had thought was a certainty was offered to someone else. With as much restraint as I could muster, I asked for a review of the process, and I was 'counselled' all over again, but this time the HR person was a bit more sophisticated and also a bit more direct. He made it clear to me that I would never rise any higher in the organisation if I didn't curb what he called my 'natural arrogance'. Natural arrogance! Wow.

While I was still processing the implications of that and wondering if I needed to apply for a job somewhere else – or even strike out on my own, which I'd been threatening to do for years – my mother died very suddenly from pancreatic cancer. It was a very traumatic period for us all and, after a bit of to-ing and fro-ing, it was decided that Dad should come to live with us. Boy, did that require some adjustment. Our previously pious daughter handled it beautifully, bless her, but I'm afraid I had trouble concealing the fact that I regarded it as a real intrusion into our well-ordered lives. Dad was showing the early signs of dementia by then, so we were having to find reserves of patience we didn't know we had. I'm ashamed to admit I resented his presence a lot of the time.

I knew I wasn't coping well. I had become crankier at home and more intransigent at work. Eventually, at my partner's urging, I went to see the HR person and asked if he could refer me to a psychologist.

So that process has begun and it's been pretty painful, so far. We've started working through a lot of history and confronted some distressing things about Mum and me, in particular. My brothers and I had always accused her of having a superiority complex and now I was facing the same thing in myself. It's pretty excruciating – humiliating, actually – to think that this might have created the chasm between me and my brothers, and to imagine them discussing me in the same way we used to talk about Mum.

One of our daughters – the saintly one – knows I am having a hard time. She just comes and sits with me and holds my hand, saying nothing.

It's like lying on a warm rock in the sun. How did she get to be so wise at such a young age? Intuitive, maybe, rather than wise.

Dad is still a great trial, but I'm working on that. It's not his fault, after all. And work? The person who got the promotion I wanted is doing a great job, I have to admit. Also, I am beginning to see why my colleagues are so wary around me, and I do feel a bit uncomfortable around them now, to be honest. I feel as if they must have spent years talking about what an arrogant so-and-so I am. I've decided to apply for a job in another firm if anything suitable comes up. It would be quite nice to arrive in a new place where people hadn't already made up their minds about me.

Can I change? Do I want to change? It's a work in progress. The therapist says we're still clearing the decks before the real work starts. Wow. As for suffering fools gladly, well, no one wants to be a fool, do they? No one *tries* to be a fool. The therapist planted that useful insight in my head.

Busyness

Staying on the treadmill means we avoid pausing long enough to face the truth about why we're running so hard.

We appear to have elevated busyness to the status of a social virtue, a badge to be worn with pride, as if being busy is the mark of the fully 'alive' person; as if the switch can only be on or off: you're busy or you're dead – or you're so useless, you might as well be dead. I exaggerate, but not by much: just watch how often proud claims of busyness are incorporated into our conversations, sometimes disguised as a complaint.

We allow our annual leave entitlements, instituted to protect our physical and mental health, to bank up in favour of fragmented and compressed 'short breaks'. The pleasures of walking or running in the open air – wind or rain in your face, birds singing, flowers blooming, leaves falling, neighbours waving – are sacrificed in favour of a concentrated burst on the treadmill at the gym. The therapeutic joy of aimlessness and the ability to relax into 'spare time' have been overwhelmed by the need for everything we do to be productive and even our leisure to be purposeful.

A sane person would regard excessive and sustained busyness as a health hazard, and not only because it contributes to our epidemics of stress and anxiety, and distracts us from the need to nurture our relationships with family, friends, colleagues and neighbours. It's also a health hazard because it robs us of sanity-restoring time for reflection on our inner life, and may even dull our awareness of the need for regular encounters with the self.

No time to read? No time to walk? No time to play? No time to nurture a neglected relationship over a cup of coffee? Surely there's something awry in a life like that, yet too many of us are inhabiting a mad world where *not* to be seen as busy is an admission of failure, and where the most dangerous propaganda of all – *time is money* – can convince you that you can't really afford to spend 'unproductive' time with friends, let alone find time for simple pleasures.

∾

Emmélie redefines 'time is money'

Theo, a corporate lawyer, is sitting at the dining table after a late meal with his wife, Emmélie. Board papers sit in a pile on the table in front of him, and he has just finished a phone call to a colleague, unaware of the look of exasperation on Emmélie's face. As he reaches for the folder on top of the pile, Emmélie says, as calmly as she can: 'Do you recall how you greeted that person on the phone just now?'

'It was only a colleague. We were tying up a couple of loose ends from a meeting.'

'I don't care who it was, or what you were tying or untying. I asked you how you greeted whoever was on the phone. Do you remember what you said?'

'No idea. I suppose I said "How are you going?" or "G'day". That's what I usually say. What is your point exactly?'

'Think back – what did you say?'

'"Good evening", perhaps?'

'Ha. If only. How civilised that would have been!'

'Come off it, Em. What's this about?'

'You said: "How are you going – *busy?*"'

'I don't recall.'

'Actually, Theo, I don't even *need* to recall. That's what you *always* say when you greet people these days – on or off the phone. As if the only thing you're interested in is whether they're busy. And all you ever seem to talk about on the phone, except when you're actually discussing your work, is how busy you are.'

'I don't think that's –'

'Listen to me, Theo. That's what you *always* say. Even my mother complains that if you happen to answer the phone and she asks how you are, you always say, "Oh, keeping busy." As if that's what she wants to know. Not some news of what we've actually being doing. Not some charming snippet about the kids. Not even a health report. Oh, no – the main thing is that you're finding things to keep you busy, as if that's your goal in life.'

'Well, I *am* busy. We're both busy. In fact, I suspect you're actually busier than I am, what with your job and the kids, and –'

'Oh, you *suspect* that, do you? You couldn't be sure, of course, and I'll tell you why. It's because you're always so busy you have no idea what's going on around you in your very own home.'

'That's not fair. I know the kids are often in bed when I get home, but our weekends –'

'*Our* weekends? When was the last time we had anything that could be described as *our* weekend? Oh, I know you go to the kids' soccer sometimes and you usually manage to find some bloke to talk to who's as busy as you are, so you can swap war stories. Last Saturday was a classic. You disappeared back to the office straight after Joey's game, and reappeared at 9 o'clock, having completely forgotten my parents were coming for dinner.'

'We've been through this, Em. Actually, I wasn't at the office – I had an important meeting with some members of the committee at the surf club. You should have called me.'

'No, Theo, I shouldn't have called you. You should have been here. But, no, you were too busy – again.'

Emmélie paused, breathing hard. For a moment, she considered getting up and leaving Theo to his papers. But then she straightened her shoulders and said: 'I haven't told you what Joey said when I put him to bed last Sunday night.'

'I'm sure you're going to tell me.'

'He said, "Will Daddy be here again next weekend?" I didn't tell you at the time because it nearly broke my heart. As if you live apart from us during the week. As if we're separated, and you pop in for child access on weekends.'

'That's ridiculous.'

'Is it? Oh, we all remember the time Joey went to school camp and you didn't even realise he'd been away until he arrived home. We tried to treat it as a family joke, but Joey wasn't amused. Maybe you need to take a look at yourself through the children's eyes.'

'I admit I'm going through a particularly busy period at present–'

'*At present?* When was the last time you took me out to a concert? Or dinner? Or for a weekend away on our own? My parents have offered to mind the kids whenever we want to go away.'

'Time is money, Em. These are precious hours I'm putting in, and I notice you don't mind the rewards.'

'Ah, I was hoping you'd say that. Again. *Time is money!* I'll tell you what that means to me. Are you interested? For me, in this marriage, in this family, in this *life* we are supposed to be sharing, time is even more important than money. If you really believed that time is like money, you'd realise how valuable our time together could be. You'd realise that the time you spend *making money* is actually impoverishing our life. *Our life*, Theo.'

'I know I should be spending more time at home–'

'Stop right there. It isn't *time at home* if you're always too busy to just *be* when you're at home. Like now. Look at you. This isn't "time at home". This is you going right on working, just in a different place – probably slightly less comfortable and convenient than your office.'

'Em, I –'

'Theo, this is totally up to you. I assume you're always busy because you want to be busy. You love being busy. It's not just work, it's all your wretched boards and committees and things. To say nothing of your addiction to texts and emails. Anything to avoid actual connection with me and the children. Who are you hiding from, Theo? Us, or yourself?'

'That's crazy talk, Em. Crazy talk.'

'Is it? Please remember that as far as your family is concerned, time *is* just like money. Just as precious. I don't want you to spend any more money on me and the kids, but I would like you to start spending more time on us. Simple as that. Next time I hear you bragging about how busy you are, I will remind myself that you're free to choose how you spend your time in precisely the same way as you're free to choose how you spend your money. Which means that, for whatever reason, you actually *want* to be this busy.'

In the contemporary culture of busyness, it's easy to hide from each other: busyness can insulate you from social encounters you'd prefer to avoid; from dealing with unresolved issues in a marriage or other relationship; from spending aimless time with your kids – the kind of down time in which strong bonding is most likely to occur. Busyness is also the enemy of social cohesion, acting like a barrier between us and those who might need our attention, engagement or support. Doesn't it strike us as tragic whenever we hear about cases of people who are not only too busy to offer help to others in need, but too busy even to notice that help is needed – never realising, for example, that a next-door neighbour hasn't appeared for a few days and might be in trouble?

But it's also easy to hide from yourself behind the mask of busyness. If we keep busy enough, there'll be no time for reflection; no time for daydreaming, drifting, or examining the state of our inner life. Some of us are too busy even to notice our own stress levels rising. In such ways, busyness distracts us from the care of our own soul.

Dr Fiona Kerr, Australian neuroscientist and founder of the NeuroTech Institute, has written and spoken about the value of meditation and abstraction as antidotes to the destructive effects of being permanently distracted. (By 'abstraction' she means those broader reflections that take us beyond specific moments or events.) She has observed that meditation produces 'lovely chemicals' that foster feelings of worth and belonging, while abstraction 'allows a quiet mind to inwardly reflect, process and sit with ourselves until we become accepting of who we are'. As Kerr remarks, 'distraction stops abstraction', and there is no easier form of distraction than keeping yourself busy.

Kerr reports that people of all ages have admitted to her that they distract themselves because they don't *want* to reflect – as we noted in chapter two, people often resist the idea of the inward journey for fear they mightn't like what they find. Perhaps busyness, then, is not only one of the easiest of all the hiding places to adopt, it might also be one of the most deliberate and conscious ways of hiding from ourselves.

'Don't disturb Mummy – she's busy.' Yes, but *why*? Is her busyness a reflection of her true priorities, or is it a form of self-defence? And, if so, defence from what?

'Now I'm retired, I don't know how I ever found the time to go to work.' Yes, but *why*? What is it about spare time – down time – that frightens you?

'We're so busy at work, I'm constantly bringing stuff home.' Yes, but *why*?

There are some awkward questions about excessive busyness we'd probably prefer to avoid asking ourselves and each other: Are we so busy because we're inefficient? Are we perhaps hogging work that should be being distributed more equitably? (The overtime worked by the fully employed at the expense of the under- or unemployed is one of the scandals of the labour market – all in the name of increased productivity and profit, of course.)

Most particularly, we carefully avoid raising the obvious question: Am I keeping myself so busy as a way of hiding from something I don't want to face? One clue that this might the case can be found in the number of times we declare that we are going to slow down (but don't), or make promises to ourselves and our families about the 'proper holiday' we'll have, one day. (Promises, promises.)

The culture of busyness has us so firmly in its grip, we rarely pause to reflect on why we keep running so hard. To borrow T.S. Eliot's question: 'Where is the Life we have lost in living?' Are we, perhaps, sacrificing too much of the quality of our life – even risking our own integrity – by going too hard at the living?

Complacency/Certainty

The warm bath of certainty lulls us into the confidence
of believing that everything can go on as it is.

Complacency is a very comfortable hiding place: it blurs our vision and absolves us of the need to question anything much, including our prejudices and the potentially yawning gap between our social identity and our private self.

Complacency can be a by-product of arrogance, but it can equally be a by-product of ignorance, ranging from ignorance of the issues swirling around us – environmental, political, social, cultural, personal – to ignorance of our authentic self. Whether wilful or not, ignorance can be such a blissful state (literally a 'fool's paradise'), that we are understandably reluctant to emerge from the complacency it engenders, especially if we think we might have to *do something* or, worse, face an uncomfortable encounter with the self that might create an obligation to respond to the needs of other people.

But complacency is at its most dangerous – and its most comfortable – when it is a by-product of certainty.

Ah, certainty. If only. Is *anything* certain?

Is it certain that the sun will come up tomorrow morning? Highly likely, but not certain, and by no means is it certain that, if it does, you'll be around to see it, since life itself is uncertain.

Is it certain that your partner – if you have one – will stick with you until you are parted by death? Confident declarations notwithstanding, unexpected splits occur; people in committed relationships fall in love with someone else and seem powerless to control their feelings; boredom sets in and you drift apart, possibly to your mutual relief. Stable lifelong partnerships are far from unusual, but they are never certain.

Is it certain that your children, if you have any, will outlive you? Tragically, no.

Is it certain that you'll keep the job you have? Or get the job you want? Or find work in the field you've trained for? No – job insecurity has become an inherent feature of the modern workplace, and with artificial intelligence looming ever larger in our lives, many jobs that now exist will one day (perhaps sooner than we imagine) be taken over by a machine.

Is it certain that your superannuation will be enough to live on for as long as you survive? Good luck working that one out.

Is it certain that our species will survive? Obviously not, especially given the accelerating rate of species extinction on our planet, and the dire predictions about what will happen to human existence if we are unwilling or unable to address the challenges of climate change with sufficient urgency. Will humans survive to the end of the century? Uncertain. Unlikely.

Most of the things we'd like to be certain about are elusive. Why are we here? What happens when we die? Why do some people have such bad luck and others such a dream run? What will become of me?

Even people with strong religious faith will admit to doubt, and why wouldn't they? Doubt is the very engine of faith. Doubt is the oxygen to faith's flickering candle. If we *knew*, there would be no need for faith. Faith is the work of the imagination; a creative act; a leap; a reaching out for certainties that keep eluding us.

Even in the realm of science, what's certain? According to astronomer Brian Schmidt, vice-chancellor of the Australian National University and co-winner of the 2011 Nobel Prize in Physics, scientific theories should be regarded as predictions, because much of what we regard as scientific knowledge is mere hypothesis. As the British philosopher and mathematician Bertrand Russell put it 75 years earlier: 'Science is always tentative, expecting that modification in its present theories will sooner or later be found necessary, and aware that its method is one which is logically incapable of arriving at a complete and final demonstration.' No hint of complacency there.

Not only do the facts change, but our understanding and interpretation of their significance also changes. In science, as in all human activity, the viewer is part of the view: a fresh pair of eyes can often see something new in old data.

If certainty is largely unavailable to us, that means learning to live with doubt is one of the great human challenges. Uncertainty, insecurity, unpredictability: that's the great trinity of truths about human existence. And each of those truths is an enemy of complacency.

Given all that, is it any wonder that some of us – let's face it, *most* of us – crave certainty so badly that we choose to live as if some things *are* certain, so we can sink into the warm bath of complacency and cross this or that item off the list of things to worry about.

At one level, that's perfectly rational: we have to assume certainty about the bus arriving to take us to work, and the workplace still being there when we reach it, just as we may choose to live as if our relationships are permanent and stable, partly so we won't go out of our minds with constant worry about 'what if . . .?'.

At another level, it means that we learn to live very comfortably in a state of denial, since certainty entails denial – except the certainty of death, though, astonishingly, many of us choose to live in a state of denial about even that.

Pretending to be certain – or assuming a high probability of something being true, or that something is going to happen – is very close to what we normally mean by 'belief'. Choosing to act as if something is certain is tantamount to saying, 'I believe in it,' or, 'I believe it is so likely to happen – or so likely to be true – I will live as if it *is* true.'

We do that all the time, of course, without a backward glance. Operationally, belief, like hope, can easily feel like certainty. If pressed, we might concede that it's all based on assumptions and probabilities, or faith, but our sanity depends on treating some of these beliefs *as if* they are certainties. Nevertheless, they are not the same thing and thoughtlessly confusing them opens a Pandora's box of misconceptions, delusions and deceptions.

Show me the person who is utterly certain of their position on God, the afterlife, politics, the pre-eminence of science in human

107

knowledge, their rights and privileges, or any other matter on which opinions and beliefs can easily morph into certainty, and I'll show you a person in denial and at risk of complacency.

Show me the person whose self-righteousness is blinding them to their own frailties and inadequacies, and I'll show you a person about to slip effortlessly into the languid waters of complacency. Once immersed, they will soon drift beyond reach of the urge for self-reflection, since certainty is the handmaiden of inauthenticity.

Doubt, by contrast, is the hallmark of authenticity and is therefore another of the enemies of complacency. Doubt would have to count as a virtue, since it preserves our humility, whereas certainty ranks self-satisfaction above self-knowledge. Next stop: hubris.

Alfred, Lord Tennyson put it rather well in his poem 'The Ancient Sage':

For nothing worthy proving can be proven,
Nor yet disproven: wherefore thou be wise,
Cleave ever to the sunnier side of doubt.

A tale of two grandfathers

My mother's maiden name was Brown and she married a Green, so when I was growing up, there were endless family jokes about the greening of Dorothy, my mum. Actually, it was really the other way around – the Green side of the family were a rather superficial, arid lot, but Grandpa Brown was a really lovely, really gentle old guy.

He had lots of sayings he would regularly trot out, but we never got tired of them. I don't know whether he was a religious man, exactly, but whenever any arrangements were being made for him to come and stay with us, or for us to go somewhere with him, he would always repeat the arrangement and add, 'God willing'. It was as if he was admitting that nothing was certain. Mum used to say that occasionally, too, kind of poking fun at Grandpa Brown, but half serious as well.

When he stayed with us, we always had really animated conversations around the dinner table. My mum obviously adored him, so the mood was always loving and positive, but he was a ferocious stickler for making people defend their point of view. He hated prejudice of any kind and always called it out – even if it was just my younger brother making one of his sarcastic remarks about kids from other schools, or confidently expressing an opinion on something he barely knew anything about.

'How can you be so sure of yourself, young man? What's your evidence?' Grandpa Brown would always say – kindly, but he really meant it.

He and my dad had totally different views on politics, but it never got heated. I can still hear Grandpa Brown saying, 'No one has a monopoly on the truth, Rick.'

He was in the army in the Second World War and I think that scarred him, but it also made him really tolerant of other people and other points of view. I often heard him say things like, 'No one really wins in war, you know,' and, 'Both sides always think they're right, but no one is ever totally right or totally wrong.'

He had a real influence on my own attitude to things. I try to be tolerant, too, and I try not to be too sure of myself. 'Nothing's ever certain,' was another of Grandpa's sayings, 'so don't talk as if it is.'

Complacency was his pet hate. 'Take nothing for granted,' he always said. 'Be grateful, and be thoughtful. Just when you think everything's hunky-dory, that's when you'll slip up.'

My father's father, Grandpa Green – totally different story. He was always the centre of attention. Very noisy. Full of jokes. Always wanted an audience. Always up for a laugh. I thought it was terrific when I was little, but as I grew into my teens it became very tedious and I realised how incredibly conceited and sure of himself he was. If there was an argument, he always had to win it. I only ever saw the two grandpas together at Christmas, and they were like chalk and cheese. I noticed GB used to take a back seat and let GG hold the floor, which he was always very happy to do. When he was around, his opinion was the only one that counted, and he could be quite nasty if anyone challenged him.

As I got older, I began to see that he was actually a really smug, really prejudiced guy. I couldn't say anything to my dad about it, but I know Mum agreed with me. She once said that Grandpa Brown had had to do a lot of soul-searching in his life . . . she sort of left that remark hanging in the air, but I knew she was saying Grandpa Green was not one for soul-searching.

I used to think of Grandpa Brown as a deep pool of calm and wisdom, and Grandpa Green as a splashy, shallow puddle, though Grandpa Brown would have berated me for saying anything so uncharitable and unprovable! 'Never assume you know what's going on inside another person's head,' was another of his favourites.

Whenever I asked for advice – about things like uni subjects and career choices, and even boyfriends – Grandpa Brown always listened to me very carefully and gave me considered responses. I would never have thought of asking Grandpa Green's advice about anything. He was so polished, there was no way in, if you know what I mean. I never felt I could reach him.

Their funerals were a study in contrasts. They died in the same year. Grandpa Green went first, and his funeral was a very brisk affair at the crematorium, with just the family and a few friends. Someone told a few of his favourite jokes, Dad briefly recounted the chronological facts of Grandpa's life and we all dispersed pretty quickly. Even Dad didn't seem particularly upset.

The church was packed for Grandpa Brown's funeral – some ancient army mates were there, plus loads of friends and neighbours, people who had worked with him in his pharmacy and even some of his loyal customers. Many people spoke, including a heartfelt eulogy from Mum, and there were lots of tears and lots of laughter. We really missed him when he was gone. I still do. And I still remember things he said – like, I try really, really hard not to take things for granted. 'Complacency is the enemy of clear thinking.' Yes, Grandpa, I know.

We admire a certain confidence in others: indeed, the Scottish actor Sean Connery, most famous for his James Bond movies, once declared that the three things women find most attractive in men are confidence, confidence and confidence. (The three things he believes men find most attractive in women were not reported.) But when confidence puffs itself up into certainty – especially the certainty that says, without hesitation, 'I'm right and you're wrong' – we are entering the dangerous territory of complacency. Once there, we can hardly admit to frailty, insecurity or doubt. To maintain our confidence, we have to stay in hiding.

Fantasy

When we allow our fantasies to detach us from reality,
we also run the risk of detachment from the self.

What an easy way to avoid an awkward confrontation with the self: just throw the switch to 'fantasy', sit back and enjoy the ride into a place where it's all imaginary; where dreams can be dreamt without any need to ground them in reality; where we need accept no responsibility for whatever material we're projecting onto the screen of our mind.

I'm talking here about *voluntary* fantasies – letting the imagination run wild – rather than those sometimes euphoric, sometimes frightening fantasies that appear as hallucinations, delusions or other psychoses requiring treatment. Similarly, I'm not talking about the fantasies that result from hallucinogenic drug use, or the vivid fantasies that may occur in dreams while we're sleeping.

Voluntary fantasising can be highly therapeutic and, of course, great fun. What could be more enjoyable than imagining a fairytale world tailored to your personal taste: the person of your dreams running towards you in a haze of slow-motion, soft-focus anticipation, the car of your dreams sweeping you off to the holiday destination of your dreams, and all done without effort, expense or the tedious business of having to *work* at a relationship?

And what of a child, in Shakespeare's phrase, 'creeping like snail unwillingly to school', who fantasises about a jet-pack that whooshes her into the air, swoops defiantly over the school roof and then deposits her, incognito, at the beach? Or the office worker, staring at a screen, who relieves the grim routine of the day by imagining himself to be the Supreme Ruler, abolishing computers by edict and declaring a three-day working week?

Where's the harm in imagining yourself scoring the winning goal on a world stage as you stand at the supermarket checkout? Or in creating a different life for yourself as you bounce home from work on a crowded bus, possibly including an elaborate fantasy about the way your partner will greet you when you arrive? Or in replaying past scenes from your life, tweaking the script to your advantage?

The central illusion of most voluntary fantasising is that we are in control of external events. There's no surprise about why fantasies might follow this trajectory: most of us are occasionally frustrated by our sense of powerlessness and by the uneasy feeling that we actually have very little control over what's happening to us. (We're right about that: in most circumstances, we are only in control of our own reactions to events, not the events themselves.) So the fantasy of control is mainly a form of compensation, as are our pleasure fantasies: who, after all, wouldn't mind having a bit more fun?

Some fantasies of control are based on the conviction that we know more than other people do, either because we have a superior worldview or because we've cracked some secret code – perhaps via a conspiracy theory known only to those with access to a particular website (dark or otherwise). Such fantasies are fed by the belief that 'knowledge is power', and *secret* knowledge is the most powerful of all.

Other fantasies compensate us by imbuing us with a pleasing sense of being in charge of the fantasy, 'calling the shots' in a way that is generally not possible in the circumstances of everyday life. The popularity of violent video games relies almost entirely on that illusion of control. The rise of fantasy media material more generally – in movies, TV series, books and music videos – is a symptom of the same need to compensate us for feelings of powerlessness: immersion in *Star Wars*, *Game of Thrones*, *The Lord of the Rings*, *Black Mirror* or any other fantasy material gives us a pleasing break from a reality we can't control, and a glimpse into a world devoid of our kind of tedium, drudgery, pressures and responsibilities: *Tame the dragons! Wipe out your enemies! Have sex with a demi-god! Enslave an obediently-programmed android!* (Rom-coms disguise their fantasies by creating the seductive illusion of realism.)

Fantasy can sometimes serve as a pathway to engagement with the self: our dreams and fantasies, as long as they stop short of dangerous delusions, can stimulate deeper thought about the nature of the world and our place in it, as well as encourage hopeful visions of a better world. We may be assisted in this process by identifying with classic archetypes typically embedded in fantasy material, from children's fairytales onwards: the flawed hero, the wise guide/mentor, the caregiver, the beautiful princess, the shadow, the innocent abroad etc. Fantasy often runs on hopefulness – though there is also plenty of dystopian material – so it can be a trigger for self-discovery and for positive reflection on the kind of person we want to become and the kind of society we'd like to create.

But mostly it doesn't work at such an idealistic level. Voluntary indulgence in fantasy is primarily a reality-avoidance strategy in which we create a sometimes harmless and sometimes dangerous hiding place where we can play with the idea that we have qualities and capacities we know we lack:

I'm powerful – denies the truth about my frailties and inadequacies;

I'm irresistibly attractive – denies the fact that, if I'm lucky, a handful of people might quite like me;

I'm able to magically dispose of the difficult people in my life – denies my responsibility to draw on my resources of generosity and tolerance in learning to coexist with them;

I'm always right – denies the fact that, being human, I'm often wrong;

I can do whatever I want – denies the moral and social restrictions imposed on my behaviour by the demands of a civil society.

Unrealistic, obviously, but why dangerous? Aren't our private, voluntary fantasies harmless? Yes, they might be harmless if they remain private and are simply an occasional light-hearted indulgence. The danger arises when we start to blur the boundaries between our fantasy life and real life, becoming more detached from reality and correspondingly more attached to the flattering persona we have constructed in our imagination. (It's hard to avoid the thought that some political leaders appear to be acting out their own fantasies.)

In fantasy, we break the bounds of normal imagination. Mostly, our imaginations stay connected to reality and rationality: we imagine how things might be different, without involving too much mayhem or upheaval. A bit of healthy daydreaming can lead to anything from an idea for a book to a different way of managing a tricky relationship. But fantasy can smash those boundaries and let us roam well beyond reality. Again, that can be harmless and even therapeutic fun, or it can be dangerously seductive.

With perfectly innocent intent, many parents fuel unrealistic fantasies in their children when they say things like: 'You can be anything you want to be.' Wow! Can they? *Really?* Well, no, of course they can't. Nothing wrong with saying to children or adolescents pondering their future, 'It's a good idea to find something you're good at and that you enjoy doing,' but to suggest that the 'something' could be 'anything' is to encourage the sort of unrealistic fantasy that can only lead to disappointment when reality sets in.

Remember Georgia and Michael, the young married couple we met in chapter one? A year after they split, but while they were still legally married, Michael contacted Georgia and asked if she would meet him at a cafe they used to frequent. Michael had moved to Melbourne for his job, but he was visiting Sydney for a few days, he told Georgia, and had some thoughts he wanted to share with her.

The 'power' of Michael's positive thinking

Michael was already seated at the corner table they had always favoured and Georgia approached him tentatively. She had been intrigued by his invitation to meet but now felt extremely wary. Michael stood up and kissed her lightly on the cheek. They sat in their usual places. Georgia didn't unbutton her coat.

'I nearly didn't turn up, you know,' she said. 'You've been totally silent for twelve months and now, out of the blue . . .'

'Totally silent? What about my texts?'

'What texts, Mike? I never got a single text from you.'

'I sent you a couple of texts in the beginning. I'm sure I did. But you never replied.'

'No, Mike. You *thought* you sent me a couple of texts. You might have composed them in your head. You might have imagined sending them, you might have even visualised me deleting them. But you never actually sent any. Fantasy, Mike. Pure fantasy.'

'Well, perhaps that's because reality has become too painful for me.'

'Reality?'

'The reality of us being apart. The senselessness of it. Anyway, you've been silent too, Georgie.'

'I think I had good reason.'

'Because?'

'You were the one who came home drunk once too often. You were the one who finally told me I was a royal pain in the arse.'

'So you've told me, but I can assure you that I have no recollection of ever saying that or anything like it. I *must* have been drunk. I didn't think it about you then, and I don't think it now. I thought you were the best thing that had ever happened to me, and I still think that. I dream of you all the time. I miss you every single day.'

'That would be 365 days, give or take, and not a word of this until now?'

'You're not listening, Georgie. I accept I used to drink too much. I accept I said some stupid things when I was drunk. And now I'm not drunk – now I'm never drunk – and I'm saying something totally different.'

'Go on.'

'I admit I got tired of all that transparency stuff. I didn't like the feeling that I was constantly under a spotlight. Remember those debriefs you said we had to have? What had I been thinking? What had I been *feeling*?'

'Debriefs? What debriefs? Is this another of your fantasies, Mike?'

Michael looked at Georgia incredulously, as if he couldn't be sure whether she was deliberately forgetting or was away with the pixies.

'Anyway, Mike, it didn't work out. Remember? There was too much pretending going on for our marriage to be healthy. Don't you agree?'

Michael shook his head. 'When I look at you, I can still see everything I used to see. I can see us with a couple of kids – girls, probably – and a real family life together. It was amazing when it was just the two of us, but I was always waiting for you to say the word about a baby. You know that.'

'Mike, I'm worried about you. You're slipping in and out of some fantasy world. I think you've spent the past year dreaming of things that never were.'

'Not dreaming, Georgie. Positive thinking. That's why you agreed to come here today. The power of positive thinking. I bet you didn't really want to come but you felt a sort of compulsion, right? Positive thinking. Power of.' Michael folded his arms and smiled. 'Anyway, we always said we were going to have kids. You know that.'

'I agree we *said* it, but I don't think I ever really believed it.'

Michael looked shocked. 'Well, you convinced me. And it's one of the things I've been clinging to.'

'Clinging to? The idea that we could still have babies together?'

'Sure. Why not? I'm well set up in Melbourne. You could come down and we could make a fresh start. I'm off the grog – almost totally. It's all become perfectly clear to me. I know we can make it work.'

'Mike, listen – I've been dating someone. It's not serious, not yet, but –'

'I assumed that's why you were ignoring my texts. I knew that was more or less inevitable. I've dated a few women since I moved to Melbourne, naturally. But you're the one, Georgie. You and me. Made in heaven. You, me and the kids. By the way, you're not pregnant, are you?'

'Michael! God, no. Why would you ask me that?'

'Sorry. It's just that I've been imagining you pregnant and the image was so intense, so real, I was half afraid the thought might have already led to the reality, or might even be a kind of telepathic reflection of the reality. So I'm relieved. I really am.'

'Mike, listen to me. I am not coming to Melbourne. I am not going to turn my life upside down because you're in the grip of some fantasy about us and babies and a future together. Get real. *Please!*'

'Look, Georgie, I realise you'll need some time to get used to the idea. But nothing's happening for you up here. At least come down to Melbourne for a week and see what sort of life I have now. What sort of life I have planned for *us*. There's even a room in my apartment that –'

'Mike, please stop! I have to go now. This has all been a bit distressing, actually.'

They both stood.

'I realise it's a shock, Georgie, but don't write me off. Give it some thought. I mean deep thought. I'll call you again in a week or two. I'm coming to Sydney pretty regularly now, so we'll meet again. I *know* we will. Positive thinking, Georgie. You should try it.'

~

Loneliness after a break-up is the perfect breeding ground for nostalgic fantasies, sexual and otherwise. But notice Michael's assumption that Georgia only agreed to meet him because she was impelled by the power of his positive thoughts. That's an example of so-called 'magical thinking' – a particular form of fantasy that takes the theme of control and ramps it up to a delusional level, leading people to believe that their thoughts actually have the power to control events, including other people's behaviour.

At its simplest, a belief in magical thinking might convince someone that they can 'will' a parking spot to appear wherever they want one, or ensure that there will not be a queue at the taxi line when they leave an airport terminal. Any actual experience of such coincidences, of course, strongly reinforces their belief in the magical power of their own thoughts. In fact, coincidence is such a powerful theme – in literature and in life – that some people regard almost any coincidence as significant: *You're an Aries? Really? My son is an Aries!*

Like Michael's fear of Georgia's possible pregnancy, belief in the power of magical thinking can be so disturbing, people are sometimes afraid of thinking any 'dark' thoughts in case they precipitate some tragedy or catastrophe, from a serious illness to a plane crash. More broadly, folklore, superstitions and cultural practices often rest on versions of magical thinking:

Don't say that, or you'll tempt fate.

I could have told her that having her desk face that way would lead to conflict with the staff.

When you're eating a whole fish, you mustn't turn it over to remove the flesh from the bones, or a fishing boat will overturn somewhere in the world.

120

Our cash flow has improved greatly since we installed the fountain in our front garden.

I don't want to talk about the audition – it might jinx my prospects.

Watch out: bad things always come in threes.

Fantasising can be fun. Fantasising can be harmless. But it can also become a hiding place. The inherent risk in any fantasies, even those that stop well short of magical or delusional thinking, is that they encourage unrealistic interpretations of reality, and unrealistic expectations of what might happen. There is absolutely no point in saying to yourself 'I can be anything I want to be': that is simply untrue, and deeply unhelpful if your goal is to be true to your real self rather than to some fantasy version of yourself.

If we allow ourselves to become attached to fantasies about being more powerful and in control than we really are (or ever can be), those fantasies may not only obscure our view of the more complex and less glamorous truth about ourselves but also discourage us from an encounter with our authentic self.

Fatalism

The mantra 'it is what it is' can distract us from opportunities to enrich our own life and the lives of others.

'It is what it is.' It's a seductive little phrase, like a signpost pointing to a hiding place, wide open and welcoming, that promises us refuge from that challenging and sometimes annoying inner voice that says: *Things don't have to be like this; you can be better than this; why not aim a little higher?*

Of course, in many situations, that may be the only rational response to the way things are: a diagnosis of incurable disease; a beloved partner whose affections have turned elsewhere; the loss of a job through no fault of our own; or the ravages of some natural disaster that has thrown our life into chaos. Who wouldn't feel defeated and discouraged by such turns of events, at least initially? Yet some people manage to square their shoulders and say: 'I didn't choose this, but this is what I have to deal with.'

A calm acceptance of what has happened to us can morph into an attitude of such passivity – such a comprehensive surrender to the forces of 'destiny' or 'fate' – that, whatever happens, we simply shrug and say: 'It is what it is.'

That's fine, if we're simply saying that the future is unknowable. But beware of the morph! 'It is what it is' – just like 'whatever will be, will be' – can encourage us to abdicate responsibility for what may become of us (or, indeed, for the consequences of our actions). It can distract us from the need to plan by downplaying the significance of will, intention and choice. It can elevate 'going with the flow' to the status of a strategy for living your life.

At the other end of the spectrum from fatalism lies the sentiment expressed in nineteenth-century English poet William Ernest Henley's 'Invictus': 'I am the master of my fate, I am the captain of my soul.' If you find yourself leaning in Henley's direction, then the gratingly popular statement 'It is what it is' needs to be rapidly followed by another one: 'And here's what I'm going to do about it.'

The famous 'Serenity Prayer', generally attributed to the twentieth-century American theologian Reinhold Niebuhr and later adopted by Alcoholics Anonymous, strikes the balance between acquiescence and action:

God grant me the serenity to accept the things I cannot change,
Courage to change the things I can,
And wisdom to know the difference.

It goes without saying that, if we are to remain sane, we must accept that our present situation, whatever it is, is the situation we're in.

But acceptance doesn't entail acquiescence: 'this is the situation' doesn't always mean that this is the only possible situation. If it is unpleasant or unsatisfactory, or puts us in moral or physical danger, we can try to change it. If it's a situation we really can't change – such as the care of a demanding, elderly parent – we might be able to change the character of our own response to it, perhaps by exercising greater compassion. And then we will discover that compassion is a pathway to serenity.

When a helpless shrug becomes our default response to whatever confronts us, when we wait for others to act so we can simply respond to their initiatives, when we close our ears to the inner voice – whether that comes to us as 'the voice of reason' or 'the voice of compassion' or 'the voice of faith' – then we are at risk of using fatalism as a hiding place.

Mervyn's rueful reflection on a wrong turn

I recall the precise moment. It was when I was parking my car and preparing to go into the wedding reception venue to confirm our booking and pay the deposit. I was young – though that's no excuse – and I was of a rather devout disposition. I was all in favour of surrendering myself to God's will without really having the foggiest idea of what that might mean in practical terms. In fact, looking back, I think my so-called faith was indistinguishable from fatalism. I imagine I thought that whatever happened would happen because God willed it. God was in charge, we were at his mercy, that type of thing.

The idea of free will went right out the window, in one way. Obviously, I had made all kinds of deliberate decisions that looked like the operation of free will. I had asked Jan to marry me, for instance (though that's a bit hazy – I think she might have asked me). But I had decided to do law, I had moved out of home and rented a flat. I had decided to buy the car – an ancient Wolseley – that I was engaged in the act of parking. So I wasn't totally a leaf blowing in the wind.

Anyhow, back to that moment. I had this deep conviction that Jan was not the girl I should be marrying – or, more correctly, I think I had the insight that I was not the man she should be marrying. So there I was, about to walk into the reception place and pay the deposit for an event I was sure should not be taking place at all. There was no one else involved. I could just see no good reason why we should get married. Wouldn't happen today, I imagine, but this was a long time ago. We were both impatient virgins.

If God doesn't want me to marry Jan, I thought, He'll intervene. Something will happen to prevent the wedding. It's up to Him. (Those were the days when I had a gendered notion of God as well as an interventionist one.) So I meekly paid the deposit, went on my way, and waited for the sign.

No sign. No intervention. Everything proceeded according to plan. We were married on the appointed day and, as we drove to the reception I had a flash of déjà vu, almost as if I was expecting an intervention, even at that late stage.

Nothing happened. God did not intervene so, I thought, the marriage must be in accordance with His divine will. (These days, any God I could conceive of wouldn't have the remotest interest in anyone's wedding plans, but that's another story.)

Thanks to my fatalism disguised as religious faith, poor Jan was stuck with me for five miserable years. And then, with admirable aplomb, she announced over breakfast one morning that she thought this had all been a terrible mistake and she was going to Europe for a month to consider her position.

Needless to say, I was deeply relieved and I complimented her on her courage. She went on that trip and never came back. She wrote to me from London – it was a long and heartfelt letter, and quite generous in sentiment – explaining that she had found a job and would be staying over there permanently.

We divorced. She married a Welshman – I actually saw them when I visited the UK many years later. She was like a completely different person. Her true self, no doubt, rather than the one she had tried to be when she was living with me and we were so desperately trying to please each other.

So, thank you, God. But you were a bit slow off the mark, I must say.

You wouldn't have to be as fatalistic as Mervyn (or as young, or in thrall to such simplistic religiosity, perhaps) to find fatalism an attractive refuge from the need to confront the self. Plenty of us do things we know to be unwise, reckless or ill-conceived *even while we are doing them*, as though to cast our fate to the winds. 'Let's see what happens' can seem like a bold and courageous gamble, though it can also be one of the most infuriating things we can say to someone who is hoping for something more definitive from us.

'I'll put it out to the universe' is another fashionable way of saying 'I won't take responsibility for this – I'll just see which way the wind blows'. Sometimes, of course, the wait-and-see strategy is perfectly reasonable: many millennials and post-millennials, for instance, have adopted 'wait and see' as a kind of generational mantra – and why not, given the unstable world they are living in and the sense of uncertainty and unpredictability they've grown up with, in everything from family life to the job market and technology.

People suffering from addictions sometimes adopt a fatalistic view as a way of avoiding the issue. Some people who choose to play the role of victim (see 'Victimhood', towards the end of this chapter) justify their position in terms of a helpless fatalism: 'What can I do? Look at the hand fate has dealt me.' And, as Mervyn's pre-wedding insight showed, some forms of religious faith can amount to fatalism, where people shed personal responsibility for their actions and attribute *everything* to 'the will of God'.

Similarly, astrology and superstition can lead to a resigned-to-my-fate mentality that minimises the role of the self in shaping the way we are.

What would you expect? He's a Sagittarian.

Mercury is in retro, so things were bound to go awry.

People say thirteen is an unlucky number. That's rubbish – thirteen has always been a really lucky number for me.

You can't fight it – it's your destiny.

Even the oft-quoted remark that something was 'meant to be' suggests a fatalistic disposition: 'It's nothing to do with me; it was just meant to be.' (It doesn't do to enquire 'Meant by whom?', lest you be seen as a person not in touch with the universe.)

Fatalism can be harmless, up to a point. But when we use it as an excuse for passivity, mindless acquiescence or irresponsibility, we risk becoming insulated from our deeper, more authentic self.

～

'What the heck!' Katie takes the plunge

Katie was a history teacher in a large co-ed private school. She had a heavy teaching load and extracurricular sport and drama responsibilities as well. She always ended the week tired out, but was sometimes rather grateful for the fatigue because her need for rest distracted her from the fact that her partner, Stu, seemed to be losing interest in her.

She was growing increasingly impatient with Stu, a physical education teacher at the school where Katie had taught before taking her present job. His teaching load was significantly lighter than hers and his idea of relaxation was to go for a long run, followed by some heavy drinking. Katie used to run with him, but he kept wanting to increase the pace and distance, and it was no longer companionable. She also declined to drink along with him.

Katie had tried to interest Stu in history – her passion – but to no avail. When they first got together, he had seemed interested, but that soon waned. Their taste in movies and music also seemed to have diverged over the time they had been together, so they each tended to go to the cinema or concerts with friends rather than with each other. Stu's drinking had also been lighter in the beginning. Her attempts to point out the incongruity between his drinking and his physical fitness led him to claim that he only bothered to stay fit so he *could* drink.

Peter had been the head of history at Katie's previous school and was a well-known womaniser. Several women on the staff had been bruised by brief but intensely passionate affairs with him, and some talked openly about their experiences as a warning to others. Katie, newly involved with Stu, had found it easy to deflect Peter's attentions back then.

When Peter texted Katie out of the blue with an invitation to join him for a drink after work, Katie was under no illusions about the implications of the invitation. In fact, she was excited to receive it. That very morning, she had told Stu that she was tired of his drinking and lack of interest in anything to do with her work. She almost gave him an ultimatum, but stopped short.

Knowing she was courting disaster, knowing she was doing some-thing she would have advised anyone else against doing, and knowing she was ignoring the voice of her own conscience, she said 'yes' to the drink with Peter, 'yes' to sex, then 'yes' to the offer of more of both.

She soon fell under the spell of Peter's charm and enjoyed long post-coital conversations with him. Their historical interests coincided. The affair dragged on for several months, with Katie convincing herself that she was being completely realistic – even fatalistic – about its likely outcome.

'For the first time in years, I'm spending time with someone who really interests me. I know he doesn't love me and I don't care. Stu doesn't love me, either – not really,' was how she described it to a close girlfriend. 'I'm just going to let nature take its course on this one.'

When her friend occasionally challenged her about the affair, Katie would only say, 'It is what it is.'

Things did not work out as painlessly as Katie had hoped. Peter suddenly announced that he was getting married and that their assig-nations would have to cease 'at least for a while'.

To her own surprise, Katie was shattered. She knew she had been absurdly reckless. She knew it was irresponsible. She simply didn't care. She was prepared to wait and see what would happen next. Peter would call again or he wouldn't.

Katie's affair and Mervyn's ill-starred marriage (how do you like 'ill-starred' for a touch of fatalism?) had this in common: they each heard whispers from their soul and chose to ignore them in favour of 'going with the flow'. Had they chosen not to hide from themselves in their surrender to fatalism, they might have avoided the damaging emotional fallout that followed.

'Forgetting'

When we misrepresent unpalatable aspects of our past,
we jeopardise our authenticity in the present.

The word 'forgetting' is in inverted commas to emphasise the fact that this hiding place relies on a self-protective distortion of memory that insulates us from something in our past we would find too upsetting – or too humiliating – to recall accurately. So, perhaps unconsciously, we deny it; repress it; act as if it never happened. We use *selective memory* to hide from the truth about our inner self.

This kind of forgetting can be good for us when it's a way of preserving our sanity or protecting our mental and emotional health. People who have been traumatised by childhood abuse, for example, or who have witnessed horrific scenes of carnage in war zones, may feel the need to push the memories away by refusing to discuss the troubling events, perhaps, or managing to forget they ever happened. That kind of selective forgetting is one of the ways our notoriously unreliable memory can appear to act in our favour. (Before the advent of more efficacious pain management, folklore used to insist that if women could accurately recall the pain and trauma of childbirth, they would never voluntarily have had a second child.)

Although such forms of forgetting, or repression, can seem necessary for our emotional survival, we generally pay some price for having had to distance ourselves from these painful memories. They may haunt us in nightmares. They may re-emerge, years later, triggered by some unexpected event. In the meantime, though conscious memory might have 'let them go', they remain part of us and their denial diminishes us by forcing us to reject an authentic part of our history.

But selective forgetting is not always so benign or therapeutic in its intent. Sometimes it amounts to calculated lying that provides us with a hiding place we would have done better never to enter.

A marriage unravels, and the history is rewritten

Over a turbulent twelve-month period, the twenty-year marriage of Sean and Zowie unravelled. From Sean's point of view, the first sign of the approaching end was when Zowie moved into the spare room and told their seventeen-year-old twin daughters that she had a sleeping problem.

To her friends, Zowie claimed that Sean had become impossible to live with, being totally absorbed in his work as a medical specialist. Sex was right off the agenda, she said, implying that Sean had lost interest in her. (Sean's version was that Zowie had perfected the art of feigning sleep before he got into bed.)

Over the next few months, Zowie repeatedly refused Sean's request that they see a marriage counsellor but began looking for a house or apartment to buy. Sean pleaded with her to rent, not buy, as he badly wanted to keep open the possibility of reconciliation. Zowie made it clear that 'reconciliation' was not a word in her vocabulary – 'and it shouldn't be in yours, either,' she told Sean in one rather bitter exchange.

As the situation deteriorated, various friends tried to get Zowie to explain 'the real problem' to them, since, from the outside, the marriage had always seemed strong and both parents were clearly devoted to their daughters. Zowie kept saying she couldn't really explain why living with Sean was impossible; it just was. She also admitted to her closest friend that it was she, not Sean, who had called a halt to any form of intimacy.

Looking back, and reflecting on various things Zowie had said to her, that friend concluded that Zowie had been considering leaving the marriage for about three years before she revealed her intentions to Sean. Family and friends, trying to make sense of what was happening, speculated that Zowie might be involved with someone else, but there was no evidence of this, and she denied it when asked point-blank by Sean.

Friends who saw them together towards the end found it a distressing experience. Sean was still trying to show affection for Zowie, but Zowie was having none of it. She was treating Sean almost like a stranger.

In due course, Zowie bought an apartment, and then announced that the girls should stay in the family home with Sean and visit her on weekends. She arranged to move into her apartment on a weekend when she had persuaded Sean to take the girls to visit his mother in the country.

They all settled into the new routine. The girls went to stay with Zowie every second weekend and she occasionally came to stay with them in the family home when Sean had to travel.

Sean gradually got his life back in order. He employed a housekeeper and tried to trim his working hours. The following year, the girls both started university and moved into a college on campus.

Five years later, Sean met and married another woman, also with twin daughters, coincidentally (though it wasn't such a coincidence, really: they had met when they were both taking part in a university research project on raising twins). All four girls had long since left home and were pleased to see their previously miserable parents in a loving relationship.

Ten years later, one of Sean's friends ran into Zowie in a city store. She looked strained, and much older than her years, but just as stylish as ever. He asked her how things were working out for her and she said: 'You know, I still don't know why Sean left me. I thought we had a perfectly happy marriage.'

The friend, having been close to Sean throughout the split, was too astonished to respond. Reporting the encounter to his wife, he said: 'I think my jaw might have actually dropped.'

At about the same time, another friend who had also lived through the whole saga with Sean and Zowie agreed to meet Zowie for coffee. He, too, was stunned by her version of events. 'He wanted me to go, you know,' she told him, 'and then he went and married someone else.'

The clear implication was that Sean had somehow pushed Zowie out so he could remarry. The friend was so shocked, and so offended on Sean's behalf, that he felt obliged to point out that Sean had not met his present wife until several years *after* Zowie left. Zowie looked at him as though she pitied him his stupidity.

'Do you think she has found anyone else?' Sean asked him later, when they were discussing the friend's encounter with Zowie.

'No idea. But I'd be prepared to bet she hasn't. She's living in a fantasy world. She seemed quite different from the way I remember her. Colder. More diminished, or something. I actually felt sorry for her. I think she has managed to convince herself that it was all your doing. I mean, *really* convince herself. It's though she's created some other scenario entirely and now she actually believes it. Maybe she's repeated the story so often she thinks it's the truth. She didn't sound as if she was consciously or deliberately lying about what had happened.'

Zowie's seemingly bizarre account of her separation from Sean is by no means an isolated case. What, after all, could be simpler: you do something you regret or are ashamed of, and so you rewrite the script retrospectively. You might even be unable to explain your own behaviour to yourself, so you create a story that 'makes sense'. A friend recently told me about phone conversations she still has with her ex-husband in which they disagree violently over matters that, to her, are very straightforward bits of their shared history.

'That's not how I recall it,' he says to her, and she terminates the conversation rather than get into yet another argument about what 'really' happened. I trust my friend's account of the story, because I was in touch with both of them during the split. Yet there are times when she doubts her own sanity: 'How can he say that black is white?' she asks me, beyond exasperated. The answer, of course, is that he would prefer black to *be* white – and might, by now, have convinced himself that it is.

Part of my friend's rage has been based on her discovery that her husband has been telling their mutual friends the same distortions and untruths he tells her.

'I've lost a few friends over this,' she told me recently. 'I can't blame them, in a way. If someone tells you something happened, and you weren't there at the time, why wouldn't you believe them? And then if someone else – me, for instance – tells you it wasn't like that at all, the natural tendency is to stick with what you were told first.'

The same phenomenon occurs in all aspects of life, not just relationship break-ups. Here's a case where a workplace incident was distorted to make the victim look like the villain . . .

The rise and rise of Teflon Trev

Trevor, generally known among his fellow accountants as 'Teflon Trev', sat on the board of a small charity, The Haven, that provided food and clothing, temporary housing and language classes for refugees, homeless people and others on the margins of society.

Jess was chair of the board. She was widely liked and admired for her work with The Haven, having previously been its CEO. Mary, the current CEO, was a good friend.

Trevor and Jess often clashed, usually over Jess having to draw Trevor's attention to potential conflicts of interest – like the time he tried to get The Haven involved in an investment scheme his accounting firm was promoting, or the time he tried to persuade Jess to appoint his nephew to the board because he was 'a fine young man on the way up', in spite of the nephew having no relevant qualifications or experience, and in spite of the board having recently agreed that they needed to increase the number of female directors.

Matters between Jess and Trevor came to a head over a dispute involving an architect. Jess had felt it necessary to point out to Trevor that he was, yet again, encouraging the board to behave unethically. (She had rather intemperately used the very words 'yet again'.) Funds had been raised to renovate The Haven's building and an architect had submitted some rough sketches for the renovation of the interior and a facelift to the exterior. The board loved the concept, though the architect's proposed fees for drawing up detailed plans and specifications and supervising the work had been something of a shock. Trevor thought the solution was simple: 'We can sack the architect and use these drawings to brief someone less pricey. I know just the chap.'

Jess was outraged – not only by the ethical implications of Trevor's suggestion, but also by the lack of support she received from other members of the board when she resisted it.

Two days later, the only other woman on the board invited Jess out for lunch and told her, with a show of great sadness, that Jess no longer enjoyed the confidence of the board and that they were proposing to appoint Trevor as her replacement. They all hoped Jess would not make a fuss.

Jess *did* make a fuss. She called a meeting of the board, but Trevor and three other directors failed to show up and no decisions could be made for lack of a quorum. She made a formal appointment to speak to the CEO, her friend Mary.

Mary looked embarrassed and awkward. She confirmed that Trevor had called her the morning after the last board meeting and explained that he would be taking over as chair.

'What exactly did he tell you?'

'Just that the board was ready to make a change and he would be the new chair.'

'Did he say why? Did he mention our little ethical dispute?'

Mary shrugged. 'I can't tell you any more than I've already told you.'

And that was that – or so Jess thought.

Jess and Mary lost contact, their friendship compromised by these events and by Jess's uneasy feeling that Mary knew more than she was letting on.

A year later, they met accidentally in a city department store, and went to a nearby cafe to catch up.

Jess couldn't restrain herself from asking how things were going at The Haven. 'Did you ever find out the real reason why I was shafted? Was it just Trevor's notorious ambition, pure and simple?'

'I'm afraid it's more complicated than that. You were removed because of religious prejudice *and* sexism. Surely you knew that.'

'Wha-a-t?' Jess was dumbfounded. 'Religious prejudice? *Which* religion?'

Mary shrugged noncommittally. 'Apparently when you called Trevor's ethics into question, he was convinced you were simply expressing a prejudice against him on religious grounds.'

'There wasn't any hint of that at the time. I never saw any sign of Trevor having any religious affiliation, let alone religious sensitivities. When did this emerge? And *sexism? Me?*'

'You knocked back Trevor's nominee for the board purely on the grounds of gender.'

'Not *purely*, Mary. You were there. You know what was said.'

Mary shrugged again. 'You know I can't comment on board decisions.'

Jess persisted: 'What about the other board members who were there at the time?'

'People just seem to have accepted that you had to go because your prejudices were interfering with your judgement. I'm sorry, Jess.'

'And Trevor? Does no one ever question his version of events?'

'No one trusts him. But he's very plausible.'

'Teflon Trev, indeed . . .'

Memory is a notoriously unreliable source of evidence. Just ask a police officer who has interviewed witnesses to a traffic accident or a crime. Ten witnesses; ten versions of events. And those versions often diverge in significant ways – the ethnic appearance of a perpetrator or a victim; the make or colour of a car; the number of people present; the time that elapsed between the beginning and end of the event.

Ace American crime writer Elmore Leonard captured this human frailty perfectly when he had Gloria, a character in his novel *Pronto*, say to a gunman who is describing how he intends to shoot his victim in a crowded restaurant: 'But people will see you.'

'Yeah, what?' the gunman replies. 'Ask them, they all see something different. One or two witnesses, they can identify you. A lot of people there, you got no problem.'

That's selective memory for you. We all have it, though we're obviously more conscious of it in others than in ourselves: we like to assume that *our* recollection of what happened on that infamous family picnic is the correct one; those who describe it differently have simply got it wrong (which is exactly what they think about our version).

One of my sons recently recounted an embarrassing incident that occurred 20 years ago at the exit to the car park of the Sydney Opera House when I was driving him and one of his younger brothers home from a concert. My exit ticket jammed in the machine and, with cars banking up behind us and impatient drivers honking their horns, the younger son who was sitting in the back seat jumped out to try to remedy whatever was wrong. He somehow retrieved the ticket, reinserted it in the machine, the boom gate flew up, and I drove off in a fluster, leaving my son stranded at the exit, waving and shouting at me.

All these years later, as my older son fell about with mirth at this recollection, I had to confess that although I could clearly recall the concert in question (the jazz trumpeter James Morrison, in fact) I have no recollection of the car park fiasco and my humiliating role in it. Gone. Totally. (Thank you, selective memory.)

Convenient 'forgetting', whether deliberate or not, takes a natural human weakness and plays it to our advantage, creating a place where we can hide from ourselves by pretending that things were different from the way we know them to have been. Once settled comfortably in the cocoon of false memory, nothing is easier than simply repeating the distorted 'recollection' to anyone who will listen.

That friend's assessment of Zowie was spot on: if you repeat the self-servingly distorted story to enough people for you to become familiar with hearing yourself tell it, it becomes your 'truth'.

But what then? What does it feel like to have rewritten your history to your own advantage and then kept retelling the false version? Assuming this is not a case of repressed memory due to major trauma but a deliberate attempt to hide the truth from others – and, ultimately, from yourself – then we are back in the territory of corrosive inauthenticity.

To know that you are not owning up to yourself about your own behaviour, let alone misrepresenting it to others, is deeply damaging to your personal integrity and quite likely to lead to health complications like anxiety and depression, or perhaps lower-grade effects like a lingering, non-specific sense of uneasiness or a vague yearning for greater peace of mind.

Whether the context is a troubled marriage, a difficult workplace situation, a fractured friendship or any other case where we rewrite history to advantage ourselves and disadvantage others, this is a highly dangerous hiding place. To become your authentic self means abandoning the comfort of the deception disguised as 'forgetting' and accepting that the damage you have inflicted on others by your misrepresentation is as nothing compared to the likely damage being inflicted on yourself.

Guilt and Shame

When we cling to guilt, refusing to accept forgiveness even from ourselves,
it can become both a hiding place and health hazard.

I'm a great fan of guilt. It's the most reliable signal we have for alerting us to the fact that we have done something that offends our own or others' sensibilities, or breaches our own moral code. Properly respected and appropriately dealt with, guilt is a powerful ally.

Guilt is like the cry of an outraged conscience. If we never experienced feelings of guilt, we would be morally bankrupt and socially reckless. It would be like being adrift on a trackless ocean, with no compass, no life jacket and not even the glimmer of a distant shorelight to guide us to safety.

It's tempting to think of guilt as something that holds us back; restrains us; limits our freedom to act as we wish. Guilt is sometimes characterised as 'the bad guy'; the ultimate party-pooper; the killjoy robbing us not only of fun but also of freedom. But is freedom simply about doing whatever we feel like doing?

In *The Needs of Strangers*, the Canadian writer and academic Michael Ignatieff, echoing St Augustine, makes a crucial distinction between the freedom to make choices and the deeper sense of mental and emotional freedom – the peace of mind – that comes from knowing we have made the *right* choice. In other words, there's 'good' freedom and 'bad' freedom: one is constrained by the values and scruples of the individual in response to the demands of a civil society; the other displays a reckless indifference to the rights, needs and wellbeing of others.

Guilt tells us that our moral machinery – the mental and emotional equipment we have for distinguishing between good and bad behaviour – is in working order. Morality is always about our interactions with other people: it is a system or code we develop directly out of our awareness of ourselves as social beings. If we no longer felt guilt, we would likely become troublesome, wayward individuals with no sense of responsibility for the consequences of our actions.

But then there is neurotic, persistent, disproportionate guilt . . .

Why does Sandy cling to her guilt?

When I was in grade six, I stole something from another girl. Well, it wasn't straightforward theft: I actually swapped her unfinished craft project for mine. We were all making identical writing compendiums for our mothers and Francine's was a bit better, and a bit closer to being finished, than mine was. They had all been mixed up with another class's work, and not all the girls had put their names on their work. While the teacher was trying to sort it all out, I simply rubbed out my name on my project, put it back in the pile, took Francine's, rubbed out her name and wrote my own name on her work. In the confusion, no one noticed.

Francine seemed unaware of the switch – she didn't even seem to have realised that hers was missing. She just grabbed some other half-finished compendium with no name on it, and got on with it. She was much better at craft than I was.

Anyway, we all finished the project and my mother was delighted with the compendium. She has used it for years as a sort of folder for correspondence she wants to keep. When I was still living at home, I felt a pang of guilt every time she got it out to look at something or put something new into it. That went on for years and years.

It's not as if I was some kind of goody-two-shoes. I was just a normal-enough kid who got into as much trouble as anyone else, I guess. But there was something about the deliberate nature of that act, the stealing and the swapping – the deception, I guess – that really shook me. It made we wonder what sort of person I must be if I could do something as awful as that.

Here I am, 30 years old, and I still feel it almost as keenly as I did then. It probably sounds trivial and childish to you, but it's very, very real to me. I know I should have owned up at the time and asked Francine to forgive me. I intended to confess on our last day at that school, but Francine and I were not close, and she was surrounded by her friends and . . . well, I thought I would look pretty silly and she might not even know what I was talking about.

I only ever saw her once more, on a train, when we were both about sixteen and she was wearing the uniform of the private school she attended. (I went to the local high school.) Once again, I thought I'd try to broach it with her; once again I thought it would just make me look like an idiot. Such a trivial thing! What would she even say? Like, 'I forgive you'? I just couldn't imagine it. She didn't even show any sign of recognising me.

So it just festers. I never told my mum – she still uses the wretched compendium, and occasionally even mentions how useful it's been all these years. That brings it all back.

Am I sick? Am I stupid? I just can't forgive myself for doing something so deliberately dishonest. It's as though I can't trust myself, even though I've never done anything like that since – except the affair with Nick, maybe, but I never got to rub out his wife's name and write my own name on him.

What are we to make of Sandy's lingering guilt? It would be easy to dismiss it as a silly carryover from childhood, something she should have shed years ago. Yet it gnaws at her in a way that seems out of all proportion to the 'crime'. It's as though she can't shake off the feeling that she's a deeply unworthy person and that one act exposed her essential frailty to herself.

The conscience is an integral part of our inner sense of self: if we are to confront our authentic self, it will certainly involve a confrontation with any lingering guilt. And yet, ironically, in Sandy's case the guilt seems to be an impediment to self-discovery. It's as if she can't face some *other* truth about herself, so she clings almost neurotically to her guilt as a way of deflecting her inward gaze from that deeper truth, whatever it might be. The affair with Nick might be a clue.

If Sandy were able to shed her guilt over the compendium episode, what might she find? We might assume she has nothing to fear by forgiving herself, all these years later. To aid the process of shedding the guilt, we might even encourage her to perform some symbolic act of penance (making a donation to charity, say, or offering to do some shopping for a sick neighbour) whose significance would be known only to Sandy.

Or would she prefer to go on as she is? If so, we can reasonably conclude that Sandy is using her guilt as a hiding place – and that's not an uncommon strategy for people who are clinging to guilt as a way of postponing an unencumbered confrontation with the self.

We'd need to know much more about Sandy to have a clear idea of what's going on here. But when guilt lingers year after year, it's a pretty safe bet that the guilt is an excuse for not coming to terms with something deeper. She alluded to her affair with Nick, a married man. That happened when she was in her mid-twenties and, at the time, Sandy insisted that she felt no guilt about it at all, even though Nick was terrified of exposure.

Has Sandy, then, clung to her 'little' guilt about Francine as a way of inoculating herself against larger guilts? 'I'm a bad girl, deep down' could easily be her rationale for not going deep down. (As we have seen, 'I don't want to know' is a classic form of resistance to the inner journey.) Or perhaps it's more complicated than that: Sandy, like all of us, has a remarkable capacity for loving-kindness and that, ironically, might be the inhibitor. Sandy might be wanting to deny that capacity in herself, because there's someone she is simply not prepared to love. (If that someone happens to be herself, her guilt is the perfect excuse.) By not letting go of her guilt, Sandy could be unconsciously looking for ways to punish herself – either by behaving recklessly, as with Nick, or by denying herself simple pleasures, or by not looking after her health, or in some other way.

Sandy might well require the guidance of a counsellor/psychologist, if she ever decides she needs to sort all this out. And it might not be a case of guilt at all: Sandy might be confusing guilt with regret, as we often do. But to conflate the two is to give regret unwarranted power, allowing it to obscure our view of the good within us. So regret, too, can become a hiding place.

Guilt becomes inappropriate when, as in Sandy's case, it has lingered too long to be healthy, or when it arises from an unwarranted cause, like the belief that 'I'm always wrong' (even when I'm not), or because someone has withheld forgiveness from me and I haven't yet found a way to deal with that by forgiving myself.

The best way of relieving our guilt, obviously, is to confess our wrongdoing to the person we have offended and hope their forgiveness is forthcoming. If it's not, then, for religious believers, seeking God's forgiveness can be a circuit-breaker; for others, the support of a counsellor can be valuable in finding the pathway to self-forgiveness.

Writing in the *New York Times Magazine*, Rachel Howard describes the guilt she clung to for three years after divorcing her husband, Bill. Puzzled by her inability to let go of her guilt, it was only after she had collapsed, sobbing, at the end of a Lenten service in a New York cathedral that she finally confronted the truth: 'I realised that I had loved Bill, but by the time he proposed, I had started to change. But I was 25 and scared and lonely. I buckled. I married Bill for the security. I married him selfishly.' As Howard told a priest who was comforting her: 'I betrayed him.'

The priest invited her to read some words from the Book of Common Prayer with her and then 'leave the sin behind'. Howard walked out of the cathedral, she wrote, 'a different person'. Guilt was no longer her hiding place.

Guilt is a private matter. Dealing with it involves a wrestle with our own conscience. There can of course be collective guilt, when we are complicit with others who have committed some wrongdoing or behaved unethically, and we quite properly share in their guilt. But guilt is essentially based on our conviction that we have done the wrong thing, whether other people realise it or not.

Shame is a very different story. Whereas guilt is personal, shame is socially driven. At is simplest, the distinction comes down to this: I feel guilty because of what I have done; I feel ashamed because my wrongdoing has been exposed and I am embarrassed or humiliated by that exposure. I can experience guilt – as Sandy does – without my action ever having been exposed. This is why people who commit crimes sometimes give themselves up to the police quite spontaneously: their guilt is too onerous to bear, and they are prepared to face the shame of exposure rather than live with unexpiated guilt.

Curiously, in the absence of forgiveness, shame can be the very thing that relieves our guilt and brings us out of hiding. Once our offence has been exposed, the embarrassment or humiliation that follows can be hard to bear but is often cathartic – in fact, Sandy would probably have dealt more easily with her guilt if she had been 'shamed' in the very beginning.

There's another kind of shame, also socially determined, that arises not from having done anything wrong, but from *feeling* vaguely 'wrong' or 'inferior' or 'outside' in a particular social context. Here are three examples of that kind of shame.

Chloe: an 'illegitimate' baby

I was put up for adoption as a baby and I didn't find out until I was a teenager. For some reason, my adoptive parents told my younger brother, who had been their own 'real' baby, and they swore him to secrecy. Once I found out, I was shattered at first, then I was furious with them for telling him and not me, and then I began to get this weird sense that I was somehow unworthy, not fully legitimate, because in those days people did literally talk about the babies of unmarried mothers as 'illegitimate'. It's a strange label to have to wear, I can tell you.

So I started to feel a sense of shame that has stayed with me all my life. I can't shake it off. I feel different – not just different, but inferior. An outsider. Not like all those 'legitimate' people.

Leo: a Russian immigrant

Most people would have no idea what it's like to leave your homeland to make a new life in another country, especially if you had to leave because of war or some other crisis. You feel very strange when your homeland isn't your home anymore. People say 'assimilate', 'learn the language'. Not so easy. I have learnt the language as well as I can. My kids both speak fluent English, or the Australian version of it, anyway: 'G'day, mate.'

But you're always an outsider, you know? You never feel right at home. People treat you differently because of your accent, your appearance, I don't know. I think it might be easier for people from the UK or

New Zealand or even Italy or Greece – places from where there have been lots of immigrants. Black African, not so easy. Russian, not so easy. Iranian, not so easy. Even some Greeks and Italians tell me it takes a while. I have nothing to be ashamed of – I am a proud Australian citizen, I work, I pay my taxes, I vote, I am paying off a house. People talk about 'otherness'. I can tell you about otherness. People definitely do look at me as if I'm 'other'. It makes you feel not quite right. Not quite acceptable. I tell my kids: *Never be ashamed of where you came from*. I know why I tell them that – because I do feel ashamed. And with no good reason except, maybe, that I am still secretly proud of where I came from.

Tom: a state school boy in a private school law firm

My big mistake was going to work in a law firm where the partners all went to the same two or three private schools. Not to brag, but I went to a state high school and did extremely well in my VCE and then at university. They welcomed me with open arms, so I thought, when I got this job. Then I overheard one of the partners saying how people like 'young Tom' were part of their 'diversity program'. That should have made me furious but – and I can't explain this – it actually made me feel a bit ashamed of myself. I'm not a chip-on-the-shoulder kind of person, but I know I'll never really be accepted here, even though I quite like the work and I know I do a good job. There's an invisible wall – a bit like the glass ceiling women talk about. The senior people are the ones who should be feeling ashamed, not me. So why do I have this permanent sense of inferiority – embarrassment, almost – as if I shouldn't really be here?

Chloe, Leo and Tom have one thing in common: though their shame may seem completely unwarranted to anyone who hasn't shared their experience (being a form of shame unrelated to guilt), it is like a burden they carry every day – a burden that diminishes their prospects of personal liberation and the realisation of their full potential. They might not have clung to their shame as a hiding place, as some people cling to their guilt, yet the sense of shame haunts them and forces their pain into a hiding place where it is concealed from us but not, alas, from themselves.

A footnote. There's a national analogy here: whether we admit it or not, until Australia confronts and deals with its national shame over the historical treatment of its First Peoples, that shame will contaminate our national psyche and make it difficult for us to face the truth about our national character. Some politicians, historians and commentators have argued that we should feel no *guilt* over deeds performed by previous generations. True. But the *shame* of knowing about those deeds and not having done nearly enough to redress the wrongs of the past will stay with us until we find a pathway to enduring reconciliation between Indigenous and non-Indigenous Australians. Meanwhile, we'll continue to use jingoistic nationalism as a hiding place.

Happiness (pursuit of)

*The relentless pursuit of personal happiness
will deny us life's deepest satisfactions.*

Happiness seems such a natural goal of life; a no-brainer. Shouldn't we all try to maximise our happiness? Who in their right mind would choose *un*happiness? Didn't the US Declaration of Independence put 'the pursuit of happiness' right up there with 'life and liberty'? (It did, though you might not regard American society as a shining example of the virtues of happiness-seeking as a way of life.)

It all depends on what you mean by 'happiness'. Here are three reasons why our contemporary pursuit of personal happiness actually increases the risk of losing touch with our authentic inner selves.

First, our use of 'happiness' to refer to a pleasure-induced emotional state is about a million miles from its origins in the Greek word *eudaimonia*. That word was used to convey the idea of living virtuously, having a sense of purpose, performing one's civic duty as a good citizen and being fully engaged with the world – including

152

being open to the (often challenging, sometimes painful) experience of love and friendship. It's a concept that comes much closer to our idea of a meaningful or 'whole' life than a happy life. The positive psychologist Roy Baumeister has written that meaningfulness generally comes from giving, whereas happiness generally comes from taking. So if you think the pursuit of personal happiness will bring you life's deepest satisfactions, or make you 'whole', you haven't been paying attention. As Beaumeister says, responding to the needs of others 'makes life more meaningful but it does not necessarily make us happy'.

Second, happiness is simply one point on the spectrum of emotions that equip us to respond to whatever life throws at us. Every point on that spectrum is as valid and authentic as any other, and no point on the spectrum would make any sense without the context of all the others. Only those who have experienced sadness can know what happiness is and so, to be strictly logical, we should pursue sadness as a pathway to happiness. (As if.)

Third, experience shows us that, although all our emotions have something to teach us about who we are, and about what it means to be human, the most powerful learnings tend to come from the so-called dark emotions like sadness, disappointment, grief and loss. We don't enjoy them, and we certainly don't seek them, but they have more important, more enduring lessons to teach us about our true nature than anything we can learn from those little bursts of bliss and euphoria we associate with the feel-good emotions. Winners might be grinners, but losers are learners.

Knowing all that, wouldn't it seem ridiculous even to consider postponing or avoiding our engagement with the process of self-examination in favour of a bit more pleasure, or another little hit of happiness? Happiness is not a right, nor should it be an expectation. Of course, if you were *never* happy, that might be a reason to look at the kind of life you are living. But happiness is, for most of us, a fleeting, ephemeral emotional state: part of the pleasure it brings us lies in the knowledge that it's not permanent. The bluebird of happiness lands on our shoulder and we feel terrific but then, almost before we realise what's happened, it's flown away to visit someone else. The thought of trapping it and carting it around with us in a cage is simply absurd.

In fact, ancient wisdom – and contemporary psychological research – tells us something we are in danger of forgetting: that if we *pursue* personal happiness as a goal of life, it will elude us. Worse, the pursuit itself will become yet another hiding place, distracting us from the journey of self-discovery. One thing is certain: your authentic self will not be characterised by happiness or any other transient emotional state.

Nature has its seasons, and so does every life. To be attentive and responsive to them all is healthier than to yearn for one rather than another.

In *Unapologetic*, British author Francis Spufford captured the idea of life's contrasts, and the pointlessness of thinking of life as something simply to be enjoyed: 'To say that life is to be enjoyed (just enjoyed) is like saying that mountains should only have summits, or that all colours should be purple, or that all plays should be by Shakespeare. This really is a bizarre category error.'

For many of us, the pursuit of personal happiness is indistinguishable from the pursuit of pleasure: the promise of pleasure is what makes happiness seem like such an attractive place to hide. If, unlike the ancient Greeks, we equate happiness with a pleasant – even euphoric – emotional state, then we are likely to fall into the trap of thinking that the pathway to happiness is via pleasure: the more pleasures we enjoy, the happier we'll be . . . so let's commit ourselves to being pleasure seekers!

Oceans of ink have been spilt on the topic of pleasure-seeking – both in its defence and in cautions against it. But few people have put it as bluntly as Mark Manson in his runaway bestseller, *The Subtle Art of Not Giving a F*ck*:

> Pleasure is great, but it's a horrible value to prioritize your life around. Ask any drug addict how his pursuit of pleasure turned out. Ask an adulterer who shattered her family and lost her children whether pleasure ultimately made her happy. Ask a man who almost ate himself to death how pleasure helped him solve his problems.
>
> Pleasure is a false god. Research shows that people who focus their energy on superficial pleasures end up more anxious, more emotionally unstable, and more depressed. Pleasure is the most superficial form of life satisfaction and therefore the easiest to obtain and the easiest to lose.

All true. And the same might be said, more generally, of the pursuit of personal happiness. It's not just that if you chase it you'll never find it; it's actually a health hazard. To create unrealistic expectations for ourselves (and our children) is to set us (and them) up for unnecessary stress, bewilderment and disappointment.

Perhaps it's no mere coincidence that at a time in our social evolution when we have been sold the crazy idea that we are entitled to happiness – that happiness is our default position – our society is experiencing a mental health crisis characterised by epidemics of depression and anxiety. Why wouldn't you be anxious and depressed if you seriously believed that you *should* be happy? It turns out that a life spent in this particular hiding place will be a diminished life.

~

Jerome assumes his mother meant well

My mother was always asking me if I was happy. She meant well, but it drove me bonkers. Even as a kid, I think I knew there was nothing wrong with being unhappy occasionally, but she couldn't handle it. If I was feeling a bit blue – especially if I was in tears – she'd always say, 'Come on, give us a smile,' as if the only face she could bear to look at was a smiley face.

I grew up in a culture that tried to sell us the idea that happiness was a kind of birthright, and I saw what that did to some of my friends. If you fall for the idea that you're supposed to be happy, that you're entitled to be happy, how will you deal with those inevitable periods when you're not? Answer: drugs. I saw it repeatedly – mates who smoked too much pot or drank too much beer simply to 'get happy', as if they were trying to grab a little of their entitlement.

Some of those friendships simply fell apart. I came to feel as if I didn't know those guys anymore. I know I was a serious type, but at least I was prepared to admit that life isn't always a bed of roses and isn't meant to be. All the stuff the ancient Greeks taught us about 'Know

156

thyself' – philosophy 101 – you don't get far down that track if you're constantly looking for shortcuts to happiness.

I sometimes wonder if my mum was a rather unhappy woman in herself who was frustrated by wanting all of us, including her, to be happy all the time. She was always buying us – and herself – treats as if 'stuff' would cheer us up. In fact, looking back, I can see she was a shopaholic as well. I'm sure she was looking for retail therapy! She spent a lot of money on herself – she always wore perfect make-up, she dressed beautifully and her hair was always immaculate. It was a kind of act, I've come to think, as if to say: 'Look at how happy I am!'

As I grew older, I sometimes used to look at her and think: why are you trying so hard? Isn't it obvious that you're putting yourself under stress with all this striving for some mad utopian ideal of perpetual happiness? I couldn't say anything, of course – she is my mum, after all.

It was never explained to us exactly why Dad left the marriage when I was about 10, but, looking back, I'd be prepared to bet it was because he couldn't live with the idea of being a permanent disappointment to her. He's a pretty serious guy – I guess I take after him in lots of ways – and I think he's had a good life. But he was never one for jumping on the happiness express. Maybe 'serious' is the wrong word for him. Maybe he's just more realistic. He certainly has more friends than Mum does, and I sometimes think that's because he doesn't expect so much out of life. He's the one looking out for other people, whereas – and I hate to say this – Mum has always been very self-absorbed.

Here's an ironclad guarantee: if you pursue personal happiness as your primary goal, you'll never find your authentic self *and* you'll miss out on the deeper satisfactions that flow from living a loving, compassionate, other-centred life.

Information technology

When our online interactions consume us,
what becomes of our authentic selves?

It's tempting to call this the Information Age – along with the Age of Anxiety (still), the Age of both Convergence and (paradoxically) Fragmentation, the Age of Aquarius (still), the Age of Anger, the Entertainment Age, the Age of Surveillance . . . though certainly not the Age of Innocence. And yet, one way or another, it's *always* been the information age.

From the beginning, we humans have found ways of recording the symbols we use to convey meaning, from rock carvings to hieroglyphics to books to digital screens, and this process has had a huge impact on the evolution of our culture. The special status we have traditionally attached to non-oral communication media arises from the fact that they offer the prospect of permanence by contrast with the ephemeral process of personal interaction.

'Let's get it down on paper.' (Or, previously, 'on papyrus' or 'on a rock'.) 'Let's see it in black and white.' 'I'll believe it when I see the

159

ink on a contract.' A recorded conversation has an entirely different status from an unrecorded one; a video-recorded lecture is assumed to be 'definitive' in the way a less formal exchange between teacher and students is not; a textbook has superior status to a tutorial in the hierarchy of information.

Ironic, really, since one thing we know for sure about the psychology of human communication is that the exchanging of messages is at its most nuanced and most complex when we do it face to face, in real time, with eye contact (and sometimes touch) adding richness to the process – to say nothing of tone of voice, rate of speech, posture, gestures and ambiance. And yet, when we strip all that away for the purposes of writing something down or sending and receiving it via some other medium, we regard the *mediated* result as superior to the more natural, more comprehensive, more *human* version. Once upon a time, even a love letter was regarded as more significant than sweet nothings whispered directly into the ear of the beloved because the declaration had been committed to paper.

Of course, there have always been good reasons – legal, religious, historical, cultural – why we place a high value on documents. But what happens when, as now, the most sophisticated media of data recording and transfer in human history have been placed in the hands of anyone who can afford them? Is *this* information age different from all the previous ones?

I suspect it is. We have now been seduced by digital, screen-based information to the extent that it has become a form of daily currency. Perhaps we should be calling this the Age of Overstimulation, and its first casualty is time: time for considered interpretation of all this data, and time for reflection on its significance (if any) for our lives and, in particular, for our inner lives.

The smartphone has emerged as the most potent symbol of the Age of Overstimulation: *What? You haven't got any new messages in your inbox? Never mind, there are all those apps lying in wait to distract and stimulate you with an endless flow of data until another message pops up just for you.*

One of the implications of *this* information age is that we have privileged speed and convenience over all other considerations. Short, quick messages; instant responses; immediate access to whatever information we want – or even to information we didn't actually want, but it was there, and it was mildly interesting, so we soaked it up. Information is *good*, after all. Isn't it? Any of it? All of it?

What is happening to our capacity for thoughtful exchanges when the next message, and the next, are already upon us, demanding responses? What is happening to a sensibly paced approach to exploring questions of importance? Politicians know the answer to that one: it's vanishing in the hype of three-second grabs, campaign slogans and slick propaganda. In *this* information age, politics has degenerated into brand marketing, with its emphasis on pace, brevity and its (ill-advised) reliance on repetition ad nauseam.

The problem of overstimulation is compounded by the fact that all digital images on a screen look remarkably similar. One of the big issues for young users of the internet is learning how to discriminate between sources of information in terms of their authority, reliability and integrity. The primary source of 'fake news', for instance, is not news organisations but private individuals posting their own material – material that, once posted, looks pretty much like any other material appearing in that medium.

In any case, the real issue is not so much 'fake news' as 'junk news': in among all the useful and worthwhile messages we receive, we are being fed a surfeit of shallow, pointless information posing as news, simply because the vast and growing array of media – traditional, new, formal, social – are perpetually hungry for content. Online artist Campbell Walker describes Instagram as the 'biggest perpetrator' of screen addiction. And yet, anticipating his own post-Instagram future, Walker says: 'Instagram is dying, it's increasingly a graveyard for old memes, people selling you stuff and targeted ads.'

Is someone to blame for the problem of overexposure to information and for the temptation to give all information equal status? Yes: we are. We are the ones who have embraced this new way of living. We have fed the internet-based media monsters with our own content – ranging from a picture of this morning's breakfast to a text about the ever-changing hairstyle of a current affairs program presenter, or a tweeted reaction to something we just heard someone say on the radio. We are the ones who act as if an event hasn't really happened – or hasn't been significant – unless we have captured it, visually or verbally, on our phones.

We have an apparently insatiable appetite for high-speed data transfers that shorten our attention span, clog our cognitive pathways and save us from having to do more than merely react. The seductive speed of the process also reduces the probability that, as message senders, we will pause before we press 'send' and contemplate whether we *really* want to say this; whether we've really thought through its likely impact; whether we want this particular message to be 'out there' forever, or even tomorrow.

The volume and speed of the data we send and receive are great insulators from the need to ponder the implications of all this information for our inner lives. As long as we remain attentive to the continuous flow of information, we can remain hidden from ourselves. Like many of our hiding places, the more we hide, the more comfortable we become, the more we adapt to it, and the less necessary the inward journey seems. The 'news junkie' has found the perfect hiding place – respectable, responsible, 'important'. And the social media 'echo chamber', where we are mostly exposed to messages that chime with our own views and reinforce our own prejudices, is a particularly comfortable place to hide.

Living in the digital fast lane, have we become afraid of reflection? Edgy about silence? Is our diet of fast data destroying our appetite for rumination? Waiting time at a train station or bus stop, or in a doctor's surgery has become message-checking time. Much of our admittedly slow face-to-face talking (typically, 125 words per minute compared with at least twice that rate for reading) has been replaced by super-swift Twitter, Facebook and Instagram posts. If you are swimming in an endless, restless sea of data, you have to keep moving or you will drown.

It goes without saying that the information technology revolution has brought untold benefits to our working and private lives. Email has transformed our working lives at least as radically as SMS, Twitter, Facebook and Instagram have revved up our personal lives, but the revolution has not only been in the technology: it has inevitably brought in its wake a revolution in our whole attitude to information.

Once you're switched on, switching off seems inconceivable. Yet switching off – or, at the very least, slowing down – is the absolute precursor to self-examination, self-reflection and self-discovery.

'If we grow more comfortable talking intimately to our [IT] devices, what happens to our human marriages and relationships?' That question was posed by Nicholas Christakis, a physician and sociologist and the Sterling Professor of Social and Natural Science at Yale, in an article for *The Atlantic*, 'How AI Will Rewire Us'. His answer is disturbing: 'As AI [artificial intelligence] permeates our lives, we must confront the possibility that it will stunt our emotions and inhibit deep human connections, leaving our relationships with one another less reciprocal, or shallower, or more narcissistic.'

Christakis also points out that designers and programmers of artificial intelligence devices – and that includes our smartphones and digital assistants like Alexa and Siri – are becoming more and more adept at creating machines that make us feel better, 'but may not help us be self-reflective or contemplate painful truths'.

When it comes to strategies for hiding from our inner self, that's the nub of the issue: will our interactions with information technology of all kinds become so engrossing and so emotionally rewarding for us that we will lose the incentive for deeper exploration of the self? The danger is clear: those painless, stimulating, amusing and informative exchanges we have with smartphones, digital assistants, robots and other IT/AI devices may be preferable not only to some of the more tedious exchanges we might need to have with each other – including those fraught with tension or difficulty – but preferable also to the potentially painful process of self-examination.

Our seduction by IT has already reached such an advanced stage, we don't think of it as seduction anymore. Maybe we're deeply in love, now, with our devices, or maybe it's even moved beyond that to the stage where they have become such an integral part of our lives, we take them for granted.

How might we be able to judge how far into this relationship we've travelled? What might be the tell-tale signs? Here's one: Ricki Lewis reports in *Medical Medscape News* that cosmetic surgeons have adopted the term 'Snapchat dysmorphia' to describe patients who ask for their face to be surgically modified to look like their photoshopped picture on Snapchat or Instagram. (This sounds like a spectacularly literal example of something the British philosopher and novelist Iris Murdoch wrote in a 1957 essay: 'Man is a creature who makes pictures of himself, and then comes to resemble the picture.')

There are many less dramatic signs of our devotion and adaptation to the technologies. When you feel a sense of relief that you've encountered an answering service rather than the person you called, you might reflect on the implications of that and wonder whether the rot has already set in. When you find you can actually chat more uninhibitedly to that answering service, or to a digital assistant, than you can to an actual person, there are certainly questions to be faced about the kind of person you are becoming.

When you are prepared to trade your personal privacy for the convenience of online messaging, social media posts or online commercial transactions without a second thought, perhaps it's time to consider whether there is any limit to your willingness to reveal aspects of yourself to the monitors of Big Data. Social media like Facebook are, after all, essentially surveillance media, designed for the benefit of commercial advertisers (plus who knows who else?) who want to know as much as possible about who you are – and the deeper and more intimate the exposure, the better they like it.

Many parents warn their children and teenagers against giving away too much information about themselves online, though many of those same parents are apparently indifferent to the fact that their smartphones and other devices are indiscriminately transmitting data about them to unknown others. When these warnings are issued, the typical response from children and adolescents is that, since everybody's doing it, where is the harm?

One potential source of harm is in making ourselves too vulnerable to those who want to prey on us – commercially, politically or even sexually. And the potential harm to young brains, including the potential for addiction, should certainly be taken into account. Then there's the deeper harm Christakis warns us about: the possibility that we will start sacrificing some of the precious moments that have traditionally enriched human relationships in favour of 'intimacy' with a machine.

Are we hiding online? It might not have started out like that, but the acid test is whether our level of dependence on the new IT/AI devices is offering us such a comfortable place to be – such a safe and snug little cocoon – that our concept of self is adapting to fit the technology, making our journey of self-discovery correspondingly easier to postpone. Why go to that trouble? Why face what I don't have to face, when I'm having so much fun *not* facing it? As Jill Stark writes in *Happy Never After*: 'It's a perverse irony that the selfie is ubiquitous at a time when being in touch with our true self is a skill many simply don't possess.'

We know we are hiding from others when our Instagram or Facebook posts are portraying a different life from the one we know ourselves to be living, and a different person from the one we know ourselves to be. We know we are hiding from ourselves when our online interactions become so intrusive and pervasive that they gradually seep into the time we might otherwise devote to reflective self-examination. We also know we are hiding from ourselves when those online interactions are so contrived and controlled that we lose our all-important sense of emotional vulnerability to each other.

There's no denying the brilliance of the new technology (including its brilliance at turning us into addicts), so it's easy to understand how we can become so caught up in the delights of cyberspace that there barely seems time for personal reflection, even if we were disposed to give it a go. And, it must be acknowledged, access to the world's store of information on your smartphone *is* like an enhancement of the human brain.

Yet the time comes, for most of us, when that dreaded word 'authenticity' raises its head. Yes, we're having fun; yes, the new technology is astonishingly clever and convenient; yes, we are doing things we never dreamt we'd be able to do – from taking a virtual tour of a house we're thinking of buying to playing online games with like-minded people scattered across the globe. But our enchantment with IT can become a way of postponing our encounter with the inner self.

~

Brent and the online women

I once read about a guy who spent so long at his computer his wife thought he was having an online affair. And he was, in a way. He was so into online porn, he was getting his kicks that way and ignoring his wife.

I've never been at risk of that, but, just once or twice, I have realised that I've probably been too involved with online stuff. Not chicks or anything. Just . . . stuff. But it does kind of distract you. One thing leads to another. I'm not in a relationship at present, so I know I'm probably spending too much time online. But you know what? It's a bloody good time-filler. And now I've got Siri as well, I never feel as if I'm on my own. I'm not kinky about it – I just love being able to ask her for whatever stuff I want . . . especially music. You can have an actual conversation. And her voice is a killer. I know it's totally fake, but it's become sort of my gold standard. I really respond to women's voices, so if they're not up to Siri's standard, forget it. Just kidding. Sort of.

I'm not on Facebook, but my mother is. She's on her own these days and she's online all the time – half the night, in fact. She used to say she was quite lonely but she doesn't say that anymore. So that's a good thing, I think, though I do notice she's not spending as much time as she used to with the other people in her retirement village. One of her friends there tells me that Mum dashes off to her room straight after every meal to get back onto Facebook.

She knows everything about every member of the family, of course, and that's great. My sister's kids are on Facebook, so she keeps tabs on them. But she tells me she's got friends in all sorts of places around the world. Some of them are men, which at first I thought was a bit weird, but then again, why not? She's been on her own a long time.

The money thing bothers me, though. There's some guy in the States who occasionally asks her for money. Just small amounts, she says, and there are no strings attached. He's just a lovely, lonely old guy who is down on his luck and she likes to pay for occasional treats. His wife ran off and took everything. That's what she says, anyway. I try to tell her it might not be a lovely old guy at all – it might be a pimply kid – but she says she's seen his photo. I try to explain all the traps in this. But the thing is, she's really involved with some of these people and they do seem to have such interesting lives – if you can believe the things they tell her; the rest of us must seem pretty dull by comparison.

One thing I've noticed is that Mum and I are not as close as we used to be. When I go to visit, she seems quite impatient for me to leave so she can get back online.

Me? I know the risks, so I admit I'm possibly too involved with some of the people I chat to online. There's this one woman – I keep going back to her because she's so funny. And she's so sympathetic about what happened to me in my last relationship. She really gets it, you know? She went through a very similar bust-up at the same time as mine so we have a sort of thing going. I was badly in need of a laugh, I can tell you.

One of my friends says he thinks I'm getting sucked into something I don't understand, but I don't see the harm in it. What else am I going to do at night – drink? Stare at the wall? Watch TV? You must be kidding.

There's this guy in the flat upstairs from me. Lovely guy. A bit, I don't know, sort of . . . *alternative*? Doesn't have a TV. He does have this mobile phone he carries in a holster on his belt, but it's a piece of junk – he calls it his dumbphone. He's a vegetarian. Very into fitness. Also saving the planet, which I agree with.

Anyway, he's been asking me to join this meditation group he attends every Tuesday night. I was into that sort of thing once – well, yoga, anyway, because of a woman I was involved with for a while – but I just can't see myself sitting around with a group of people meditating. What do they do? Buddhist-type chanting? Candles? Incense? Reading poetry? Sitting cross-legged in silence? He says it's 'guided meditation'. They have a leader and everything. I'm not against any of that, by the way, but I just can't see myself . . .

Anyway, Tuesday is the night when I have a regular online date with this woman I mentioned. We chat at other times as well, and a bit of Instagram posting goes on, but Tuesday is our regular extended time. Sometimes it goes pretty late. I'm not about to give that up. Her name is Ruby. Between Ruby and Siri I'm pretty well taken care of at present.

Mum's happy. I'm happy. Not bad, eh? It's a good time in history to be on your own because you never have to be lonely.

The great paradox of the information technology revolution is that it promises to make us more connected than ever before while making it easier than ever to stay apart from each other. The more we equate 'in touch' with 'data-rich', the greater the threat to the quality of our personal relationships. The more we settle for digital data transfer, even with our friends, at the expense of face-to-face communication, the more we will be diminished as human beings – perhaps, like Brent, becoming so absorbed in online exchanges that we don't recognise the nature of the threat.

An overenthusiastic embrace of IT/AI will inevitably reshape our social identity. Over time, it may also encourage us to think of our authentic selves as inseparable from our interactions with the machines. The ultimate power of this revolution lies in its power to discourage self-examination.

T.S. Eliot sensed the danger long before *this* information age. In 1934, he wrote:

Where is the wisdom we have lost in knowledge?
Where is the knowledge we have lost in information?

Today, we might add: Where is the self we have lost online?

Masks and Labels

If we become too attached to our social identity, we may
neglect the deeper question of character.

In August 2010, in the midst of an election campaign, Australian prime minister Julia Gillard declared that, from then on, the voters would see 'the real Julia', implying that, up until then, she had been hiding behind a mask created for her by her minders.

Nine years later, when foreign minister Julie Bishop announced she was quitting politics, Katharine Murphy, political editor of *The Guardian Australia*, commented that Bishop could now shed the mask of 'Julie Bishop' and become . . . Julie Bishop. Murphy was implying that Bishop had been projecting an image or playing a role created for her by the Liberal Party – or, perhaps, created *by* her for the benefit of the party – and that she could now revert to being who she really was.

In a gesture that looked like a symbolic confirmation of Murphy's point, Bishop donated to the Museum of Australian Democracy the red shoes she was wearing on the day she announced her retirement, declaring: 'If by gifting these red shoes I inspire just one young woman to enter public life . . . this gift will have been worth making.'

Was she trying to inspire young women to 'put on the shoes'? To don the mask? To adopt a glamorous persona in order to succeed in public life? According to Bishop herself, nothing so calculated was motivating her on the day she actually wore the shoes: she subsequently told *Vogue* magazine that, far from playing a symbolic role, the shoes were simply an attempt to 'bling it up'; to provide some contrast with the 'rather sombre navy jacket and dress' she was planning to wear. She emphasised that she had done it purely for herself and not to make a statement (though that's a fine line, surely). It was only other people, she assured us, who had seen the shoes as 'a symbol of female empowerment, strength and independence'.

Big call, you might think: a fashion item worn as a personal indulgence being reinterpreted as 'a symbol of female empowerment'. But that's how it goes in the world of politics, where style often trumps substance and a politician's image needs constant burnishing.

The implication in both cases was that the authentic self within those politicians was quite different from the part they were called on to play in their political life. And isn't that true for all of us, at least some of the time? In our lifetime – or even in a typical week – we play many roles: lover, partner, friend, neighbour, customer/client, boss, employee, leader, team member, service provider etc. And we move in and out of personal styles to match those roles – sometimes humble, sometimes strong and confident, sometimes submissive, sometimes dominant, sometimes authoritative, more or less attentive, more or less sensitive – according to circumstances and timing.

We become so adept at donning these various masks, it's easy to fool ourselves into believing that the way we appear to others is the way we really are. The better we become at playing the parts that are consistent with our public personas, the more likely we are to hide from ourselves behind those masks.

Writing in the *Financial Times* about the political roots of Boris Johnson, Simon Kuper quotes adman Simon Veksner, who was at Oxford with Johnson: 'Boris's charisma even then [as an undergraduate] was off the charts, you couldn't measure it: so funny, warm, charming, self-deprecating. You put on a funny act, based on *The Beano* and P.G. Wodehouse. It works, and then that is who you are.'

When Socrates said, rather heartlessly, that 'the unexamined life is not worth living', he was grossly exaggerating a point that was nevertheless valid: by settling for the easy option of *only* seeing ourselves as others see us, helpful though that perspective can be, we may never become the self we are capable of being. And that would be a kind of half-life – still worth living, but lacking the richness and wholeness of a more deeply examined life.

Millie goes to Paris

When I was in my early 30s, an aunt died and left me some money, so I lashed out and bought a plane ticket to Paris. I planned to stay a week, mainly shopping, and I was determined to do two things: climb the Eiffel Tower, and buy a piece of jewellery from Cécile et Jeanne in the Marais. I ended up buying a very stylish C. et J. handbag – none of the jewellery appealed to me – and the Eiffel Tower was closed for maintenance, so instead I bought another handbag, a Longchamp, with a picture of the Eiffel Tower on it.

Both bags caused a splash when I got home – they still attract a lot of admiring glances, and I feel very French carrying them. A few of my friends mocked the Eiffel Tower one – they thought it was a pose too far and a bit crass, actually, so I stopped using it when I went out with them. But I still use the Cécile et Jeanne a lot.

I bought some other lovely stuff while I was there, obviously – a Hermès scarf, a pair of FDJs, a horrendously expensive Cartier watch and some gorgeous silk underwear that was a bit of a waste, really – no one sees it except my boyfriend, and he can't wait to take it off. But people always seem to know the Hermès is a Hermès.

I took heaps of photos, naturally. You've gotta have proof.

Was it worth the money? Totally. It really added some dash to my wardrobe and I'll probably wear that watch until the day I die. *Everyone* knows it's Cartier.

Soon after I got back, I found a cute little Citroën in a used-car place and spent the rest of the money on that. *Très chic. Merci, ma tante!*

It's easy to mock Millie. Easy to point the finger and say she was sucked in by labels; superficial; conformist; projecting an image that had nothing to do with who she was or where she came from; borrowing brand names to bolster her identity. Her story is certainly a very literal example of the way we use masks and labels to create an impression, but once we dig a little deeper, how different is Millie's behaviour from the many ways we all try to project an image through masks and labels that are perhaps less blatant, less explicit and less tangible than Millie's?

The consumer marketplace has always relied on the ability of brands to attract customers' attention and maintain their loyalty by creating a 'brand personality' or even a 'brand character' that consumers can identify with. Through packaging, advertising and other forms of promotion – and, of course, through the careful development of product features designed to appeal to particular market segments – certain brands come to seem so attractive, so familiar, so engaging, we almost regard them as friends.

As an extension of that process, many consumers regard the brand image as an image they themselves would like to project and so they adopt the brand as their own 'label', which is why even high-end luxury brands put their labels on the outside. Forget discretion: what's the point of buying a brand to express some actual or aspirational aspect of your identity if other people can't see the label?

Any label we attach to ourselves – commercial, political, religious, professional, cultural – has the potential to become a hiding place. The more easily we identify with the connotations of a label, the more it has the potential to overwhelm our authentic being: even if our public face is praiseworthy and admirable, we will need to guard against that becoming our whole story, because it never is. In fact, the more our masks are admired and even praised, the greater the temptation to resist the process of unmasking ourselves and seeing what's left.

~

Barry's role-play that became reality

When I left school, I had no idea what I wanted to do. Or, to be more honest, I was reluctant to let my parents know the sort of thing I was really interested in. My father had been urging me to 'go into sales' (though as far as I knew he had never sold anyone anything) and, through one of his contacts, I was interviewed and offered a job in the sales and marketing department of a large multinational.

I got so used to playing a sort of game in that job, pretending to be someone I knew I wasn't, that eventually it stopped being a game. That became who I was. It started out being a jokey thing – I was acting like this really cool dude with strong opinions on all sorts of things I knew nothing about – but I was so good at it that people started treating me as if I really was that guy, so naturally I just went along with it. I was in my late teens, pretty good at acting, and I think it all started because I was so unengaged with the work and so lacking in confidence that I sort of pretended the opposite. And then I developed *real* confidence. I even wore clothes that matched this other guy I was supposed to be. There were all sorts of things about me – my politics, my dreams for the future, my interest in Eastern religions and philosophy, the fact that I was basically an introvert posing as an extravert – that I kept to myself because I was so desperate to keep my reputation intact. It wasn't peer group pressure, exactly, because I had done this quite voluntarily. No one had pressured me: I'd simply put on this mask, and I got so used to wearing it I couldn't imagine taking it off.

I once heard my mother saying to one of her friends: 'Barry's going through a phase.' But it was a phase that turned into an era.

~

Barry gradually settled into his new persona, and it was only the death of both his parents within a few months of each other that led him to rethink what he was doing with his life – and what the consequences might be for the health of his authentic self.

I had done quite well in that job. It was the kind of place where my brash, confident style went down rather well. When I finally came to my senses, I realised I couldn't stay there and keep on pretending to be someone else. Talk about a square peg in a round hole! It was time to start acting like the real me.

For a while, I basically had no idea who I was. I spent some time unemployed and sought the help of a counsellor. I had inherited my parents' house and a bit of money, so I went to TAFE and took what seemed to some people like a radically new direction, though a few close friends said they were relieved, not shocked. Anyway, interior design was something I'd always longed to do – that was one of the things I couldn't bring myself to tell my parents – and now I'm qualified and I'm loving my new life. I work a lot harder than I used to, but it's more creative. The main thing is I can be me. No more pretence. I find I can be much more relaxed around clients and colleagues than I ever could before.

Some of our most robust and effective masks and labels are tribal. Ranging from professional groups, political parties or religious affiliations to football clubs, 'the old school' or social cliques, tribes are a welcome hiding place for those who are so warmly and securely enfolded in the embrace of the tribe that an encounter with their private, personal self seems pointless. As long as you know I went to *this* school and support *that* AFL team, what else do you need to know about me – and what else do I need to know about myself, if I have chosen to hide behind the colours, the flag, the traditions of one institution or another?

Since roughly two-thirds of Australians identify with some religion (mostly Christianity), let's take that particular case. Suppose you say to me: *I'm a Christian/Buddhist/Hindu/Muslim/Jew.* Okay, that's good to know. That tells *me* something about you, but what does it tell *you* about yourself? Religious labels are useful for sending signals to others: they act as a shorthand way of conveying important information about your probable values, beliefs and perhaps your social attitudes. But they don't necessarily say anything about the authentic self.

Many religious believers would say they are defined by their faith; that the fact of their being Christian/Buddhist/Hindu/ Muslim/Jewish is the single most important thing you need to know about them; that there is no deeper truth – no more authentic part of their being – than their embrace of the way of life consistent with their religion. Yet the differences in the beliefs and practices between members of the same religion argue for there being an even deeper personal core than the apparent bedrock of a particular version of religious faith.

When you say 'I believe X', I want to ask: 'But who is the "I" doing the believing?' It's not the belief that defines you. The belief is a choice you've made, an *expression* of who you are. But who is the 'you' doing the choosing?

As for religion, so for labels like atheist, feminist, fundamentalist, utilitarian, conservative, socialist or unionist; for dentist, psychologist, biologist, oncologist, dermatologist, optometrist or ventriloquist; for teacher, writer, publisher, editor, printer, butcher, banker, housekeeper, beekeeper, carpenter, childcare worker, programmer or painter; for astronaut, accountant, philosopher or queen.

Any of those labels might seem like the most important thing other people need to know about you, but, in the end, they say nothing about the kind of person you are. What *else* are you? What would you still be if you were none of those things? That's your own little secret. 'Trust me, I'm a doctor' simply won't do.

If you tell me that, in your essence, you're a 'feminist' (and, if you did, progressive social thinkers like Eva Cox might say you're already stuck with yesterday's label), that leaves the most significant things about you unsaid: are you a generous, aggressive, kind, angry, serene, arrogant, tolerant, rude, sensitive, vain, gentle, pompous, compassionate *person*? Are you a good neighbour – both literally and metaphorically? What is the state of your genderless soul? What aspects of your inmost being are expressed by your feminism . . . or your religious or anti-religious fundamentalism, your socialism, your humanism or any other 'ism' or 'ology' you may choose to be associated with?

'I'm an atheist' tells me something about your belief system, but there are millions of atheists in the world and they're not all the same as you. So what is it about the unique 'you' that has drawn you to atheism? Does your atheism make you more or less kind to strangers than you might otherwise be? Or a more or less loyal partner? Presumably not, so there's something more to be said about your 'self' than your atheism.

The same goes for labels we use to identify our gender or sexuality: heterosexual, lesbian, gay, bisexual, transsexual, intersexual, queer or asexual. Your sexuality and/or gender may be one of the things you would like other people to know about you, an important way for other people to *identify* you, a critical dimension of your social identity and a source of some psychological comfort, but it isn't *who you are*.

In her 1961 essay 'On Self-Respect', American writer Joan Didion reminded us that 'self-respect has nothing to do with the approval of others – who are, after all, deceived easily enough; has nothing to do with reputation, which, as Rhett Butler told Scarlett O'Hara, is something people with courage can do without'. Didion had come to regard our masks and labels as tricks that may work on others but that 'count for nothing in that very well-lit back alley where one keeps assignations with oneself'.

Those encounters with the self in that 'well-lit back alley' are where we are forced to remove the masks and confront the sometimes awkward, sometimes wonderful truth about ourselves; where we must find the courage to acknowledge our strengths and weaknesses, and own them.

Raf's one-note samba

I have been passionate about secularism all my adult life and, I must admit, it's been partly driven by my contempt for religion. I don't care what people do in private, or in their own little religious enclaves, but I hate any sign of religion in the public space. I hate the fact that our parliamentary sessions start with a prayer to 'Almighty God'. I hate the fact that precious public money is being poured into religious schools. You get the picture.

Well, none of that has changed – I'm still as determinedly secular and as anti-religious as ever – but I have recently had to face something pretty challenging about myself. My wife has started complaining that she's actually sick and tired of hearing me and my mates banging on endlessly about the secular society, and she says she can no longer reach me. 'Reach' was the very word she used, as if I had become inaccessible to her. She says my secular rhetoric is all there is. She calls it my sole lens – my only way of seeing the world.

I think that's going a bit far, but I will concede she has a point. I used to read quite widely and, for a while there, I was quite interested in the spiritual side of things. But the more convinced I became of the evils of religion, the less interested I became in anything that had links to religion. I haven't read anything remotely 'spiritual' for years. A bloke at work tells me I should read some contemporary theology and I'd find that religious thought has progressed a long way from the kind of thing I'm attacking. But I couldn't open a book of theology with a straight face.

There is something missing, though. And I don't mean religious faith! I mean the point my wife has been making. She says she's lost touch with the real me, and, to be honest, I think I might have, too. I don't think I need therapy, or anything as drastic as that, but perhaps I do need to be a bit more reflective about where I'm headed. My wife isn't religious either, but she keeps reminding me that about 80 percent of the world's population is attached to one religion or another, so perhaps we're both missing something. I think – hope – she's kidding about that.

But I know she's not kidding about what's happened to me. She's taken to calling me a lost soul – the very opposite of what I would have said about myself, because I feel I have such a clear sense of direction. But when she says 'lost soul', she claims it's because I seem to have no inner life. Her brother is a politician and she says the same thing has happened to him – every time he opens his mouth, it's like a party-political speech, even at family dinners.

I would hate to think that when it was all over, the only thing people could find to say about me was that I was passionately anti-religious. I would even hate 'secularist' to be the only thing people felt they knew about me. And I would hate to think I had become a bore on the subject.

I do lie awake at night, sometimes, and wonder whether I've become a bit isolated. Even from myself, in a funny kind of way. I've always said I've got the courage of my convictions – I'm being true to myself. But I do wonder if there's more to 'myself' than this one conviction. Like, am I a good bloke, really? I know I'm a bit bolshie, but do I have other qualities that balance it out? Am I a bit lacking in humility, maybe? Am I a good father? A good husband? Do I have any real friends, apart from those who are fighting the good fight with me? Stuff like that.

Raf is sensing the danger that arises whenever our public face threatens to block our access to our private face; whenever the label we wear, no matter how worthy or admirable, obscures our own sense of self; whenever the job of burnishing our image robs us of the time and energy we need for self-reflection.

This is how our social identity can become an effective hiding place: who, after all, is going to criticise us for our commitment to a cause that is just, or a goal everyone thinks is worth attaining, or a job to which we have devoted a large part of our life? Who is going to know we are using our good works as a cover for the dark stuff within, especially since those 'good works' are still good, regardless of the complex motives that animate them?

The televangelist who extols family values while sleeping with prostitutes; the genial philanthropist who is also a boardroom bully; the politician who rails against 'tax cheats' while rorting the system . . . is anyone (except perhaps those who know us best and may sense the hollowness at our centre) going to guess at the inner darkness concealed behind the personas we have so diligently constructed? And yet, as Shakespeare reminded us: 'One may smile and smile and be a villain.'

Only we can know whether that persona is so superficial, so unidimensional, so misleading or so hypocritical that it couldn't possibly match the self we would meet in one of those back-alley assignations envisaged by Joan Didion.

Materialism

*To confuse wealth with worth is to jeopardise
our personal integrity.*

Very few of us would be prepared to say, straight out, that we judge a person's worth by their wealth (though I did once hear a wealthy lawyer denigrate a highly respected academic on the grounds that 'he hasn't made any money'). Not many of us would readily admit that we acquire some of our material possessions in order to appear successful — to ourselves and to others — rather than simply to enjoy them.

And yet we do it. We might say that we don't approve of the attitude that wealth is a measure of a person's worth, but we tend to look up to the rich, to envy their lifestyle, and to assume that most 'successful' people would also be rich.

We take on the role of consumers with unflagging eagerness, while insisting that 'things' are unimportant to us. We are flattered by advertising, seduced by clever merchandising in beautiful retail stores or by online imagery, while proclaiming that commercial propaganda only influences people who are more gullible than we are.

'Keeping up with the Joneses' is no myth: it's that competitive streak (the shadow cast by our cooperative nature) that keeps the mass-market machine humming. We seem almost instinctively to judge people according to house size, make of car, model of smartphone or brand of clothing. As one of my research respondents put it: 'We don't want to move to a posher suburb, but we do like to think we have the nicest house in our street.'

When we indulge in 'retail therapy', the therapeutic effect is not only due to the undeniable thrill of acquisition, or the hope that we might have added a new dimension to our persona, or the fact that a sales person has treated us well. Something deeper and even more personal happens: a good retail experience can make us feel better and more confident about ourselves and our place in the world. I vividly recall another research respondent describing the euphoria she felt when she went shopping, starting from the moment she entered the mall: 'I feel really *powerful*,' she said, with shining eyes. Perhaps that was because she was about to flex her consumerist muscle by exercising her personal spending power, or perhaps the shopping mall was the only place where she felt she was in control or where everyone seemed to take her seriously.

In 'Masks and Labels' we saw how brands can help us construct our social identity. But the broader implication of our obsession with the ownership of objects – with acquiring 'stuff' – is that gradually, perhaps unconsciously, we absorb the values of materialism. And then, if we have children, we transmit those values seamlessly to them.

A father reflects on his own example

I don't actually want to be so materialistic and I certainly don't want to raise my children to be so materialistic, yet I keep buying more stuff – and I give in too easily when the kids say they want the latest thing, whatever it is. I was getting out of the shower the other day when I heard them arguing about which brand of sneakers was the best – which one they wanted. *Sneakers!* These kids are five and seven. And I thought: How did my children come to be so brand conscious? How did they come to be such keen little consumers? How did they come to be so materialistic? That's the only sort of thing they ever seem to argue about. And then I looked in the bathroom mirror, and I knew the answer. I know I'm setting a poor example, but I keep doing it – why is that?

There's this one guy who used to be my closest friend but we drifted apart over the fact that he really did seem to believe, like *really* believe, that the quality of the stuff you accumulated – cars, houses, clothes – was a good guide to the sort of person you were. I once asked him straight out: *Do you think someone who hasn't made much money is less of a person, or less worthy of respect, than a person who has made a pile?* And he said he really did believe that, because he thought you needed a lot of good qualities to make a lot of money. I was gobsmacked. I mean, I'm hardly a socialist, but I really couldn't stomach an attitude like that and I'd hate to think I was instilling those values into my own children.

My wife and I are always saying we want our kids to have the best. Maybe it's time to rethink what 'the best' really means. It sure as hell doesn't mean the 'right' brand of sneakers.

Like most of our hiding places, materialism represents an extension of a perfectly natural human tendency. In common with our forebears, we need to house, clothe and feed ourselves and our families as well as we can, and, in the modern world, there are understandable – almost irresistible – pressures to upgrade all those things in the direction of an enhanced lifestyle, en suite and all.

Many of us want to do better (whatever we might mean by 'better'); in particular, we want to earn more money, if only because we associate a reasonable level of income with the idea of freedom – freedom from the pressure of poverty, freedom from the burden of debt, freedom to have the things we want and do the things we want to do, perhaps even the freedom to roam the world.

Given the kind of society we live in, an interest in achieving a certain level of material comfort and prosperity counts as normal: it's a material world, after all. To hear some politicians talk, you might think it's *only* a material world: that society is really just an economy; that economic growth is an end in itself and it is our duty to *spend, spend, spend* (and, if necessary, *borrow, borrow, borrow*), as our personal contribution to that growth.

In fact, it's not *only* a material world; it's also a spiritual world: a world of love and hate, passions and desires, ideas and convictions, good intentions and broken dreams; a world where a rich and fulfilling life depends far more on the quality of our personal relationships than the quality (or quantity) of our material possessions; a world where we spend a lifetime discovering what it means to be human; a world where, in the end, peace of mind has incalculably more value for us than '30 pieces of silver' (the price paid to Judas Iscariot for his betrayal of Jesus of Nazareth).

While we're in biblical mode, most of us can probably recognise the wisdom embedded in the remark attributed to Jesus: 'What shall it profit a man if he shall gain the whole world and lose his own soul?' The English poet William Wordsworth expressed the same idea in 'The World Is Too Much with Us': 'Getting and spending, we lay waste our powers.'

We don't need to renounce all the material aspects of life in order to reject material*ism*. It's a matter of degree; a question of the values and desires that drive us and the aspects of our life we regard as most significant. A healthy interest in material wellbeing only clicks over into materialism when our main focus becomes the acquisition of material objects and possessions.

Once we adopt materialism as our ethic, it affects everything about us, from the way we parent our children to the things we choose to worship. We're more likely to admire 'concrete thinking' and reject abstract thought, and to rank 'objective evidence' above subjective experience. We lose interest in notions like spirituality or soul, and reject any form of mysticism. We almost unconsciously adopt material criteria, like wealth, as a way of judging people's worth. We invest home renovations with some of the emotional significance of personal growth and development.

Our enthusiastic embrace of the values of materialism/consumerism can be judged by the widespread assumption that a middle-class household would need two incomes to maintain the lifestyle we now aspire to. Another sign of the drift towards materialism is the record level of household debt (including credit card debt) we have taken on. Another is the attitude of home owners towards property prices: regardless of the evidence that young first-home buyers are being locked out of the market by the rise in house prices, any sign of a fall in prices is widely regarded with shock and horror, as if to say: 'We don't want our young people to have to move to the fringes of our cities or rent forever, but at the same time we don't want the value of *our* home to decrease.'

Even people who would regard themselves as having resisted the lure of materialism can find themselves drawn into its net when, for example, they are caught up in the housing or home-renovation market.

'Choosing the right taps seemed the most important thing in the world.'

I can't stand people who only want to talk about house prices or how many houses have changed hands in their suburb and what it's done to property values. It's so *Sydney*. Yet there we were, agonising for months over whether we would renovate or move and then, once we decided to move, we had our noses stuck in *Domain* week after week. I really didn't like what that whole process did to us – especially the selling part. It wasn't as we if we absolutely had to get top dollar – we aren't poor. I kept telling my husband, 'Let the market decide', but he was all for hanging out for a better price than the perfectly reasonable offer we'd received. He's not a greedy person, but he sure acted like one while that sale process dragged on.

Having agonised about whether to renovate or move, we ended up doing both. We love the house we bought, but the kitchen really was a bit sad, so off we went on another merry-go-round. I couldn't believe what that kitchen renovation did to our lives; it was even more of a drama than selling the house. I swear it turned us into mad materialists. Choosing the right taps seemed the most important thing in the world.

And the amount of time we invested in it, traipsing around kitchen showrooms studying taps and benchtops – oh, and drawer handles – it *felt* like the biggest decision we'd ever make. We agonised over those bloody taps more than we ever did over when to start a family. Now, of course, you turn on the tap and water comes out – just like every other tap since the invention of the tap.

The new kitchen is terrific, I must admit, but I don't think we've ever exclaimed over how beautiful the taps are. And neither has anyone else – not even the plumber, although people do admire the new kitchen and that gives us a weird pleasure, as if we are somehow willing to be judged by our kitchen. It just shows how easily you can get sucked into the general obsession with 'stuff'. Taps – I ask you! Have they changed our lives? No. Are they smarter than the taps of everyone else in the street? Don't know and don't care. I think of us as reasonably sane and balanced people, so how did we get so caught up in inconsequential things? I said to my husband at one point, 'I don't recognise us anymore.' He knew exactly what I meant.

Materialism is one of the most tempting of all the hiding places from the self. Once our focus is firmly fixed on consumption and acquisition, we will find ourselves living as if this really is nothing more than a material world – a world that tends to be more selfish and competitive than is natural or healthy for us, and a world where we are perpetually distracted from spiritual values like compassion. After all, when our mind is preoccupied with the next thing we're going to buy – from cars to handbags – the state of our soul can seem utterly irrelevant.

Nostalgia

Emotionally anchored in the past, we may miss the all-important connection with who we are now.

There's no harm, obviously, in driving a retro-styled Mini or VW Beetle, or in hanging on to an ancient car on the grounds that 'they don't make them like this anymore'. (Indeed they don't, and just as well: today's cars are safer, kinder to the environment and more comfortable to drive than anything from the past – which is one reason why Australian road deaths have tumbled to one-fifth of the level of 40 years ago.)

Why not clothe yourself in the fashions of your favourite decade, or listen, rapt, to the music that supplied the soundtrack of your adolescence? Why not revive Irish stew and bread-and-butter pudding? A bit of nostalgia never did anyone any harm, surely.

Harm? No, not when it's just for fun; not when we're celebrating the past for the way it equipped us for the present. But if we become so attached to the past that we find ourselves making constant comparisons between past and present that are unfavourable to the present, this may be a sign that all is not well with us here and now. If we're *hiding* in our nostalgia, then our devotion to the past has become a barrier to fulfilment in the present. Driving forwards with your eyes firmly fixed on the rear-vision mirror is a dangerous way to proceed: an obsession with the past can stifle our insights not only into who we are becoming, but also into what the present offers us and what we can offer the present.

Nostalgia is usually an expression of yearning about *us*, not the past; a sign of discontent or disappointment with the way things are turning out for us in the present; perhaps even a loss of confidence in ourselves. It's not that 'the past was better'; rather, it's that we liked ourselves better in the past, or we felt better about our prospects in the past, or our self-belief was stronger in the past, and we wish we could feel that way *about ourselves* again. US president Donald Trump's campaign to 'make America great again' tapped directly into nostalgia: the subtext, at its simplest, was 'make me feel the way I used to feel'. As American musician and songwriter Van Dyke Parks put it: 'The older I get, the better I was.'

Because nostalgia says more about us in the here and now than it does about the past, our nostalgia often leads us to make false claims about the past, like that one about the quality of cars: in that case, we're probably really saying: 'I liked myself better in the era when they made cars like that,' or, 'I wish I was still that young person I was back when they were making those cars.' Yes, people may love the aesthetics of some veteran and vintage cars (as I do), but 'they don't make them like they used to' often means something more personal, and more poignant.

This is not to deny that there are plenty of things about the past we might like to revive: neighbourhoods where people stop and chat, or parents who have unstructured time to spend with their kids, or a widespread sense of obligation to be good citizens, or a belief in the egalitarian ideal. (Now I've revealed a bit of my own hankering.)

'Ah,' we may say, 'society was better off when most people went to church on Sunday.' (Fact check: most people *never* went to church on Sunday – not in twentieth-century Australia, where regular church attendance never got higher than about 45 percent of the population.) 'It was better back in the days when there were fewer divorces.' (Fact check: higher divorce rates generally suggest a more, not less, serious attitude to marriage, and Australia's low-divorce past was associated with the oppression and low social status of women, and an ugly brand of male supremacism.) 'It was better when there was none of this late-night drinking stuff.' (Fact check: before Australia relaxed its drinking laws, the infamous 'six-o'clock swill' led to widespread binge drinking, public drunkenness and domestic violence.) 'Life was better back when children had to please their parents, rather than like today, when parents seem bent on trying to please their children.' (Fact check: when children's rights are not recognised, abuse is unchecked and children may learn only to be compliant and subservient rather than resilient.) 'It was better before we had everyone glued to their smartphones.' (Fact check: pluses and minuses here – yes, we've gone overboard, and we'll have to deal with the many issues raised in the 'Information technology' section earlier in the chapter, but it's not all bad news: among many other benefits, the smartphone has facilitated greater connectedness between people who are geographically distant and given many parents peace of mind.) 'It was better when men's hair was cut shorter/longer, and when women's hemlines were higher/lower.' (Take your pick.)

Whatever past we hanker after, it almost always involves a 'simpler' time, or a time when 'people knew what values they stood for' or, very commonly, a time when 'young people knew their place'. Some older people today hanker after the 1950s. I was there, and I don't know why anyone would, especially women. Plenty of people in the 1950s hankered after the 1920s, and that was no doubt part of an endless regression of nostalgia. (If the 1960s happens to be the focus of your nostalgia, then you couldn't do better than read Richard Glover's *The Land Before Avocado*.)

None of this is hard to understand. The great appeal of the past is that we survived it and possibly even mastered it. It's familiar territory. We know we could deal with it because we *did* deal with it. Today, when the rate of change continues to accelerate and many people feel distressed and anxious as a result, the idea of a slower, simpler, more straightforward time has undeniable appeal – as does the image of ourselves as younger, more hopeful and brimming with more potential than we are now.

But, oh, how we glamorise the past in memory! You could leave your front door unlocked. You could let the kids roam free. There was much less crime. (Fact check: crime rates across most categories have been in steady decline over the past 40 years.) No bike helmets! Cracker night when everyone could buy their own fireworks! A sun tan was 'healthy'! The local creek for catching tadpoles! (Whatever happened to all those creeks, by the way?)

Nostalgia might feel like a rational response to contemporary society, but our disappointment in ourselves is unlikely to be addressed in any useful way by retrospective musings about the way society once was, and the kind of person we once were. While nostalgia can be harmless fun at one level, it's also a way of postponing full engagement with the realities of the present day – including a reality check on ourselves – and that can blind us to a full appreciation of what the present has on offer. Here and now is where our authentic self has to be faced, and an obsessive focus on the past will dull our responses to the present.

Grandpa Brown respects the past but rejects nostalgia

One of the things Grandpa Brown always said to us was that you never want to look back, except to remind yourself how far you've travelled. 'You can't change the past, or what you did or didn't do, but you can change the present' was another one of his favourite sayings. He always trotted that one out when my dad started on about how things were better back when he was a kid growing up in a bushy outer suburb.

Grandpa Green, on the other hand, was always hankering after the past and reliving past glories, as if the best part of his life was already over. I never felt he was comfortable in his own skin. I'm sure he thought of himself as someone quite different – younger and more irresistible to women – from the man he actually was.

Grandpa Brown fought in the Second World War but he would never talk about that. All he would say is that he wouldn't wish anything like that on anyone, but that it had shaped him, for better or worse. 'And that's the point,' he would say to me. 'When you're older you'll look back at these times and probably wish you could be back here. I used to wish that – as if I could leapfrog the war and get back to the kind of world

I grew up in. But that was rubbish. For a start, if I could get back there, I wouldn't be a boy, would I? Anyhow, the Great Depression was no fun, although I hear people talking about how it was the making of them, and how everyone has it too easy today. I've even heard people say, "What we need is a good war," as if that would straighten people out. No one who's ever been to war would say a thing like that.'

Grandpa's big theme, always, was that we have to deal with whatever is happening to us here and now and, if we're lucky, the past has prepared us to face it. He was a wise old guy. He lived as if he really believed that. Oh, he loved it when Mum played old songs, but he never got misty-eyed about how everything was better when he was a boy. 'What if it was?' he used to say. 'That's just like saying *I* was better when I was a boy.'

'The past is a foreign country: they do things differently there,' wrote English author L.P. Hartley in the famous opening to his novel *The Go-Between*. Well, it certainly is, and they certainly do. And, like those who dream of moving to a foreign country (a year in the Cinque Terre, anyone?) to escape the pressures, responsibilities and tedium of their daily life, those who seek an escape from the present in the remembered joys of the past may simply be avoiding an encounter with their authentic self.

In the end, that encounter is inevitable. The tension we create in ourselves by avoiding it can, paradoxically, intensify our desire to be somewhere else, and the past may strike us as the easiest of all the foreign countries to visit. Yet we would be as out of place there as we would be in any more obviously 'foreign' clime: the past we fondly remember was a place where we were very different from the person we are now. As Grandpa Brown said, if he could revisit the time when he was a boy, he would no longer be a boy there.

Migrants who return to the village they came from often report feeling disorientated and disappointed, sometimes because things have changed so much since they lived there, but mainly because *they* have changed so much since they lived there. In precisely the same way, the exercise of winding back the clock, if it were possible, would be bound to upset, confuse and disappoint us.

Wrapping ourselves in a blanket of nostalgia might offer us some consolation for life's disappointments, embarrassments or humiliations, but an unflinching encounter with the person I am right now is the best way to establish a new sense of purpose as a basis for a new sense of self-respect.

The present is tomorrow's yesterday, and before long, people will be nostalgic about now. But let's not miss the real message of nostalgia: it's telling us something about ourselves. To avoid that message by assuming we're only talking about the past is, like all these hiding places, a mental health hazard.

Perfectionism

Striving for unrealistic or unachievable perfection is an attempt to distract us from the imperfections we all must live with.

In his searingly honest and often hilarious account of his midlife crisis, *Fat, Forty and Fired*, Nigel Marsh describes his relief at realising that perfection was not a possibility. 'I haven't got any answers,' he writes. 'I do, however, look at things in a different way now. I have stopped looking for perfection. Having spent my life so far only seeing black and white, I am now more comfortable with grey.' Admitting to himself that life will always be a struggle, Marsh decided to focus on the struggle 'rather than attempting to create a mythical stress-free nirvana', praising himself for small victories rather than beating himself up for 'the bigger failure of not having a perfect life'.

Perfection. We sometimes glimpse it in a flower, or a rainbow, or perhaps in a musical phrase that won't leave us alone. I sometimes read a sentence and think: 'I wish I'd written that – it's perfect.'

But life itself is never perfect. Relationships are never perfect (though we may tell each other *this* one is). Life is messy, unpredictable, complex, brief . . . and often wonderful. It's full of ambiguities, contradictions, paradoxes, ironies, heartache and moments of joy. But *perfect?* Only in your dreams.

The truth about us is that we are all frail, flawed, fragile and feeble, as well as many more flattering things. Yes, we are sometimes bold, funny, thoughtful and even wise. Yes, we can succeed in all kinds of endeavours; we can prosper. Yes, we can be wonderfully compassionate and caring; we can fight for justice and win; we can create beautiful objects, words and pictures; we can offer unstinting service to others and expect no reward for it; we can give and receive love and be enriched by it.

We are all that and more, and the 'more' contains as much darkness as light. We are bound to fail sometimes. Life will frustrate us. Family and friends will disappoint us. Some of the lessons we learn about ourselves will be hard to take. We won't always want the truth to be told about who we really are and what really drives us.

Being human *entails* imperfection. We are all good guys and bad guys, rotating in and out of the light. When we act alone, we have to live with our shortcomings and irrationalities; when we act together, those complications are compounded. We are all torn by competing desires, like the desire for love and the desire for control (which can never be simultaneously satisfied in a healthy relationship, by the way). We desperately want something until we get it, and then wonder what all the fuss was about. We crave certainty and stability, yet our brains thrive on uncertainty and unpredictability. If we were perfectly rational, we might be able to create a perfectly ordered life, though it would be an excruciatingly dull one.

The Irish poet and writer James Stephens summed it up in his comic novel, *The Crock of Gold*: 'Finality is death. Perfection is finality. Nothing is perfect. There are lumps in it.'

Lumps indeed. When you find the perfect job, the perfect partner, the perfect house with a perfect kitchen (with perfect taps), the perfect holiday destination, and when you have all those perfect children (perfectly parented by you) and send them to the perfect school . . . there will always be lumps.

The toothpaste I use proudly proclaims on the pack: 'Perfection'. (It also promises something called '3D White', which would be start-ling if it were true.) After prolonged use, I'd say my teeth look about as old as they are, and no closer to perfection that they ever were. I'm not disappointed, though: I never really expected anything other than clean teeth, with a fresh taste in the mouth a pleasant bonus. My car isn't perfect either, though it's among the best I've ever owned, and neither is my apartment, though I wouldn't want to change a single thing about a place that feels so warmly and wonderfully like home.

I'm not suggesting for a moment that, because perfection is an illusory *personal* goal, we shouldn't strive to do the best we can in everything we do, or that we shouldn't work hard at making our rela-tionships sing. I'm not suggesting that the fashionable 'excellence' is unattainable, or denying that a job done well can give us great pride and satisfaction. (I sometimes feel like that about cleaning the kitchen bench.) Obviously, we expect something pretty close to perfection from the work of dentists, airline pilots, engineers and others whose work demands a high degree of precision, though we know they'll be human like the rest of us when they go home from work and prune the roses, raise their children, retile the bathroom or lose the car keys. I'm simply stating the obvious: imperfection is inherent in the experience of being human.

Knowing all that, why would anyone seek perfection? Answer: because it's a very clever hiding place. As long as we aim for perfection and feel a rush of pleasure when someone calls us a perfectionist (receiving it as a compliment), our focus can remain determinedly external. We know, with a terrible certainty, that we ourselves are far from perfect . . . so let's not go there. Let's find the perfect latte, instead. Or a perfect geranium in a perfect pot. Let's not have a single fallen leaf spoiling the perfect neatness of our front path. Let's keep our lawn, and our hair, trimmed to perfection. Let's set the table with the cutlery perfectly parallel, the mats absolutely straight and the serving dish dead centre.

Was George a perfectionist or merely a pedant?

After 30 years of marriage, Helen was finally running out of patience.

'When I was growing up, my father was constantly correcting my English, and then I married George, and he does the same thing,' she was complaining to a friend over coffee. 'If I say "George and I" when it should be "George and me", he points it out. Every time. *Objective case, Helen. Following the verb.* Regardless of where we are or who we're with. I probably should have said "whom" just then, should I? I used to think it was quite amusing until our son Max cottoned on to it, and he also started correcting me. It's quite a relief that Max is living away from home at present. It's not as if I don't try.'

That night over dinner, Helen mentioned to George a phone conversation she'd had with their son: 'We've been invited to spend a few days at Max's friend's family's beach house.'

After a brief silence, George looked at his wife and said: 'Awkward construction. Three consecutive possessive nouns doing adjectival work like that. Not wrong. Not these days. But awkward. Perhaps "at the family beach house of a friend of Max"? Better, but still awkward, those two "ofs". I see your difficulty. Perhaps we could just say "the family beach house of Max's friend", though I see how that might imply that Max only has one friend.'

Helen, used to these spontaneous tutorials, pressed on: 'I realise you'd probably rather stay at work, but I'm sure the invitation would apply equally if it was only Max and I going.'

George looked shocked. He was at a genuine loss to understand how, after all these years, Helen couldn't grasp the difference between the nominative and objective case. He knew she'd left school at fifteen, but still . . . It wasn't as if he hadn't tried.

'Max and *me*,' he said, in the measured tone of an automaton.

Helen snapped. 'George! Do you know what? I couldn't care less if it's nominative or objective or possessive or subjunctive or . . .'

George smiled, impressed by Helen's command of these terms, but she was not to be distracted.

'I am sick of being corrected all the time. Sick of it! I was sick of my father doing it, I'm sick of you doing it, and I'm extremely irritated that you've inducted Max into the secret society of pedantry.'

'It's hardly a secret society, Helen. And, by the way, I think pedantry is an unnecessarily pejorative term. We're just interested in getting it right. Language is one of those rare things in life where perfection is actually possible: the right word – there's always a right word – and the right grammar, the right syntax. Not hard, Helen. No harder to get it right than to get it wrong.'

'George, you're missing my point. I think you're far more interested in my grammar than you are in *me*. You scarcely notice me. You never comment on my appearance. I can't remember the last time you kissed me except for those perfunctory pecks you give me when you leave for work. I doubt if you can even remember what I just cooked us for dinner. I think you're totally disinterested in me, if you want to know.'

'Far from disinterested, Helen. I think you might mean uninterested. Disinterested, as I think I might already have mentioned once or twice, suggests impartiality – no conflict of interest – not *lack* of interest.'

Helen threw down her napkin. 'George! Enough! I'm not sure how to say this, but I think there are some big question marks over our marriage. *Big* question marks.'

George was still enjoying the fact that Helen had said 'perfunctory', but he couldn't let this latest assault go unremarked.

'I suspect you mean *questions*, Helen. A question *mark* on its own would be a rather meaningless thing to have hanging over a marriage, or hanging anywhere, really. I know where you got that from. Journalists are saying it all the time. "There's a question mark over the minister's travel claims." Ridiculous. There's a *question*, surely, but the question *mark* is merely the punctuation that signifies a question has been asked . . .'

George paused, but there was no response. Helen had left the room and was in their bedroom, changing into her walking shoes in preparation for a very long, very thoughtful walk.

I'm sorry to have made you suffer through a mealtime with George, but I'm very familiar with the type. My own mother complained, just as Helen did, that first her father, then her husband, then her sons corrected her English, though none of us ever sank to George's depths. (I hope.)

Pedantry is just one of the many manifestations of perfectionism, like people who are obsessively neat and tidy, or those who can't rest until the hems on the curtains are perfectly level, or those made anxious by *other people* wearing colours that 'don't go'. A friend's marriage finally broke up over her husband's insistence that magazines on a coffee table should be 'neatly stacked, not strewn'. That was the last straw, of course, not the sole cause of the break-up.

Perfectionism works so well as a hiding place because it portrays us as having high standards, wanting things to be done properly, being sticklers for order – all admirable and even enviable qualities. It's as if the persona of the perfectionist is an outward sign of some inward purity, like highly polished shoes being interpreted as a sign of moral strength.

Not all perfectionists are in hiding; some of us seem to have been born with that neurosis. But when perfectionism is rampant and obsessive, or even aggressive, it's a pretty safe bet that we are hiding from some threatening, unpalatable or otherwise messy truth about ourselves.

The autocratic workplace perfectionist who, verging on bullying, demands unreasonable compliance with his/her own standards is almost certainly fearful of having personal inadequacies and frailties exposed:

My way or the highway!

Get it right first time!

A job worth doing is a job worth doing not just well, but perfectly!

Tidy desk, tidy mind! (The manager who used that one as a mantra always had an immaculate desk. The people reporting to him were fond of muttering: 'Empty desk, empty mind.')

There's no need to surrender to chaos in response to our under-standing of human nature in all its imperfection, though Persian carpets are generally woven with a deliberate, symbolic imperfection as an expression of the Muslim belief that only Allah's handiwork is perfect.

But, at the same time, it's unrealistic to strive for perfection in ourselves or others – *so* unrealistic, in fact, that it's tempting to say the perfectionist always has something to hide.

Projection

*The faults we find in others are sometimes a reflection
of our own unresolved issues.*

Projection is an almost universal tendency, though what it tells us about our reluctance to face ourselves is a rather dark story.

Sigmund Freud introduced the term to psychology as a way of describing how we 'see' in others qualities we are trying to conceal – or refusing to admit – in ourselves. For example, we might try to hide from our own anger by aggressively questioning our partner about why she/he is so angry. We might accuse someone of being a 'control freak' as a way of deflecting attention from our own urge to control others. We might mask our feelings of guilt over our own intense feelings of jealousy by accusing someone else of being excessively jealous. We might attack someone for their arrogance as a way of denying that very tendency in ourselves. Or we might criticise someone for being 'too attached' to their children because of our unadmitted anxiety about the intensity of our own attachment.

Bullying is one of the ugliest faces of projection. Bullies are almost always projecting their own sense of inadequacy, inflicting on their victims the punishment the bullies, perhaps unconsciously, believe they themselves deserve.

We generally think of projection as a negative and potentially destructive process, but it can also work in a positive way. The English philosopher and theologian Don Cupitt sees God as a projection of the human desire for faith – 'an imaginary focus for the religious life'. And the misplaced faith we sometimes invest in political leaders is generally nothing more than a projection of our hopes for a fairer society and a better world. The same kind of hopeful projection often occurs between people newly in love, with their perceptions of reality clouded by their wish for 'true love' and a perfect relationship. In all such cases, an element of defence is present: we are attempting to protect ourselves from disappointment.

The phenomenon of projection was described in a famous passage from the Gospel of Matthew in which Jesus of Nazareth is urging his followers not to be judgemental:

Why do you see the speck in your brother's eye, but you do not notice the log in your own eye? Or how can you say to your neighbour, 'Let me take the speck out of your eye', while the log is in your own eye? You hypocrite, first take the log out of your own eye and then you will see clearly to take the speck out of your neighbour's eye.

Jesus proposed that, having removed your own 'log' you could then attend to your neighbour's 'speck', but analytical psychology would say that the speck might not be there at all: it could well be a mere projection that serves our need to hide from some unattractive aspect of ourselves, though there might sometimes be enough of a speck to justify our projection.

Either way, that passage captures the essence of projection: we are so anxious to avoid confronting the guilt or shame we feel about our own inadequacies or misdemeanours, we seize on another person as a screen onto which we can project those feelings and thus relieve ourselves of the need to deal with them.

~

Andrew encounters a 'pointless' uni course run by 'inadequate' people

When Andrew left school, he had no ambition to do or be anything in particular. He spent a year backpacking around South America, came home and worked in his father's online printing business for twelve months, was uninspired, and travelled again – this time to Europe with his girlfriend. After that, he returned to his father's business for another year, became bored with the work and decided it was time to do a university course. His girlfriend was already well advanced with an arts degree and seemed to be enjoying it, so that was a good sign. Andrew liked his girlfriend well enough, but confided in a mate that he sometimes found her a bit boring.

A degree in information technology, he felt, could be the way to go, given how the world was embracing artificial intelligence. He thought driverless cars were a great idea, for instance. And virtual reality.

He duly enrolled and began the course. He was surprised – shocked, really – to discover how much work was involved, and how early in the course the students were expected to undertake their first major assignment. He was also surprised by how young most of the other students seemed – his four years out of school made him feel not only older than the others, but also more mature. In fact, he found the other students rather childish.

He was underwhelmed by the quality of the teaching, too. Some lecturers were fluent enough, though not very engaging. Others seemed ill-prepared and scarcely coherent, though he had been assured that they were all highly qualified. In fact, the worst one appeared to have the most impressive qualifications – no doubt one of those brilliant researchers who hate having to teach, thought Andrew.

His impatience with the whole process grew but he submitted his first assignment – as a draft, really, because he felt the need of some guidance about what standard of work was expected so early in the course.

He soon found out. He was summoned to a meeting with his tutor and asked to explain the assignment he had submitted.

'Explain what?' he asked.

'Well, it's hardly an assignment. It's more like a series of notes you've cobbled together before starting work on the assignment.'

'Exactly. Well spotted. As this is the first assignment I've done, I thought we could use my notes as the basis for a conversation about how to proceed. It's a while since I've done anything like this. I've been out of school longer than the others.'

His tutor was tempted simply to fail him, but there was strong pressure in the department not to fail anyone, at least in the first semester. She asked him if he'd like to have a second chance – to submit something more satisfactory in another week.

Andrew reluctantly agreed to that, but gave the matter a lot of thought: the teaching was crap, the other students were immature, the course seemed to be going nowhere . . . why was he bothering?

He briefly entertained the idea of hiring a learning coach to see if such a person could give the whole thing a bit more focus. *Focus.* That was what was missing. This lot had no focus. *And* they were an arrogant bunch, as well, with very little to be arrogant about, in Andrew's opinion.

He spoke to a student adviser about the possibility of switching to another course – he was thinking philosophy might be more to his liking than this hodgepodge. The adviser assured him that he could switch to arts and enrol at the start of the next semester, and he suggested Andrew might like to sit in on a couple of philosophy lectures in the meantime.

'Would they count towards anything?' Andrew asked.

'No, I'm just thinking you might like to see how you feel about it before actually making the change.'

'Forget that,' said Andrew, amazed at how unrealistic some of these people were. Go to lectures that weren't compulsory? He was fast coming to the conclusion that this place really was an ivory tower.

He spoke to a learning coach, but she made it clear that working with her would increase, rather than ease, his workload. She also irritated him by commenting on the excellent reputation of some of his lecturers.

Eventually, he emailed his tutor, pointing out just how disorganised the department was, how inadequate the teaching, how low-calibre the students, and how unfocused the program. He cleaned up his assignment a bit and resubmitted it, with no real interest in the outcome.

He showed the email to his girlfriend. 'I think you're projecting, Andy,' she said with a laugh.

He had no idea what she was talking about but didn't take kindly to her amused tone. 'Why do you always have to find everything so funny? I'm treated badly and you *laugh*? I'm not sure you're a very nice person under that veneer of maturity and sophistication.'

Projection is not always as simple and straightforward as 'seeing' our own faults in others, as in a mirror. Projection can also occur when, for example, we avoid dealing with our own feelings of guilt by trying to make someone else feel guilty instead – almost as if we are letting them bear our guilt for us.

In *Why Do I Do That?*, American psychotherapist Joseph Burgo relates the story of Jim, who has forgotten to collect the dry-cleaning on his way home. His wife asks where it is, Jim admits he forgot to pick it up and apologises. Instead of accepting his apology, his wife sighs in irritation and complains that she would now have to collect it herself tomorrow. His wife's refusal to accept his apology sharpens Jim's guilt and gives him an opening for a counterattack: he accuses her of always being judgemental. Jim knows that he is at fault but, by projection, he has convinced himself that his wife is really 'the bad person' in this situation.

That might seem a rather trivial domestic example, yet it is in such settings that projection often occurs. A wife may berate her husband for his sloppy table manners or 'embarrassing' wardrobe choices in such exaggerated terms that he is puzzled by her vehemence. If she is hiding something she would rather not admit about her own behaviour (perhaps a moment of extravagance at the cosmetics counter, or a foolish flirtation with a colleague), she might be trying ease her guilt by projecting it on to some completely unrelated aspect of her husband's behaviour in order to portray *him* as being in the wrong.

Carl Jung's view was that projection was not simply a matter of avoiding confrontations with specific feelings of guilt or shame, but rather an attempt to deny the 'dark side' of our nature by projecting it onto others. Jung believed that we can't be whole until we confront our dark side and incorporate it into our view of ourselves, however painful that process may be. As he wrote in *Contributions to Analytical Psychology*: 'There is no coming to consciousness without pain. People will do anything, no matter how absurd, in order to avoid facing their own Soul. One does not become enlightened by imagining figures of light, but by making the darkness conscious.'

Australian academic and writer David Tacey notes in *The Darkening Spirit* that 'this viewpoint is never popular . . . since it asks us to accept what we do not want to know about ourselves'. Tacey reminds us that 'wise people of all times have kept emphasising this insight' because it is so easy for us – consciously or unconsciously – to discharge our guilt or anxiety by pretending someone else actually has the problem.

You don't have to buy into Jung's or any other version of analytical psychology to appreciate the appeal of projection as a hiding place. We all know we are a complex mixture of noble and base desires and motives. We all experience tension between good and bad impulses within us. Any serious journey of self-discovery is therefore bound to involve some encounter with 'darkness', and an awareness of our tendency to project can be a fruitful starting point, an opportunity to examine the state of our own mind/heart/soul via the projections we make onto other people.

Here is the great paradox of projection: the very defence mechanism we are using to help us hide from ourselves can become a source of revelation about the self. In *Radical Forgiveness*, Colin Tipping explains it like this: 'If you want to know what you dislike about yourself and have largely disowned, simply look at what annoys you about the people who come into your life. Look into the mirror they provide.'

This does not, of course, mean that every criticism of another person is necessarily a projection. What it does mean is that when we are forced to confront the possibility that we are being inappropriately or disproportionately judgemental (perhaps because others can't even see the problem we claim to find so annoying), it's time to turn the focus inwards.

Similarly, when we find that someone close to us is feeling manipulated or humiliated by our attacks on them that seem unjustified, some quiet contemplation of the motives or emotions that lie behind our attacks may be called for.

'Scapegoating', where one person is blamed for the wrongdoings of others, is a societal version of projection. In some cases, the scapegoat is simply the 'fall guy' – taking the blame for others' misdeeds. In other, more dramatic cases, a group, a community, or an entire society may project their feelings of guilt or shame (often converted into anger) onto a single individual who is then called on to make some sacrifice to assuage their collective guilt.

The term originated in ancient Jewish culture, when a priest would ritualistically lay the sins of the people onto a goat which would then be sent out into the wilderness to carry those sins away. The same idea is sometimes attached to the crucifixion of Jesus by those who choose to interpret his death as having been a sacrifice for 'the sins of the whole world'.

In Australia, the 2019 conviction of Roman Catholic cardinal George Pell on charges of child sexual assault took on some of the projective aspects of scapegoating. Many Australians were so convinced of Pell's guilt and so jubilant about his conviction, without any direct knowledge of the facts of the case, that it appeared as if more general feelings of anger and hostility towards the Roman Catholic Church – and even, perhaps, towards other tarnished institutions such as banks, politics, the media etc. – were being projected onto that one individual.

Pell's case was not 'pure' scapegoating, since he was convicted of a heinous offence (though later acquitted). Nevertheless, the widespread projection of anger was so intense, there seems little doubt he was being asked, symbolically, to bear an even greater burden of guilt than might otherwise have been the case.

The rise of anti-immigration sentiment across many Western societies looks suspiciously like a version of scapegoating: we seek relief from our barely admitted feelings of guilt and shame about our own lack of compassion, tolerance and generosity – our own failure to respond to the plight of those less fortunate than we are – by condemning immigrants and refugees (and, most especially, asylum seekers). We blame them for the trouble they cause us and the damage they are alleged to inflict on our economy. In effect, we are transferring our guilt to them – asking *them* to feel guilty, as if *they* are the ones who have behaved badly. If it's not a case of scapegoating, then it's a projection of guilt that comes very close to it.

Of course, *all* projection involves some degree of scapegoating, since we are attempting to deal with our own guilt, shame, anger or regret by asking someone else to bear that burden for us. When we experience outrage at the very idea of scapegoating, we need to remind ourselves that our own attempts to hide from ourselves through the process of projection are as unfair to our 'victim' as scapegoating was to the goat.

As a defence mechanism, projection often works brilliantly. The ancient Israelites were, presumably, relieved of their guilt by the sight of that sin-bearing goat heading for the desert, since the ritualised relief of guilt is sometimes necessary for a sense of forgiveness and redemption to be achieved. And if we manage to project our own underlying state onto someone else, we *do* feel better, at least for the time being, though the root cause is being displaced rather than confronted.

The danger is that if we 'get away with' our projections, we will simply have further postponed our ultimate encounter with whatever aspect of the self we are hiding from. In the end, it would be healthier for us to accept that we are merely projecting and to turn our attention inwards to the source of the projection.

Religion and Science

Worship of the artefacts of religion, like science worship,
can distract us from spiritual truths about ourselves.

It might strike you as odd to be bracketing religion and science together, yet they afford remarkably similar hiding places for fanatics who are looking for somewhere to hide from the truth about themselves.

Both science and religion are demonstrably valuable in themselves. Both have contributed immeasurable good to humanity. Both offer systems of meaning that encourage exploration of the very frontiers of human thought and imagination. Both can stimulate deep reflection on the nature of the self.

Yet history is littered with tragic examples of the misuse of both religion and science to excuse various forms of evil. In the case of religion, that abuse is most evident in the intense hatreds that have led to the persecution of 'heretics', wars, acts of terrorism (in recent history, think Northern Ireland and the Middle East) and

217

other offences against humanity. Considering that most religions claim loving-kindness, peace and harmony as their foundations, the attempt to justify evil deeds by suggesting they are being committed 'in the name of God' represents a breathtakingly arrogant affront to those religious ideologies. Similarly, stories of child sexual abuse at the hands of priests and others in positions of authority in religious institutions – to say nothing of financial corruption and exploitation of the poor – point to those institutions themselves as hiding places for unethical and even criminal behaviour.

In the case of science, Nazi Germany's human 'experiments' at the hands of the notorious Dr Mengele are perhaps one of the vilest examples of the proposition that anything that *can* be done in the name of science *will* be done. The development of nuclear weapons – or, indeed, any weapons – is another nasty example of the principle, and the dropping of atomic bombs on Hiroshima and Nagasaki demonstrated that, once we have the technology, we are inclined to use it (unless deterred by the knowledge that 'the others' also have it). The misdeeds of so-called Big Pharma in exploiting people's vulnerability for profit, or in withholding drugs that might be more efficacious but less profitable than others, or in developing drugs and then looking for 'diseases' they can treat; the use of science to create products that encourage addiction or to satisfy corporate greed in other ways; the technology that has created greenhouse gases on a life-threatening scale, and polluted our rivers and oceans with chemicals and plastic waste; the galloping development of increasingly smart artificial intelligence that invades our privacy, turns us into the slaves of technology, and might (if the fears of people like Stephen Hawking, Bill Gates and Elon Musk turn out to have been well-founded) ultimately lead to our destruction . . . these manifestations of the dark side of science point to the danger of assuming that science is 'morally neutral' and that every scientific frontier is worth exploring.

Justifying appalling behaviour 'in the name of God' or 'in the name of science' is one way of hiding from the truth about the dark side of our nature. A more common misuse of religion and science is as a distraction from engagement with the inner life.

In the case of religion, you can find examples across the theological spectrum of people who have lost sight of the point of religion – which, I take it, is to inspire and encourage a life of compassion – and have focused, instead, on what Australian theologian Bruce Kaye calls its artefacts. This might involve a retreat into hardline dogma as a way of denying the doubt that properly accompanies faith; it might involve treating scripture as worthy of worship in itself, divinely inspired and literally true in every word (an attitude regarded as idolatrous by more liberal-minded believers); or it might involve such strict adherence to certain liturgical forms that those forms become more important than the spiritual responses they are intended to evoke.

American writer and former clergyman Mark Galli says that 'it should not surprise us that the liturgy is one of the best places to hide from God', likening it to the Genesis myth of Adam and Eve savouring the delights of the Garden of Eden while hiding from the One that provided them.

The phenomenon of artefact worship is well described by American theologian Marcus Borg. In *Reading the Bible Again for the First Time*, Borg draws on a Buddhist metaphor – when a wise man points his finger at the moon, a fool looks only at the finger – to warn Christians against literal belief in the Bible (a mere 'finger') rather than seeing the Christian life as 'a relationship to that to which the finger points'.

When worshippers become infatuated with religious practices, rituals and objects – icons, banners, processions, incense, holy water, stained-glass windows, kneeling, the sign of the cross or the raised arms of the Pentecostalist – the symbols can become ends in themselves rather than ways of stimulating spiritual reflection. They become the finger that distracts us from – rather than points us to – the moon. In the process, they tend to externalise the focus of religious experience, isolating us from spiritual insights as surely as rampant materialism can.

Gabi and the Palm Sunday service

I'm sometimes asked to take part in processions and other rituals at our church. It takes a lot of preparation and training to get it right, and you do tend to get caught up in the theatrics of it all. I often hear people at morning tea after a particularly 'big' service complimenting everyone on how well it went. Sometimes they say it was 'inspiring', but I'm never quite sure whether they mean it was inspiring like a feel-good movie or a particularly uplifting concert, or inspiring in a way that motivates them to live a more compassionate life.

I sometimes get obsessed by the trappings myself. If someone puts a foot wrong in a procession, I can feel myself getting angry about it, or if someone slips up in a reading or a prayer, I think how slack that is, as if they are actors playing a part. Well, they are, in a way, but it's all supposed to help us in our own devotions and reflections, isn't it? I mean, if we turn on a spectacular procession and everyone goes home feeling smug and satisfied, I'm not sure we're doing our job.

Anyway, all this came to something of a head for me on Palm Sunday last year. It really was a wonderful service – lots of visitors, a big procession, people waving palms, the full thing. The music was sensational.

And then came the sermon. It was a visiting preacher who talked about refugees, which has become a bit of a Palm Sunday thing. He seemed very knowledgeable, and started talking about the difficulties being faced by refugees living in our part of Melbourne.

There was a bit of shuffling and clearing of throats as he spoke and I thought, 'This is terrific. People are really listening. They're really getting it.' And then we got on with the rest of the service, back to the rituals, the choir sang like angels, we had another procession and I was scared people would just forget what was said.

Some did, of course. Some were outraged by it, because of their politics. Some had their usual cups of tea and raved about the wonderful music or the procession and the banners, and when they said 'inspiring' I don't think they were talking about the address. But a few people got together straight after the service and decided to start up a refugee support group, and that's really taken hold. Who knew we had refugees living in our very own suburb?

In the same way as religious faith is narrowed by a focus on artefacts, and by the excesses of clericalism or fundamentalism, so the mystery of science is narrowed by scientism, defined by American philosopher Tom Sorrell as 'a matter of putting too high a value on natural science in comparison with other branches of learning or culture'. At its extreme, scientism claims that science is the only valid source of knowledge – the same claim religious extremists make for religion. For people in thrall to scientism, science seems like a kind of god and, just like the artefacts of religion, scientific theories and discoveries can assume almost sacred significance.

Indeed, the French philosopher Bruno Latour argues in his provocative book, *On the Modern Cult of the Factish Gods*, that scientific theories are just like leaps of faith, and scientific 'constructions' like religious artefacts. As Latour points out, religious people embrace beliefs (the religious equivalent of theories), and then construct artefacts (icons, fetishes etc.) designed to represent those beliefs, based on their understanding of the world as they experience it. This, he suggests, is precisely what scientists do with facts that seem real and stable at the time, even though such facts – like the tenets of religion – might be subject to revision or reinterpretation in the light of new understandings at a later time.

In his essay 'What is Scientism?', published by the American Academy for the Advancement of Science, Thomas Burnett of the John Templeton Foundation traces the origins of this kind of infatuated science worship to seventeenth-century Europe and the Scientific Revolution, when a 'torrent of new learning' led to a movement proclaiming a new *foundation* for learning, 'one that involved careful scrutiny of nature instead of analysis of ancient texts'.

A century later came the Enlightenment and a deepening of intellectuals' love affair with natural science. During the French Revolution, a number of Catholic churches were converted into 'temples of reason' where quasi-religious services encouraged the worship of science. (More recently, Swiss-British philosopher Alain de Botton proposed a contemporary initiative along similar lines in his book *Religion for Atheists*.)

Such worship has well and truly survived. Carl Sagan: 'The Cosmos is all there ever is or was or will be.' E.O. Wilson: 'We can be proud as a species because, having discovered that we are alone, we owe the gods very little.' As Burnett comments, such bold claims blur the distinction between 'solid, evidence-based science and rampant philosophical speculation'.

For serious scientists – like serious theologians – the work of challenging everything goes on as more research brings new data to light. Even the theory that nothing can travel faster than the speed of light has been challenged, and the recent photograph of a black hole was greeted with excitement and some relief by scientists who were sure black holes existed, as predicted by Einstein, but were reassured by photographic evidence (rather like receiving a picture of your sister's baby on Instagram – you knew she'd had it, but seeing the picture was the confirmation you needed).

~

Jake's partner is unmoved by black holes

I confess I'm a science nut. I read everything I can lay my hands on. I listen to all the science shows and watch everything on TV – Brian Cox is my current hero. What a guy!

I find space the most interesting. I guess I'm in love with space, really. When I was a kid, I was in love with dinosaurs. But I also love learning everything I can about the tiniest microbes. Both my parents were quite religious, but I can't see how you could ever believe in God – even the rather vague kind of God they seemed to believe in – once you pay attention to what the scientists are saying (except those weird scientists who say religion and science are perfectly compatible . . . *really*?).

Anyway, the most exciting event of the year, so far, has to be that photograph of a black hole. I've got it blown up to poster size on my study wall and a smaller copy stuck on my pinboard at work. I heard all kinds of science people saying this was the greatest thing since the moon landing – or it might have been the Mars probe. Anyway, I agree.

My partner doesn't. Oh, she's impressed by the technology, and she actually knows quite a bit about the science. She's a closet Einstein fan, I think. Anyway, when that photo was all over the news – and I admit I couldn't talk about anything else – she said to me: 'How is this going to change your life, Jake?' Or she might even have said, 'How is this going to change our lives?' She always says things like that. She once accused me of using science as a way of avoiding proper engagement with the here-and-now – including her. She actually said science was a threat to our relationship, though I didn't really get what she meant, and I still don't. Sure, I get absorbed in science stuff – I guess you could say I'm sometimes a bit extreme – but I do love my partner. If only she could share my passion for science!

The next time I mentioned the black hole, she said: 'Speaking of black holes, next weekend is a black hole in my diary – let's go away some-where, and *not* to that deep space communication thingy in Canberra. Okay?' I laughed at her little joke but, really, I find just going off some-where aimless a total waste of time, when there's so much science stuff we could be doing.

Sometimes my partner says, 'Just switch off and contemplate the meaning of life, Jake.' But I say to her – because I truly believe it – that the only pathway to the meaning of life is through science. Scientists are the great explainers of the universe. What else matters as much as that?

If we allow ourselves to become infatuated with the signs and symbols of piety or with the latest scientific discovery – or bedazzled by the charisma of a religious leader or celebrity scientist – we are less likely to feel the need to examine ourselves. Stargazing sometimes encourages soul-searching, but never if our hearts and minds are totally fixated on the stars, or even on the finger pointing to them.

Victimhood

Don't blame me for the way I am;
blame my circumstances.

Having spent most of my working life sitting in people's homes, listening to the stories of their lives and their views on every imaginable subject, I can say two things with confidence. The first is that everyone's story is interesting: you have only to listen patiently enough to realise that. The second is that everyone has had their share of tragedy; everyone walks with shadows; everyone has been wounded, disappointed, wronged or misjudged. Everyone.

And perhaps there's a third thing, though it's less universal: almost everyone resists the temptation to take themselves too seriously, or to fall into a trough of self-pity; almost everyone knows that there's someone worse off than they are.

What you can never predict is how individuals might deal with misfortune and setbacks. Some of the most serene and gentle-seeming people turn out to be harbouring a seething resentment of 'fate'. Some people who seem relaxed and charming turn out to be restless rogues or bullies constantly plotting revenge against real or imagined adversaries. (Indeed, I'm tempted to propose a law of human nature: charm is the preferred disguise of the rogue and the bully – that's how they get away with it.)

Others, whose experiences would move you to tears of sympathy for their loss, their sorrow or their tough luck, shrug their shoulders and look at you with a half-smile, as if to say: 'What can you do? What can anyone do?'

Some people lead lives of quiet heroism – as carers for disabled children or parents with dementia, as visitors to lonely people in hospitals or nursing homes, as spouses who sacrifice their own career to support their partner's aspirations or to raise their children – without even realising how heroic they have been. Others complain bitterly about the sacrifices they feel they have been forced to make.

Some people have experienced life-threatening illness and never once asked: 'Why me?'; others have railed ceaselessly against the injustice of it all, throughout their illness and beyond. Some people have been bullied, harassed, abused or belittled by parents, teachers or people in positions of authority in the workplace, and maintained their dignity and courage; others have been discouraged and diminished.

All unpredictable. All part of the broad range of normal human behaviour. And none of it apparently connected with whether people seem generally optimistic or pessimistic by nature, what religious or other beliefs they might or might not hold, or what stage in the life cycle they might have reached.

It's unpredictable partly because of the crucial role played by luck in determining the trajectory of our lives. Yes, some of us can improve whatever situation we find ourselves in, through education, training and hard work. But some of us simply can't do that because our genetic inheritance has left us with insufficient cognitive ability or emotional resources to rise above our difficulties, or because it has proved impossible to escape from a poverty trap or other crushing disadvantage.

Where and when we were born, who our parents were, the kind of family we belonged to, the quality of education we received, the kind of opportunities that were available to us . . . we have no control over such things. It's tempting to think that whatever success we've enjoyed is due to our own effort (perhaps with a nod to genetic heritage), but the truth is always more complicated than that.

Unless we are irretrievably disadvantaged, being dealt this or that hand by the fates does not entail being *defined* by the hand we've been dealt. As Carl Jung put it: 'I am not what happened to me; I am what I choose to become.'

Yet 'what happened to me' is one of our favourite hiding places. *Look what a hard life I've had! Look how hopeless my parents were! Look how badly I've been treated!* If we allow ourselves to be consumed by self-pity, that may well turn into a hiding place, allowing us to settle for a superficial, reflexive victimhood rather than taking a deeper look at what we might yet become.

In *Fat, Forty and Fired*, the account of his midlife crisis, Nigel Marsh described the process of coming to terms with his past – starting with his parents enrolling him in an English boarding school at the age of five. Everything about that experience was inauspicious: social isolation and other privations, loss of the comforts of home and family life, the emotional torture of daily humiliations.

As Marsh wrote, 'a nation's prison and school systems say a lot about the country that devises them. Suffice to say, in this instance Britain obviously got the two confused.'

The point of the book was not for Marsh to wallow in his tough upbringing nor to dwell on the appalling effects on health and wellbeing of his hard-driving career in advertising and his equally hard-driving alcoholism. Quite the opposite: it was to show how, having been retrenched at the age of 40, Marsh examined his life, reordered his priorities and set off on an entirely new course. The story is a frank reminder of the truth behind Jung's assertion: Marsh was determined not to *be* what had happened to him but to choose what he wanted to *become*.

To reject victimhood is to be liberated from our history so we can connect with our inner life and seek more authentic ways to express the self we truly are.

Lucy's father suffers a mild stroke and makes the most of it

After our parents separated, my brother and I spent very little time with our father. Our mother kept dragging us from place to place – trying to find herself, I guess – and it was hard to stay in touch with Dad.

When I was in my twenties, I did a postgraduate degree at a university in the city where he was living, so we sort of reconnected. Gradually, I drifted away from Mum – she was still pursuing this crazy hippie image she had dreamt up for herself – and that made contact with Dad a bit easier.

Then, in his mid-fifties, he suffered a mild stroke. I had a call from the hospital to say he was there and that everything was basically okay, but he would need a light program of rehab to get his speech and walking back to normal. I visited him a few times, of course, and I was amazed by the change in him.

To be totally frank, Dad had always been something of a phoney. He hid behind this facade of the successful businessman: hard-living, hard-drinking, 'take no prisoners', very into top-label casual gear, always the latest smartphone, flash cars. I used to think it was a bit of a joke, really, like such an obvious pose. I'm sure that was one of the things Mum found impossible to live with, in the end.

The point is, he always projected himself as this really strong, successful guy. But when I visited him in hospital, he had totally changed. It was like a surrender. He was talking as if the stroke was much more severe than it really had been. I know any stroke is a serious thing – at least a serious warning sign – but, really, this one was pretty mild. At first, his speech was a bit slurred and he needed someone to steady him when he walked, but the speech therapist and the physiotherapist were on to it, and they assured me everything would soon be back in good working order.

But Dad wasn't convinced. He simply dropped his bundle. The other thing was, he started on about what a struggle it had been since Mum left him and how tough it was living alone. (He hasn't always been living alone, by the way: there have been a few live-in girlfriends over the years. Anyway, I was living alone myself at the time.)

It was real victim-talk. He even started referring to himself quite explicitly as 'a stroke victim', as though that was how he was going to define himself from then on. I was shocked. In fact, I told him never to use that word, 'victim'.

He just said I didn't understand what a blow this had been.

Anyway, the various therapists did their jobs beautifully and, after a bit of rehab, Dad was back in his home and coping pretty well. For a couple of weeks, someone came in each day to check on him and bring him a meal, but this was mainly precautionary. He had to attend a day centre for some ongoing rehab, and he asked me to drive him to and from those sessions, even though he'd been cleared to drive himself. He really was okay.

But from then on, he repeatedly used the term 'stroke victim' to justify anything he did or said. 'Go easy on me – I'm a stroke victim, remember,' he would say. Once, when I lost my temper with him, he held up his hand and said, 'Stop it, Lucy, or you'll give me another stroke.'

He seemed to have adopted this persona of the frail old guy and it really affected his life. He went back to work part-time and started talking about early retirement and going on cruises. It all struck me as a bit of an excuse for opting out, as though he was almost frightened to face up to the truth of what had happened – not just the stroke but the fact of where his whole life was going. He actually seemed to prefer the victim version.

Many people who experience illness or other misfortunes ranging from retrenchment or divorce to poverty or disability manage to display remarkable resilience, including a capacity to remain in touch with their essential loving self. But people who embrace victimhood in any of its guises tend to have an inflated sense of entitlement, are more likely to expect others to tolerate their rudeness, insensitivity or self-centredness, and are more prone to anger based on a sense of 'the injustice of it all'.

What are such people hiding from behind that veneer of victim-hood? What is it about portraying ourselves as victims that appeals to some of us? Given that the desire to be taken seriously is the most fundamental of all our social desires, is it that we believe victimhood to be the only way to get other people to take us seriously?

None of this is intended to downplay the misery of people trapped in the coils of tragedy or misfortune. Such people need all the sympathy, all the kindness, all the understanding and all the practical support we can muster on their behalf. But when they elect to play the victim role, that diminishes their capacity for self-reflection, as well as our capacity for sympathy: after all, if someone is wallowing in self-pity, it's a bit hard to muster much additional pity to add to the existing swamp.

A rough New Year's Eve for Susan

Rather against my better judgement, I agreed to attend a friend's NYE party. I wore my favourite black top with a new pair of pink silk pants (which turned out to be a big mistake) and sallied forth. My friend lives with her husband and too many children in a harbourside house and I knew it would be a big, boozy affair.

A sour note was struck early on, though: I ran into my ex and he suggested we repair to the garden for a private talk.

'What do you want to talk about?' I asked, rather defensively. We hadn't laid eyes on each other for two years, and it had been a particularly bitter split. I hadn't been a paragon of dignity and restraint myself at the time, but my ex had behaved excruciatingly badly. Even now, I feel damaged when I recall it.

'Oh, come on, tell me how the dogs are getting on, if nothing else. We haven't seen each other for a long time.' Blithe as you like.

I'm afraid I was somewhat terse: 'Aren't you going to apologise for what you did?'

'Huh?' he said. (I then recalled how often he used to say 'huh'. It was as irritating as ever.)

'Your behaviour. Taking all the furniture. The books. The sound equipment. Clearing out while I was on an interstate trip. Leaving me that bizarre note.' I quoted a few words of it.

'Oh, you've kept my note?'

'I didn't say I'd kept it.'

Silence.

'So, don't you think, now we've all cooled down, maybe an apology is in order? I'm certainly sorry for my extreme reaction at the time, but I do think I was provoked, don't you?'

'I don't have to apologise for something I wasn't responsible for. I was depressed at the time. I can't be blamed.'

'Really? Depressed? I didn't know you were depressed. That was never mentioned. So you're saying you accept no responsibility for what happened? For your own behaviour?'

'That's precisely what I'm saying. Anyone could see that it wasn't my fault. Anyone who's suffered, I mean.'

'So are you still depressed?'

'Oh, no. That was an episode. Always lurks, of course. You're never free of it, really.'

'So the fact that you were allegedly depressed at the time absolves you of all responsibility for what you did *then*. But now . . . now you're *not* depressed, and looking back, would you think it might be appropriate to apologise *now*?'

He just shrugged, and smiled the sort of smile that reminded me of why he had turned out to be such an infuriating person to live with.

I headed back inside at that point and avoided him for the rest of the night – easy to do in such a surging mob. My ex, of all people, Mr Charm himself, playing the victim. What a thought!

The night wore on. You can't escape until the midnight ritual is over. So, when the time came, there we all were, trying to cross arms and link hands in a shape that had no geometrical name – a sort of winding snake eating its tail, half of us inside the house, half outside.

As the singing neared its teary, tipsy end, the man next to me, a total stranger, Auld Lang Syne-curved me out of the ring and into a quiet corner, where he put his arms firmly around me, kissed me full on the mouth, and began kneading my butt. I extricated myself with a minimum of violence and as much dignity as I could muster and, looking him straight in the eye, I hissed at him: 'Don't you dare do such a thing ever again.'

To my amazement, he began weeping and apologising in the most abject manner. I think he was actually wringing his hands. Instead of just walking away, I felt I had to hear him out. It was an apology, after all – the kind of thing my ex was clearly incapable of.

'It all started when I was sixteen,' he said. 'This girl –'

I held up my hand. 'I don't want to hear about your adolescent fantasies. I accept your apology, but I warn you that if you ever try anything like that on me again, I won't be so restrained.'

'No, you don't understand,' he said. 'It was no fantasy. Adolescent boys – the first time, I mean – well, fetishes develop. Those pink pants, just like the ones that girl was –'

'Stop,' I said again.

'I just couldn't control myself. Especially after a few drinks. You just turned me on. You were irresistible in those pants. Pure and simple.'

'I think "impure and complex" would be a better description,' I said, wishing I was already in my car and halfway home.

He started to speak again, to defend himself, to explain, but I'd had enough for one night. I wasn't going to get into an argument with a drunk fetishist about which of us was the victim. I found my friend, wished her a happy New Year and fled into the night.

We sometimes adopt victimhood as a hiding place even when we are the architects of our own problems. We may complain about the inroads of IT into our life, as though 'it's nothing to do with me – I'm just the victim of all these messages I need to respond to'. Or, having crowded our lives with too many commitments, or failed to be strict or sensible about our priorities, we may sound just like a victim: 'Oh, I'm so *busy*. I don't know how I'm going to cope. People make so many demands on me!'

Sometimes, victimhood poses as martyrdom – not in the classical sense of a person dying for a cause they believe in, but in the more mundane, everyday sense of a person who has fallen into the trap of self-pity because of the demands being made on them. It might be the competing demands of work and family, or the burden of caring for (or even just worrying about) frail elderly parents, or the self-imposed stress brought about by taking on too much. By playing the martyr, we try to convince ourselves that there's something heroic about our situation, that we are worthy of praise and admiration, and that people are not giving us sufficient recognition or sympathy.

Yet when we call someone *else* a martyr, there's often a mocking edge to it, as though we can see through the pose to the reality. Perhaps this is a person who has either taken on too much but refuses to delegate some of their responsibilities to others or declines offers of help. Or perhaps it's a case of someone who has refused to acknowledge (or has not yet learnt) that all of us will sometimes be called on to make sacrifices in response to the demands of other people – family, friends, neighbours, strangers – for emotional support, encouragement or practical assistance, and that has nothing to do with being a doormat. Responsiveness to others' needs is simply an expression of one of the deepest truths about what it means to be human: we are all in this thing together, and there will be many times when our own priorities will very properly be swept aside by someone else's more urgent need.

To perceive ourselves as having been 'martyred' or victimised by our responsibilities to others is to have become deaf to the whispers of the soul.

There are a great many victims in our midst, all of them worthy of our attention and support: victims of natural disasters, of illness, of relationship break-ups, of retrenchment, of prolonged unemployment leading to poverty and, yes, even of incompetent, neglectful or abusive parents. In whatever situation they find themselves, victims are entitled to expect compassionate responses from us. But the person who embraces the role of victim and wears it like a badge of honour is a person in need of a different kind of help.

Work

Preoccupation with work can become
the enemy of self-reflection.

The psychology of work is fraught with at least as many contradictions as any other aspect of human psychology. When we try to theorise about the role of work in our lives it's easy to make generalisations that overlook the vast range of individual differences in motivation, attitudes and experience. Our social and cultural context affects our attitudes to work; so does our level of intelligence – cognitive, emotional and otherwise; so do our aptitudes, opportunities, ambitions . . . and, of course, our luck.

We can glibly say that work is a primary source of dignity and identity. We can point to the long march of history and say we have all evolved, socially and culturally, from ancestors who had to hunt and forage – and, later, farm and cultivate – to survive; who had to build their own shelter and make their own clothes. That's where work came from: survival (and once survival was assured, comfort).

And that's where the work ethic came from: the need to do your share of the work required to ensure the survival and comfort of your social group.

Gradually, it all became more sophisticated and fragmented, and we began dividing the tasks between us and paying each other to specialise in particular parts of the total workload: you could grow crops or farm animals, I could educate children, someone else could manufacture clothes, cars or entertainment machines, someone else could build houses or run the money system. The shift from work-for-survival to the outsourcing and redistribution of work has been radical and profound, and has made possible the operation of a modern economy (including the burgeoning field of work that simply involves moving other people's money around). Yet our attitudes to work have changed remarkably little.

'Why do we work?' seems like a silly question, though contemporary answers are so diverse it's still worth asking. Many of us feel that some form of employment is essential to the life of a complete person; that everyone should be pulling their weight in the workforce, whether their work is paid or unpaid, even when (as is now obvious) we no longer have enough work for everyone who wants a job. Some people feel that unemployment diminishes us by robbing us of a work-based identity, as well as severely limiting our income. And, of course, work also creates the possibility of leisure: if we don't have work, we don't have leisure, since 'time off' is meaningless if there's no 'time on'.

Usually (but not always), we work because we need an income. We might work because we crave the satisfactions that work can bring. We might work to add a significant (perhaps the *most* significant) dimension to our social identity. After all, 'What do you do for a living?' is one of the easiest conversation starters and most obvious ways of locating someone's place in society.

We might work because we fear the social opprobrium of *not* working. We might work because other people are relying on us to support them. We might work (especially in a two-income household) because we can't otherwise afford to maintain the lifestyle we aspire to. We might work because, though we may never admit it out loud, we equate wealth with worth, and we want to be rich enough to be taken seriously.

I once knew a senior public servant – divorced, no children – who had embraced her work with such fervour that she described her job as 'my spouse and children'. Having given work such a priority in her life, she never complained about the punishingly long hours she worked. Later, after she had remarried and forged a completely new way of life, she looked back on those years of being married to the job with the clarity of hindsight and admitted: 'It was actually my great escape from having to face what my life had become.'

Fran resists becoming a 'job bore'

When you're hammering in a nail, your mind is on only one thing. And then there's the next nail, so to speak, and then the day's over, you're buggered, and maybe there's time to join the boys for a drink, especially on a Friday. Then you pick up the kids – my partner Zac works later than I do – and go home. You're tired, but you need to throw yourself into family time: you start getting things ready to cook dinner when he comes in, you eat, one of you will read to the kids before bedtime, then you flop in front of the TV and hope there's something worth watching. I usually fall asleep at that point, so Zac has to wake me up to go to bed.

Up early, help out with breakfast, and it's back to work. More nails to hit on the head – literally and metaphorically. I love this job. I get enormous satisfaction out of seeing a house take shape and then, when it's all done, knowing what went into it and what I contributed to that. I'd recommend a trade to anyone – girls as well as boys – because it's one of those jobs where you're constantly solving problems and you regularly get to finish things. Job well done, type of thing.

My brother's in an office. He sits in front of a screen most of the day. Totally different kind of life. He reckons you *never* finish – it all just sort of rolls on. He gets tired too, but in a different way. More mental than physical. Mind you, on building sites we have the radio on most of the day, so we get into some pretty heated discussions about politics and other stuff. You talk while you work.

The point I'm making is that you get totally caught up in this job. It becomes your life and that's a good thing in lots of ways. Weekends off, sure, but you want to spend that time with the kids – sport and that – plus household chores and a bit of socialising, and then it's back to Monday, off early, ready to strap on the tools at seven-thirty.

But I've noticed a change lately. A couple of years ago, I started going to a yoga class once a week. One of the guys I work with used to go, and he said it was terrific for his flexibility. I thought I was pretty fit already, but I started going and now I wouldn't miss it. I've even persuaded Zac to come, and he's loving it too.

The thing is, there's more to yoga than you might think. You start out, like I did, doing it for flexibility and learning to relax – the breathing and everything – and then you find there's a kind of spiritual thing that

240

happens. I wouldn't say this to everyone, but I can see that it opens you up to other stuff. Like stuff about your place in the world. How we're all connected. Not meaning-of-life stuff, exactly . . . but it certainly makes you think about what you're doing with your own life. Zac and I have had some terrific discussions in the car on the way home from yoga. Other times, we don't speak at all – you just get this amazing sense of peace.

So I'm having a bit of a rethink. There's no way I'd give up carpentry – I really do love the work. But there's more to life – and there's more to *me* – than a power drill and a hammer and trying to balance a household budget. Know what I mean? There was a risk I was becoming a bit superficial. A bit narrow in my thinking. Even a bit boring . . . It can easily happen when you're doing something you love and you get totally involved in the job. I want to go a bit deeper – I think that's what I'm saying.

I'm not sure where this is going, but it's going somewhere. And I like it.

Not everyone who is engaged with their work is able to switch off at weekends. Though Fran feared becoming a 'job bore', she still managed to attend to other facets of her life – especially her family. Work, for her, was a source of pride and satisfaction rather than an obsession, let alone a hiding place.

But many people do 'hide' in their work, as they do in other forms of busyness, using it as an insulator from the demands of life beyond the job: working long hours, thinking of work as the *only* source of worthwhile accomplishments and gratifications in life, identifying exclusively with their workplace culture rather than with any other groups they might belong to – all at the expense of their engagement with family life, neighbourhood life, or the maintenance of friendships with people unconnected with their work.

Of course, if you don't have a job, or you don't have the job you want, you are likely to be understandably preoccupied with the challenge of finding the right job, to the exclusion of anything as marginal-seeming as 'finding yourself' – though, in fact, finding yourself might be the crucial step you need to take in the process of deciding what's the best job for you. The classic compendium of attitudes to work, Studs Terkel's *Working*, contains a graphic story of a miserable bank officer ('It's just paper; it's not real') who, feeling inauthentic, threw in that job to become a firefighter and was later able to reflect on the satisfactions he obtained: 'It shows I did something on this earth.'

Work – even if it doesn't feel like the ideal job for us – can satisfy most of the basic social desires that drive us, so it's hardly surprising that some of us are deeply reluctant to let go of our paid work. Here's one of my research respondents reflecting on the moment of his retirement: 'It was such a hollow feeling. Most of your life was bound up with the job and then, suddenly, that wasn't you anymore. Where I come from, if you haven't got a job, you're a bit of a non-person – a bit useless.'

That's not everyone, of course: some of us can't wait for retirement to release us from the grind and drudgery of a job we never much liked or that has worn us out. But as long as our work is reasonably satisfying, it's easier to hide from ourselves at work than almost anywhere else.

Two of my long-term acquaintances – I'll call them Paula and Marc – have both done that very successfully. They have both had stellar careers and have steadfastly resisted leaving their jobs at the point where most people would have retired, not because they wouldn't know what else to do with themselves, but because – well, here's their story . . .

~

Why Paula and Marc will go on and on and on . . .

Paula and Marc were both born in Adelaide. These days, they live on opposite sides of the world. Both have risen to the top of their chosen professions – Paula is an academic urban anthropologist and, for many years, has been a prominent public intellectual; Marc is an investigative journalist with the BBC.

Paula has always sought the limelight. For as long as anyone can remember, she has wanted to be more than a successful academic: from the beginning of her career, she has courted the media assiduously and has been ready with an opinion on almost anything she's asked about, even when it lies outside her area of expertise. She is shameless in wanting to be famous as well as brilliant and successful, and she has always believed that public intellectuals don't get discovered, 'they work bloody hard at it'. Jean-Paul Sartre is her favourite example: Sartre apparently gave up a teaching post to concentrate on the self-promotion that did indeed turn him into a public intellectual. Paula never gave up teaching, but, at one stage, she did have an agent whose job was to get her as much media exposure as possible.

Marc's working life began in public relations and he had a successful parallel career as a fashion model. In that capacity, he was 'discovered' by a TV producer who was looking for a host for a new game show. Marc auditioned, got the job, and thus began his lifelong love affair with the idea of himself as a media celebrity.

Within a few years he had become the stand-in presenter for a commercial current affairs show and then, wanting to do something more substantial, he began researching some of the stories himself.

While Marc was in the process of remaking himself as a serious investigative journalist, Paula's academic career had followed a more predictable trajectory. Short of a vice-chancellorship, which she'd always said she would hate, she had risen as high as she could in academia. She'd had a couple of serious books published but, to the chagrin of her colleagues, she has always preferred writing for the popular press to grinding out papers for academic journals. These days, she has her own blog.

Marc's reputation as a fearless reporter became so strong, he could pick and choose the stories he would work on and, these days, he is often asked to do opinion pieces as well as reportage. He has been offered a number of more senior appointments at the BBC and back home in Australia, but has always declined, citing his horror of management and administration. He's determined to stay at the coalface, as he puts it, though the coalface increasingly means air-conditioned studios rather than the wilds of Afghanistan . . . or even the streets of London.

His TV career ended long ago, once his poster-boy looks faded, his hair turned lank and grey, and he needed spectacle lenses so thick as to be disconcerting to the viewer. But he has clung to that radio microphone as if his life depends on it.

Paula has had several short-term visiting fellowships overseas, and some of her colleagues have unkindly wished one of them might have turned into a permanent post. She is not a popular figure among her peers, partly because her ambition has always been so naked, and partly because her personal manner is acerbic.

Now well into her 70s, she complains that, as a commentator, she is still fighting the same battles over urban planning she fought – and thought she'd won – 40 years ago. But media exposure is still the oxygen that keeps her going.

Will either of them ever retire?

A friend and colleague of Marc's recently had a heart-to-heart with him over a glass of red after Marc had finished recording a story. It was the week before his 69th birthday.

'Do you think it might soon be time to ease back, Marc?' she asked. 'You can't go on forever.'

'Ease back? No way. I want to die at the microphone.'

With as cheeky a grin as she could muster, the friend said, 'Actually, with all due respect, mate, it sometimes sounds as if you already have.'

Perhaps fortunately, Marc seemed not to catch the full import of that remark. He was still pondering her question.

'I couldn't retire,' he said. 'I'd have to face who I really am.'

It was Paula's sister who raised the same question with her: 'How about joining me on a trip somewhere? You always travel for work, never for fun. We could even do the year-in-Provence thing. How about it? You can't go on forever. There must be some younger people itching to get their hands on your job.'

Paula looked at her sister as if she was mad. 'I couldn't retire,' she said. 'Then I'd have to find out who I really am.'

Two strikingly different career paths. Two very different personalities. Yet both Marc and Paula chose almost exactly the same words to explain their reluctance to retire. In fact, reluctance is the wrong word: it's more like a steely determination to stick with their self-defining jobs rather than contemplate, so late in life, the nature of their authentic beings.

No doubt each of them would say, 'It's too late to change,' or, 'Why should I bother taking any action that would threaten the smooth path I've been on all these years? It's a very satisfactory life.' And, rather like my public service friend, they might equally admit that the job is like a spouse and family to them, since they are both unattached.

There's a tragic aspect to both stories. Neither Marc nor Paula has tried to imagine what other possibilities might have emerged if they'd stepped back from their respective treadmills for long enough to attend to their inner life or simply devoted more attention to their personal relationships. Neither is sensitive to the concern of friends and family about their mental and emotional wellbeing: they are both obviously miserable away from work. And neither has fully faced up to their personal contribution to the emotional wreckage wrought by multiple sexual liaisons in one case, and cruelly abandoned friendships in the other. 'It's always been all about the job,' has been a common complaint of former friends and even family members who have been made to feel they are no longer significant.

There are many people, in and out of the public eye, who resist retirement for precisely the same reasons as Marc and Paula. Afraid of what they might find if they were to have a frank encounter with the self, they soldier on, convinced that their successful career is enough, or perhaps that it is all they are capable of doing or being. Success at work can be the great enemy of self-reflection.

Perhaps, like most people who use work as a hiding place, they fear the personal inadequacies or frailties they might have to face if they were to come out of hiding. And because they have both been so widely admired for their work, it has been easy to convince themselves that nothing else mattered.

The irony is that many other people are clearly capable of doing the jobs Marc and Paula have done, but no one else was ever capable of becoming the person – as distinct from the public persona – they might have become.

Anyone whose job has made a significant contribution to the common good would be justified in asking: 'Isn't that enough?' But that, of course, is a question for them alone to answer.

There are many other hiding places.

In aggressive **individualism** we hide from the truth of our dependency on each other.

In the emotional profligacy of **lust** we hide from the risky vulnerabilities of love.

In our determination to put a '**positive spin**' on everything, we may be hiding from a confrontation with our authentic feelings.

In the comfort of our **prejudices** we remain hidden from fresh insights that might transform us.

In **relentless socialising** we distract ourselves from the inner life.

In constant **travel** we might be learning useful lessons about who *we* are compared with who *they* are, but we might also be hiding from ourselves behind the facade of 'interesting places', using the distraction of a constantly changing scene to avoid being trapped in one of those Didionesque well-lit back alleys.

In **violence**, whether physical or emotional, and whether intended to inflict harm or only to discharge feelings of aggression, we may be hiding from the truth about our frailty and vulnerability, since violence is usually a compensation for weakness, insecurity and fear. It's also a way of hiding from our inability to communicate by more socially acceptable means.

Sometimes, we hide from ourselves by too-zealously embracing strategies that encourage us to **stay in the moment** and focus on the externals of the here and now. All good advice. But our deep inner self is part of the here and now and any serious attempt to be 'in the moment' demands that we ourselves be authentically present.

We hide to avoid – or deny – the truth about who we really are, and the more comfortable the hiding place, the harder it is to give it up. Yet for most of us there will come a time – perhaps a personal epiphany; perhaps a trauma; perhaps the classic 'midlife crisis' – when, in the interests of personal integrity, fidelity and authenticity, we need to escape from our self-imposed captivity. We need to be 'found'. When that time comes, what will beckon is the prospect of becoming the fulfilled, loving person we are all capable of being.

FOUR

Soul-searching

Who looks outside, dreams; who looks inside, awakes.

Carl Jung

If you recognise any of the hiding places in chapter three as *your* hiding place, now is the moment to consider whether you're ready to make your bid for freedom, or whether you'd prefer 'the real you' to remain hidden.

Some hiding places capture us as effectively as they do precisely because they cocoon us in the comfort of denial, protect us from possibly painful confrontations with the self, and become so familiar to us that we regard them as being integral to who we are:

Oh, I know I'm a perfectionist. That's just me.

Yes, I'm a control freak – I admit it.

I know I keep travelling to avoid having to think about the purpose of my life – but doesn't everyone?

I'm only a workaholic because I love my job so much – are you going to criticise me for that?

I'm a creature of habit. I just want to go right on doing exactly what I'm doing now.

Suppose you decided that your social, external identity was enough, and that you'd rather not go too deeply into the idea of a more authentic self that might challenge you to live differently; suppose you decided that you would prefer to remain in the protective shadows rather than expose yourself to the glare of the sun; then what?

I have already referred to the 'half-life' we would be condemned to live if we never came out of hiding. It would be a half-life because it would mean we were denying or suppressing a huge chunk of our potential by choosing to live within restricted emotional and psychological boundaries – boundaries mainly set for us by the perceptions and expectations of others rather than the dictates of our own conscience and the demands of our own character. Above all, we would be diminished as humans if we failed to respond to the warmth of the sun at our centre, ignoring our species' demand that we live lovingly.

Many of us do fall into the trap of letting other people's expectations determine how we will live, because it often seems easier to conform than to have the courage of our convictions (and, in some circumstances, it's appropriate: 'When in Rome . . .'). But if we never reflect on who we really are, and who we could become, we may find ourselves responding not only to what others expect of us but even to what we think they *might* expect of us. Second-guessing others' expectations is a very unreliable basis for finding your personal bearings!

The Danish philosopher Søren Kierkegaard saw our tendency to live as if we were someone other than our true self as a particular form of despair – the despair of weakness and passivity. He believed that this kind of despair often goes unnoticed in the world because you can hide from yourself and still put on a flawless performance, be successful in material terms, attract praise and honours. He wrote scathingly of those who may 'amass wealth, carry out enterprises, make prudent calculations . . . perhaps [be] mentioned in history, but they are not authentic selves. They are copies. In a spiritual sense, they have no self.'

No self? The picture Kierkegaard is painting is of a person who has chosen to hide in the shadows – in spite of a public performance that suggests otherwise – by refusing to answer the deepest and most searching questions that ever come to us from the depths of our own being: Are you living for yourself, or for others? Have you understood the oceanic breadth and depth of the love that is available to you; the love that can transform your own life and the lives of those you touch? Do you think of your relationships mainly in terms of what you're getting rather than what you're giving, or *could* be giving?

Kierkegaard's use of the word 'despair' may strike you as too bleak. Yet despair is indeed the likely consequence of a life that is lived in ignorance or denial of our true nature; a life not illuminated and energised by loving-kindness. The source of that despair may not be obvious to us, and it may show up in such guises as perpetual restlessness, listlessness, depression, anxiety or a gnawing sense of dissatisfaction expressing itself as an insatiable appetite for more of whatever we most desire. Much contemporary despair can be traced to the rise of self-absorbed individualism – the so-called Me Culture – that encourages us to focus on our own happiness and entitlements rather than on the contributions we can make to a better world through our engagement with the lives of others.

Steve Biddulph, the Australian psychologist and parent educator, speaks of the 'wounded helpful' to describe the fact that people who have suffered some tragedy or trauma in their own lives are more likely to be empathic in their dealings with others. Here's an example of that in the life of Teflon Trev, whom we met in chapter three when he was undermining and then deposing Jess as chair of The Haven.

Teflon Trev picks up the phone

'Jess? It's Trevor here. Please don't hang up.'

Jess pauses, conscious of the strong urge to do just that. But her natural courtesy, and her curiosity, prevail.

'Hello, Trevor,' she says, hearing a little tremor in her own voice. 'This is a surprise.'

'I know it is. And the reason for my call may come as a surprise as well. I won't beat around the bush. I've called to apologise for what I did to you at The Haven a couple of years ago, but I'd rather do it face to face. Would you be free to have coffee with me in the next week or two? It's not urgent, obviously, but it's something I need to do as soon as it's convenient for you.'

Jess briefly wonders if she is dreaming. She has heard nothing of The Haven, or of Trevor, since her rather unsatisfactory chance encounter with The Haven's CEO, Mary, and she has tried to put the entire episode behind her. But every now and then, it rises up in her and renews her feelings of hurt and anger.

'You still there, Jess?'

'Sorry, Trevor. Go ahead.'

'So – coffee? I find saying these things much easier in person than over the phone. Or texts, God help us. My daughter recently broke off a romance with her boyfriend by text. I ask you.'

Was this really Teflon Trev? Jess was asking herself. *Where did this warmth come from?* She didn't even know Trevor had a daughter. Her first inclination was to ask him to say what he had to say over the phone, but she happened to agree with his point about the value of face-to-face encounters.

'Yes. Okay. What about this coming Monday?'

An arrangement was duly made. Stunned, Jess immediately picked up the phone again and called Mary at The Haven.

'Mary? Jess. I've just had a call from Trevor. What on earth is going on? Has he had a religious conversion of some kind?'

'Hello, Jess. Nice to hear from you. I almost called you myself, but things between us ended on a rather abrupt note last time and I wasn't sure how I'd be received.'

'Yes, well, sorry about that. So tell me about Trevor.'

'There's been no religious conversion that I'm aware of, but he is a changed man. I won't say a broken man, but he's deeply shaken. His wife is extremely ill and a few weeks ago he thought he was going to lose her. She's been his rock, and the thought of her dying was almost more than he could bear. He was in my office weeping about it.'

'Weeping? Teflon Trev? He's certainly reduced a few other people to tears in his time. So what's happened to his wife?'

'She's still very ill. It's a rare form of cancer. She may or may not recover. But Trev feels he's been given a reprieve and is determined to put all sorts of things right – including with her, I gather.'

'He's been remarkably frank with you, Mary, I must say.'

'He has. That's part of the new Trevor. He's still right on the ball, and just as productive as ever, but his whole manner has been – well, I was going to say transformed and, actually, I think that is the right word. There's a warm, human side to Trevor – I'd almost say a 'soul' – we never knew about. He's simply a far nicer person. More genuine. Transparent. Less driven, too. You'll see when you meet him. The apology will be genuine and he'll ask you if there's any way he can make it up to you.'

'Well, I don't want my old job back, if that's what he's thinking. But I'm amazed by all this and – well, of course I'm sorry about his wife. I'll hear him out, and if he's become the man you say he is, I'm sure I'll be able to forgive him.'

~

'Life begins at 40!' (or 50, or 60)

Many young people reflect deeply on who they are, on their reason for being, on the kind of person they want to become. Indeed, the tendency for young people to ask searching questions about their life's meaning and purpose is likely to increase as they, like all of us, come to recognise the existential threat to our species from the impact of global warming on sea levels, fresh water and food supplies, and the prospect of sharply reduced scope for human habitation.

But the preoccupations of adolescence and early adulthood are not typically focused on reflection and rumination about the nature of our essential self. We are more likely to spend our early years doing things and acquiring things that help us establish our personal identity within our particular milieu: a certain level of education, a job, a house or apartment and its furnishings, a car, a pet, a style of clothing, IT devices . . . all the ways we communicate to those around us that we are *this* kind of person and not *that* kind; the ways we identify and express our personality, our style, our interests, our place in the world – or, at least, the place we aspire to occupy.

The narrator in Sally Rooney's *Conversations with Friends* says: 'At 21, I had no achievements or possessions that proved I was a serious person.' And the American poet Anne Sexton told Barbara Kevles at *Paris Review* that 'until I was 28, I had a kind of buried self who didn't know she could do anything but make white sauce and diaper babies. I didn't know I had any creative depths. All I wanted was a little piece of life, to be married, to have children.'

Crucial to that early identity-building process are the relationships we choose to nurture with people – lovers, friends, work colleagues – who help us clarify our personal identity by reassuring us that we are recognised and accepted by them.

To the extent that love figures in our young imagination, it is likely to be mainly focused on romantic love. The distinction between love and lust is often unclear, and the desire for sexual gratification can easily blot out other, more selfless considerations. As a gross generalisation, it's probably fair to say that, one way or another, younger people are more *driven* than older people – more determined to *make something happen* – and this is an understandable distraction from more spiritual, inward reflections.

In *Finding Meaning in the Second Half of Life*, Jungian psychoanalyst James Hollis describes this 'first-half' process of separating from parents and establishing an identity of our own as being a response to the question: 'What does the world ask of me, and what resources can I muster to meet its demands?'

That process of accumulating external, visible signs and symbols of who we are typically starts to lose some of its momentum as we settle into the social contexts – family, work, friendship circles, neighbourhood – that help establish our identity. It is at this point that many people become restless for a different, deeper awareness of self. Hence, one of the favourite sayings of people in their middle years – *Life begins at 40!* – with its hopeful connotations of new horizons and fresh possibilities.

In a lighthearted vein, Carl Jung asserted that 'Life really does begin at forty. Up until then, you are just doing research.' Most people who have made it into their forties will be familiar with the phenomenon of the 'midlife crisis'. It sometimes presents itself as a vague yearning for a deeper sense of meaning and purpose; sometimes as a sudden urge to jump off the treadmill of current work and other responsibilities and explore alternatives. Sexual affairs and the purchase of symbolic red sports cars are the clichéd manifestations of such urges (though joining a choir, a ukulele band, a book club, a Zumba dance class, a gym, or a painting or poetry class are less reckless and potentially more therapeutic options). The prospect of cosmetic surgery – perhaps a little botox touch-up – becomes more attractive; a radical new hairstyle carries connotations of rejuvenation or even rebellion; overseas travel seems alluring as a way of escaping the burdensome familiarity and relentlessness of the daily grind.

Sometimes, the feeling is more like a gradually accumulated sense of oppression rather than a sudden crisis, particularly for people who claim to feel trapped in an intergenerational 'sandwich' – responsible for dependent offspring but also for ageing parents – while trying to live a full life of their own. The 'sandwich generation' is a modern phenomenon, mainly born of longer life expectancy and a dramatic rise in the average age of parents at the birth of their first child, but amplified by the radical culture shift in attitudes towards paid work as a symbol of identity and independence for women as much as for men.

The midlife crisis often emerges from a rather chaotic, half-formed sense that 'there must be more to life than this', or a wistful speculation about what we have achieved in the first half of life and whether we might 'do better' in the second half, perhaps by achieving more, or perhaps by doing something altogether different. The question of our legacy – the enduring influence that outlives us – might also occur to us around this stage of life.

But sometimes it goes deeper. For many of us, the midlife crisis is about a confrontation with some rather challenging facts about ourselves – perhaps that 'I am not the kind of person I had hoped to become, and would still like to become', or that 'the gap between how I look to others and how I feel inside is too wide for comfort'.

Such ruminations are rarely about externals. 'I am not the kind of person I had hoped to become' is unlikely to be a reflection on my career path ('I wish I had become an astronaut after all'), let alone my wealth or status. Almost always, the sense of a gap between who I am and who I want to be is a response to an opening up of our inner sense of self.

In my own case, the twenty years between my early twenties and early forties now seem like a sleepwalk, even though I know that in those years I married, fathered three children, started a business, built three houses, moved to the country, lost my father and three close friends, divorced and remarried. Looking back, I suspect that twenty-year period is shrouded in fog because it was, in many ways, a period of denial of the self I truly am. Or perhaps, as Hollis would argue, it was simply a period, typical of young adults, when I was more concerned with identity-building than self-examination.

In her 1977 bestseller *Passages*, American writer Gail Sheehy identified 'midlife' as the time when we typically move 'out of roles and into the self'. She also noted that this discovery of the self is associated not only with 'an enlarged capacity to love ourselves' but also a greater willingness to embrace others.

Yes, I am uniquely me, but in my innermost being I acknowledge our interconnectedness and I recognise the emotional risks of rampant individualism and the bleakness of social isolation. Perhaps one of the many joys of the middle years is this realisation that the line between self and others is blurrier than we once thought.

Adrian stops pretending

When I turned 60, I knocked back my wife's enthusiastic suggestion of a birthday party. 'I'm sick of playing games,' I told her, and she looked mystified. I realised I'd hurt her feelings, but I'd decided the time had finally come to say what I really thought.

In fact, that's the best thing about growing a bit older (I like to call it 'growing old disgracefully'): at last you reach the point where you really *don't* have to play games. You don't have to pretend you like birthday parties, for instance. (I've hated them – mine and other people's – ever since I was a little kid.) But it's more than that. It's like deciding that people really can take you or leave you as you are. No point in pretending.

I have a few really good friends – we've learnt to rub along together over many years. I have a wonderful family, and I've always embarrassed my kids, which I guess is par for the course. I've usually got on reasonably well with neighbours, and I have some decent colleagues at work.

But I've been guilty of my share of bullshit over the years. Saying things I don't really believe, just to sound good. Even wearing clothes that made me feel uncomfortable, as if I was 'dressing up'. I've been to too many functions where I had to bite my tongue to fit in. Been too polite. My wife says that was all very good for me, by the way. Makes me more civilised. Okay, but there is a limit.

Now I find I can be more like myself – more like the simple straightforward bugger I know myself to be. And you know what? The sky hasn't fallen in. I'm not rude to people. I'm not doing anything crazy. But I just feel a whole lot more relaxed about saying what I really think – not to offend, but just to be honest. It can be done courteously and respectfully, of course. But it's a huge relief to just let go and not be so worried about other people's reactions.

The other day, my wife actually told me I was easier to get on with – easier to have around the place. How about that! Actually, it led on to quite a serious conversation. We don't normally go in for deep-and-meaningfuls, Judy and me – she can get that from her book club – but this was really interesting. It turns out she has felt for years that I was hiding something; holding something back. Now I'm more open and honest about everything, it's come as a huge relief to her.

I asked her if I seemed less civilised than I used to be, and she let that one go through to the keeper. But she did say I'm easier to love.

259

James Hollis suggests that, when we become conscious of having moved into the second half of life – a point typically reached in the decade between the ages of 40 and 50 – we become more aware of our mortality and begin to ask different questions of ourselves: 'What does the soul ask of me?' 'What does it mean that I am here?' 'Who am I apart from my roles, apart from my history?'

Apart from my roles? *Apart* from my history? Now *that's* an interesting test of the difference between a socially determined sense of personal identity and an inner sense of 'self'. To experience the difference most starkly, ask yourself 'Who am I?' and then refuse to supply an answer that has anything to do with your roles or your history.

My own sense of personal identity says I'm a father, a grandfather, a brother, a son. *Strip all that away!* I'm a husband. *Strip that away!* I'm a social psychologist and a writer. *Strip that away, too!* I sing in a choir. *Strip that away – that's what you do, not who you are!*

Can I say, then, that I'm a man? I *am* a man, of course: that's biologically and culturally true of me, and it's a significant dimension of my personal identity. But gender identity is completely irrelevant to our deeper sense, our inner sense, our essential sense of self.

Who would want to argue that the essential *you* – the stripped-down, inescapable sense of your private inner self – depends on your sexuality, your gender, your politics, your religion, your marital history, your work or any other of the myriad factors that contribute to your social identity? Think of all those things as masks we wear – the faces we need to put on to play our various roles. If you're a partner *and* a parent, then you know that you must act differently in those different roles. But you're still *you*.

Don't be afraid of the word 'soul'

Hollis's question 'What does the soul ask of me?' is not a religious question (though it can be, for some people). It is not a question that depends on some mystical idea of 'the soul' as being the immortal aspect of our otherwise mortal existence. No, that question can be asked in the context of an entirely pragmatic, secular, everyday use of the word 'soul'. After all, the word 'psychology' derives from the Greek words 'psyche' (soul) and 'logos' (study), and the universal distress signal, SOS, stands for 'save our souls'.

Just as we use words like 'mind' and 'heart' to describe aspects of our human nature – 'mind' for thinking; 'heart' for feeling – so we use 'soul' to stand for the spiritual dimension of our lives. We don't try to point to places where these things exist: indeed, we don't think of them as tangible 'things' at all. We use such terms as metaphors to stand for concepts that are intangible, but real to us.

'He has no soul' is not a puzzling description – we take it as a comment on a person's lack of feeling, or integrity, or values; perhaps a lack of empathy. 'A city with no soul' is a statement most of us can interpret quite easily: that would be a place that lacks the live-liness and buzz of social interaction; a place dominated by concrete, devoid of the richness and vibrancy of human presence. When we feel the need for some 'soul-searching', we know this will be more intense, deeper, more *inner* than objective, rational analysis. When we identify someone as a 'soulmate' we are referring to an affinity and an emotional intimacy that runs deeper than conventional friendship.

A choral conductor once chided his singers, on the eve of a performance, by saying, 'All the notes are there, but there's no soul.' The choir knew exactly what he meant, and what he was looking for. On cue, they drew on their emotional resources to add the requisite richness and nuance – the necessary *vitality* – to their performance.

When we say things like 'a restless soul', 'a troubled soul', 'a tortured soul', we are pointing to something deeper, more inward, than mere personality traits, perhaps responding to something we sense about a person's inner life; their character; their spiritual core.

Spiritual? In her contribution to the book *For God's Sake*, Australian writer and social commentator (and self-declared atheist) Jane Caro reveals an inner life that many people would recognise as 'soulful' or even 'spiritual'. Her struggle with mental illness, her sense of the numinous, her openness to awe and wonder in the face of life's mysteries, her benign acceptance of whatever life throws at her, her underlying spirit of gratitude, her faith in people and her determination to contribute positively to the lives of others . . . that's all soul-work, and it gives us a glimpse into the character of Caro. She writes like a person in touch with the self behind the public identity. The fourteenth-century German mystic Meister Eckhart described this as 'seeing with the eye of the heart'.

'Soul' doesn't only refer to beautiful and noble aspects of our nature. When that choral conductor called for 'soul' from his singers, he didn't just mean bright, smiley stuff. 'The dark night of the soul' is a concept familiar to anyone who has suffered through seasons of grief, doubt, fear or existential angst that sear us in ways that seem to go beyond mere emotion.

Since philosophers, psychologists and neuroscientists don't yet even know how to define consciousness – American psychiatrist

Robert Berezin describes it as 'the brain's beautiful illusion' – it's not surprising that we struggle for the words to explain precisely what we mean when we refer to such concepts as 'soul' or 'spirit' or 'mind' . . . or 'self'. We know the brain and central nervous system play a big part in all human experience, but our sense of the spiritual, the numinous, the essential, the *inner*, seems to call for more poetic, less rational, less objective, more metaphorical language.

We might eventually account for our sense of self – or our soul – in terms of the neurons and synapses of our electrochemical circuitry, but I wouldn't hold your breath. As Anne Harrington has recently demonstrated in *Mind Fixers: Psychiatry's troubled search for the biology of mental illness*, psychiatry has come a cropper in its vaunted attempt to prove a chemical-imbalance theory of mental illness, though that hasn't affected its popular acceptance: American psychotherapist Gary Greenberg points out in his review of *Mind Fixers* that 'the chemical-imbalance theory of mental illness may fail as science. But as rhetoric it has turned out to be a wild success.' (The same might be said of Sigmund Freud's scientifically unproven assertion that dreams reveal our hidden truths or secret wishes.)

For the time being, when it comes to the soul – or the self – we shall have to settle for metaphors.

The courage to be who I really am

If we are to undertake an unflinching examination of the state of our soul, courage is the quality we will most need, especially as we face the possibility – both beguiling and daunting – that becoming our fully realised, fully authentic self might also entail becoming a more compassionate version of who we are now.

Think about studying for an exam. Think about learning a musical instrument. Think about starting a new job, or being promoted to a position you're nervous about taking on. Think about embarking on a new relationship. That's the league we're in when we decide to move in the direction of greater authenticity, fidelity and integrity. It won't happen overnight, and, like most rewarding experiences, it will sometimes feel like a struggle.

Adrian again

I'll tell you what really brought me to my senses and made me think it was time to become what my wife would call a more authentic person. It was when I heard a bloke at work say the only way to judge what's the most important thing in your life is to calculate how much time you devote to it.

I thought to myself: okay, work is important because I have to earn a living. Outside work . . . what? The people I love, obviously. My family especially.

And then I got to thinking how much time I actually spend with them. Even my wife. I don't just mean time spent kicking around together – I mean time really spent engaging with her – listening properly to what she's saying. She's always going on about that: *Are you really listening to me?* The truth is, half the time I wasn't.

If I answered the phone when our daughter rang us from Bendigo, I'd always ask her how everything was and she'd say, 'Fine, thanks, Dad,' and then I'd pass the phone to her mother and they'd talk for an hour or more. I couldn't imagine what they talked about. And that was the point – I was so far out of the loop that I literally couldn't imagine what they found to talk about.

And it wasn't just our daughter – our son was pretty much the same. Over the years, I guess, they'd both learnt to confide in their mother. I was always too busy, or too distracted, or too tired. Or, to be brutally frank, too unsure of myself as a father. I knew how to operate at work. I was okay with my friends, I guess. But the people I cared about most – and I really did care about them the most – were the very people I seemed to have most trouble relating to.

Things came to a head when my wife had to remind me, yet again, that it was my sister's birthday and I should give her a ring. My sister lives in London, married to a Pom. I made the mistake of glancing at my watch, and my wife said: 'Are you seriously going to tell me that you're too pressed for time to ring your sister on her birthday? Do you even know what birthday it is?'

It was her 60th, as it turned out, and I should have twigged to that. We're only a year apart.

Anyway, I started to do a bit of thinking and I realised I wasn't really that busy. That wasn't the problem, and if it had been, that would have been disgraceful. No, it was just a matter of letting go all the pretence of being the Big Man – too distracted, too important, too much in demand – and accepting that what I really wanted to be, deep down, was a very different kind of guy from the one I seemed to have become.

So after I heard that bloke at work talking about how to decide what's really important in your life, I started calculating how much time I was devoting to the things I claimed were the most important – the things that really mattered to me. And it was frightening. So that was the trigger, really, for becoming the new me; the real me; the me my wife says she likes better than the other one.

Since I've started looking and listening properly, I've even discovered that there are some really interesting people in our street, and a couple of lonely older people who are badly in need of an occasional chat. That's the sort of simple thing I mean. How hard is that? I'm much more comfortable in my skin these days. I can even look in the mirror and smile occasionally.

I still can't fill an hour on the phone with my daughter, but I know a helluva lot more about her life than I did before. And I can hear a different tone in her voice. Warmer, maybe? She's a lovely woman – I mean, apart from being my daughter – and I don't think I fully realised that before.

Authenticity, fidelity, integrity . . . these are lofty ideals and most of us fall short of attaining them as completely as we might wish. But aren't they inspiring banners to have fluttering hopefully at our masthead? Don't we aspire to live like that?

And yet, we keep hiding.

Here are three questions that, when honestly faced, might encourage you to see your hiding place in a different light.

What am I afraid of?

Most of us fear rejection, or humiliation or ridicule. It's natural to fear your friends' disapproval, your partner's withdrawal of affection or your employer's dissatisfaction with your performance. You might even be beset by fears on a larger scale: fear of ageing, or homelessness, or terminal illness, all the way up to fear of the catastrophic effects of climate change or nuclear war. Some of those fears will seem rational; some will seem – even to you – to be irrational because they are so unlikely to be realised. Yet the irrational ones are as real to us as those we like to think of as rational.

Rather than worrying about whether your fears are rational or not, try categorising them in a different way. Think of any fear as being either anticipatory or inhibitory.

Anticipatory fear galvanises us into action to minimise or avoid whatever threat we are facing. It motivates us to anticipate the threat by doing something positive – the classic 'fight or flight' response to fear.

Examples of anticipatory fear include things like our fear of an approaching storm, or a bushfire, that might either cause us to pack up and leave our home (flight), or take all necessary precautions to minimise the possibility of damage (fight). Fear of an intruder who has broken into our home might lead us either to confront the intruder (fight) or hide (flight). Anticipatory fear that our partner might be losing interest in us could lead us to seek ways of rekindling the romance (fight) or to plan a swift exit from the relationship (flight). Anticipatory fear of the effects of climate change could lead us to buy an electric or hydrogen vehicle, or give up non-essential flying (since dumping CO_2 emissions straight into the stratosphere is one of our greatest acts of environmental vandalism), as well as reducing our energy consumption, being more conscientious recyclers and curbing our consumerist profligacy (five 'fight' responses), or it could lead us to move to Tasmania (flight).

By contrast, *inhibitory* fear paralyses us; the threat it poses seems so utterly beyond our control, it makes us feel helpless. For example, our fear of a nuclear war that could wipe out the human race; our fear of the consequences of a global financial meltdown; our fear of the impact of artificial intelligence on the industry we work in; our fear of the ravages of a terminal illness that has just been diagnosed. The sure sign that a fear is inhibitory is that we feel powerless to do anything about it; we may even feel 'resigned to our fate'.

Here's a curious thing about fear: whether its effect on us is anticipatory or inhibitory depends at least as much on us as on the threat. Fear of the effects of climate change is a good example of that. While some people are galvanised into action by the threat of global warming, others regard the whole issue as so enormous, so complex and so far beyond their personal control, they simply throw up their hands and say, 'It's up to the government,' or, 'Nothing I do will make a scrap of difference to the big picture,' or, 'It's too late to do anything.' Inhibitory fear of that kind can easily dissolve into a paralysed fatalism.

The threat of nuclear war in the past has led some people to build fallout shelters and others to decide that any anticipatory or evasive action would be pointless. Fear of 'economic headwinds' can lead some people to become more prudent, especially with their borrowing, and others to decide that 'since it's out of my hands, I might as well just carry on as I am'. Fear of the impact of artificial intelligence on the workplace can lead some people to freeze with inhibitory fear, just waiting for the axe of redundancy to fall, while others may decide to retrain for different work. Fear of an exam can galvanise some students and paralyse others.

At a domestic level, fear of a partner's violence can be anticipatory, leading us to seek advice from a counsellor, or support from our family, or to confront the partner with our fear, or even to plan our escape. Or it can be inhibitory, leading us to shrug with a helpless resignation, to 'freeze' in the face of the partner's anger, or simply to shut down our emotional responses.

Fear of death can be either anticipatory or inhibitory. Reflecting on our anxieties in the face of the incomprehensibility of our very existence, British Buddhist Stephen Batchelor noted in *Flight* that 'we hardly seem well equipped for this phenomenon called "life" especially when we contemplate that it leads to an irrevocable process of ageing and death'. Given that death is, indeed, the only certainty in life, our anticipation of it can galvanise us into making the most of the life we have. Alternatively, if we respond with inhibitory fear, we can be ground down, turned into nihilists who refuse to see any meaning in anything, and overwhelmed by such hopelessness and despair that we are dispirited and diminished by the very thought of our own mortality.

When we face the prospect of leaving a hiding place, two contradictory fears might be operating – one pushing us out and the other holding us back. There's the fear of the corrosive effect we are having on our own integrity by living inauthentic lives (especially if we have managed to convince everyone else that we are exactly who we appear to be). But there's also the fear that an encounter with our essence might involve some difficult or even painful changes.

It's up to us to choose whether such fears will be anticipatory or inhibitory. Will I be galvanised into action or allow myself to be frozen into inaction by the realisation that I have been settling for less than my fully authentic self? Will I feel better or worse about myself, in the long run, if I make a bid for psychological freedom – not only by being more honest with myself, but perhaps also with a partner or a friend or my family? (Is that really a question at all?)

What am I trying to prove?

When we ask each other, 'What are you trying to prove?' we generally imply some doubt about the purity of the other person's motives. It's a bit like saying: 'Come on, I know this isn't the real you. Why are you pretending? Why are you trying so hard to create an impression?'

It's a good question to ask *ourselves* when we suspect we have retreated into a hiding place like excessive busyness or perfectionism, or when we have surrendered to the ambition to be someone, or do something, mainly as a way of attracting praise or admiration.

'What am I trying to prove?' can be a useful corrective against hubris or arrogance . . . or even stupidity! If you're already on three committees and you agree to join a fourth, it might be time to ask yourself: What am I trying to prove? That I'm superwoman? That no one else could possibly do these things as well as I can? That my self-respect depends on having other people ask me to do things? Or that I'm hoping people will like me more?

If you've declared that you seriously intend to slow down or simplify but you keep speeding up or complicating your life, try asking yourself: What am I trying to prove? If you are determined to get on with that book you've always wanted to write but you keep accepting invitations to do things that distract you from writing, ask yourself: What am I trying to prove?

Closely related questions: Who am I trying to impress – and why do I want to impress them even more than I want to be true to myself? Why am I unable to say no, even when it's clear to me that that's what I *should* say? Why am I pretending to be someone other than myself?

In the end, all such questions boil down to this one: What am I hiding from?

What am I compensating for?

This is the toughest question of the three. It asks us to acknowledge that it is part of our nature sometimes to do and say things to compensate for our own sense of frailty or inadequacy; to compensate for unresolved guilt; perhaps to compensate for our reluctance to embrace the compassionate life of a decent, civilised human being.

At 'the big end of town' you can see how compensation sometimes works: a philanthropist might be compensating for ruthless business practices by making a show of generosity to a charity. This is often expressed as 'giving something back', as though that is a morally praiseworthy sentiment. In fact, it often sounds like a tacit admission that 'I took more than I should have, so now I'd better give some back'. (Simply 'giving' would surely be a purer motivation than 'giving back'.)

But it's not only the rich and powerful who try to compensate for dark secrets or dirty dealings behind a genial philanthropic facade (and, hey, their philanthropy is a still a good thing for those on the receiving end, even if it was partly propelled by motives of self-aggrandisement or compensation). All of us are capable of concealing our own inadequacies behind some kind of facade: hoping our 'good works' will lead others to be more generous in their assessment of us than they might otherwise be; pretending to be more sincere or more humble than we know ourselves to be; cultivating a 'good guy' image to distract people from the less savoury aspects of our nature. (Groucho Marx: 'The secret of life is honesty and fair dealing. If you can fake that, you've got it made.')

Concealing my true self from others by compensatory behaviour can be a risky strategy, because it creates an impression that might subsequently be exposed as false: 'I really thought she had my best interests at heart, until . . .' But there's a greater risk: it tempts us to believe our own propaganda and, in the process, to conceal *from ourselves* the fact that our potential to live more lovingly remains unrealised.

In *Playing and Reality*, the English paediatrician and psychoanalyst Donald Winnicott wrote: 'It is a joy to be hidden, and disaster not to be found.' To catch Winnicott's meaning, think of the game of hide-and-seek, beloved of children everywhere. The challenge of finding a place to hide, the thrill of being hidden and the mounting excitement of hearing the seeker on the prowl all intensify the climax of *being found*, which is the whole point of the game. Imagine if the other players lost interest in finding you, and wandered off to do something else: to be 'not found' would be like being abandoned.

Like many children's games, hide-and-seek reveals a deep truth about us: although we love hiding from others, and even from ourselves, being 'found' – discovering who we really are – is one of life's great joys.

FIVE

Out of hiding

The truth will set you free.

Gospel of John

In these early years of the 21st century, we are becoming accustomed to the idea of fake news, hollow promises, dodgy research and the rest of the paraphernalia of political, commercial and cultural propaganda. We expect to be lied to by politicians; we assume we're mostly being fed misrepresentations and half-truths; we laugh at the posturing and insincerity of political campaigning – the hard hats, the yellow jackets, the kissing of hapless babies, the awkward consumption of strange food, the false bonhomie of raised beer glasses in the company of total strangers, the precarious perching on kindergarten chairs, the street walks and the slogans, the slogans . . . always the slogans.

We become cynical about it, inevitably, which is one reason why our esteem for politics has plumbed new depths (along with our esteem for many other institutions, ranging from banks to churches). Cynicism is not the sign of a robust, healthy democracy but there's another, more personal problem arising from this increasingly acceptable currency of half-truths: we are being conditioned to accept deception as a rather ho-hum fact of life; to treat 'image' as more significant than substance; to present *ourselves*, especially in social media, as if we are brands in need of promotion. Given this cultural context, it's hardly surprising that we have become more adept at concealing the truth about ourselves even from ourselves.

There are circumstances in which we understandably fear the truth: some of us don't want to hear a totally frank assessment of the likely pain and suffering associated with a terminal illness; some of us might prefer our partner to refrain from a completely frank description of our less endearing qualities; we might prefer to hear only the good things about our performance at work. (And no author welcomes adverse reviews. As the English writer Anthony Jay once said: 'All any author wants from a review is six thousand words of closely reasoned adulation.')

But most of us know, deep within us, that lies or even half-truths are like prisons where we become captive to the lie – especially if we ourselves are its author. Once we've pretended that something is the case when we know it isn't, we are obliged to stick to the story and construct whatever other lies are necessary to prop it up.

Hiding from ourselves is just like that. We deceive ourselves into believing we are the person other people think we are, or the person we would like them to think we are. Then, having convinced ourselves that our hiding place is safe, we fear that facing the truth about who we really are might jeopardise that safety.

In fact, the only pathway to escape is via the truth. Hence, 'the truth will set you free' – the quote at the top of the chapter, attributed to Jesus Christ. That statement was made in a religious context, but its self-evident force has been deployed in many other contexts, from the engraved marble at the entrance to the headquarters of the US Central Intelligence Agency to the halls of academia. The implied proposition underlying all teaching and research – from astronomy to zoology – is that we seek the truth because only the truth can liberate us from the prejudices, misconceptions and misapprehensions that limit our understanding of the world and our place in it.

Robert Berezin writes of the negative effect on us of the dissonance between our deepest (private) sense of self and our social (public) identity, leading to an understandable confusion about our nature. Often, he says, we ask that searching question 'Who am I?' precisely because we are experiencing some underlying tension between our public and private faces while not fully understanding the source of the tension. Coming out of hiding means we can resolve that dissonance, clear up the confusion and relieve the tension.

What if the 'real me' is dark or ugly?

Anyone who has ever spent a moment contemplating this thing called 'human nature' will tell you that we are a complicated blend of good and evil, nice and nasty, noble and base. That blend is part of the *potential* we all share as humans. It doesn't mean we all do dreadful things; it means that the impulse towards doing the wrong thing can sometimes be as strong as, or even stronger than, the impulse towards doing the right thing.

Those rotating, orbiting planets of our personal solar system move inexorably through dark phases that test our capacity for compassion and expose us to some rather unattractive aspects of ourselves. And even on the sunny side, there are plenty of deep shadows where we can hide from the light and heat of that metaphorical sun at our centre. We know the shadows are there, because we have all sought refuge in them at one time or another: we have hidden from our capacity for love in the shadows of hate, jealousy, revenge or prejudice.

Psychotherapists are familiar with the fear sometimes expressed by their clients – and occasionally felt by most of us – that if my real self were to be unleashed on the world, I might lose all my friends and become a less pleasant, less socially acceptable person: reckless, irresponsible, unrestrained, even dangerous. This was a view Carl Rogers encountered in almost every client he treated: 'If I dare to let the feelings flow which are dammed up within me, if by some chance I should live in those feelings, then this would be catastrophe.' In a similar vein, I have heard people say that, if it were not for their religious faith, they would be much less civilised, as if the demons within them would become uncontrollable.

There are two powerful arguments against the idea that confronting our dark stuff will be harmful to us, let alone catastrophic. The first is that we are not *only* dark stuff – the planets rotate! Once we begin to explore our inner life, we will discover at least as much beautiful, loving material within us as any dark stuff. No one is all dark; no one is all light. Every saint is also a sinner; every sinner also has a saint in there somewhere, who, given half a chance, could help us rise to a loftier plane. Whatever phase we're in, however 'dark' we may feel ourselves to be, the sun of human love shines on, right at the core of our being, and it's usually helpful to acknowledge that

that's where the shadows come from. We have a dark side *because of* our capacity for love.

When we begin to explore who we really are, it is the *combination* of good and bad within that will strike us – not the existence of dark thoughts and impulses alone. It's a contest that takes place in all of us: we want to be civilised and compassionate, but occasionally we give in to jealousy or hatred or rage. Or we might wish to unleash the full force of our fury, but kinder, nobler impulses restrain us.

That contest can play out in large ways and small. A person may wish to euthanise a terminally ill parent out of compassion and pity, yet be restrained by doubt about whether they are also being driven by impatience and resentment of the demands being made by the ailing parent on their own emotional and financial resources. A person may decide to enter parliament in a safe seat to contribute to a better society, but stay past their use-by date in order to maximise the financial benefits of a parliamentary pension. A person may declare they are not having any children because of the appalling state of the world and its uncertain future, but secretly acknowledge that it's mainly because they fear children would be a drag on their affluent and comfortable lifestyle. Or a person might appear to behave altruistically merely to impress a potential partner ('Oh, I *love* kindness in a man'). Motives are rarely simple or straightforward, because the various facets of our character create inevitable tension within us, as do our competing desires – like the fundamentally incompatible desires for control and for love.

The second factor in favour of confronting and accepting our dark side is that if we try to ignore or repress or deny the dark stuff within us, *that's* when it's most likely to be dangerous. To understand this process, you don't have to uncritically embrace the psycho-analysts' concept of the unconscious mind; you only have to observe what happens in life when natural impulses are frustrated. When children are too restrictively controlled or too harshly disciplined, they become sneaky and devious in order to get what they want. When rules and regulations become too severe, we tend to look for the loopholes that allow us to beat the system. When laws are so draconian that people feel their freedoms are being unduly restricted, they will start demonstrating in the streets. When minorities are persecuted, repressed and denied the rights of other citizens, their frustration leads them to become more militant.

All our desires, when frustrated, can turn ugly. Refusing to acknowledge another person, for instance, may be a sign of our own unfulfilled desire to be taken seriously. Mockery of others' beliefs is often a sign of our own frustrated desire for something to believe in. A frustrated desire to belong – to be accepted – can lead to poten-tially radical feelings of alienation and hostility that may erupt in violence. The withholding of affection may signal an unfulfilled desire to be loved.

If we try to pretend that our dark impulses don't exist, we will soon discover that frustration can be a powerful force: our resultant bad behaviour might take us by surprise. Violence, infidelity, devi-ousness . . . these can all be expressions of dark emotions like anger, disappointment or jealousy that have been frustrated by not being acknowledged, identified and dealt with openly, honestly and safely.

How many times have you heard someone say of a relationship breakdown, 'I didn't see it coming'? Such cataclysmic events can appear to have come out of a clear blue sky because the warning signs were deliberately kept hidden: when internal states ranging from an accumulation of minor irritations to festering, malevolent resentments or frustrations are not addressed, the danger of a major eruption steadily increases over time. And yet, as many of us can attest, the people about whom we harbour our darkest thoughts are often blithely unaware of the maelstrom raging within us, because we learn to pretend otherwise rather than admit to such hostile feelings.

The only way to curb the power of frustration is to face our demons and accept them as part of us, not something to be denied or swept under the carpet. Once the dark stuff is brought into the light of self-examination and evaluation, we can deal with it more temperately than if we wait for it to erupt under pressure. We can better control our anger, for example, if we have learnt to recognise its causes and symptoms. We can more easily contain our potential for violence if we have confronted and reflected on its presence within us, preferably at times when we're *not* feeling violent. We can handle our fears and anxieties more easily if we have acknowledged that, like everyone else, we are destined to live with fears and anxieties.

All of this 'dark side' of our nature can be more easily dealt with once we have acknowledged that it only exists in us because of the capacity for love that is our essence. (We deserve no praise for acting lovingly, by the way: this is more about species survival than virtue.)

Kim confronts her arrogance

It's been a pretty painful process, actually. The therapy, I mean. Coping with Dad's dementia is pretty painful, too, but I think I am getting better at that. It's not his fault – which is such an obvious thing to say but, until I discussed it with the therapist, I think I had been unconsciously blaming him.

Anyway, we've been endlessly through the arrogance thing and I think I'm finally beginning to realise how destructive it's been – bad for me, and bad for all the people around me. The therapist thinks it all comes down to my deep-seated competitiveness – my desire to win, to always be best at everything, even to be doing better in the workforce than my partner is doing. When she put it like that, I felt pretty small and silly, to be honest, though she keeps saying it's not my fault – it's the fact that I was the second-born and spent my childhood trying to get past my super-cool, super-talented older sister. She was always top dog, right from the start. She was the one who had our parents all to herself until I came along.

I realise this is all straight out of the textbook, of course. It's almost pathetic, it's so predictable and so typical! I actually laughed when she explained it to me. It felt like such a cliché. No point in blaming my older sister; she was just being herself. Actually, she was pretty kind to me when I was a kid. She had more to complain about than I did – after all, I was the one who had invaded her very comfortable little patch.

And my two younger brothers – well, they were just my little brothers. I always felt kind of superior to them.

It wasn't helped by the fact that Mum was a huge women's libber, so my sister and I got the full thing about 'girls can do anything they want'. I don't think the boys received anywhere near the encouragement we did. Anyway, Mum's dead and Dad has dementia, so blaming them would be a bit cruel, wouldn't it, as well as pointless?

My therapist thinks I was emotionally stuck at the adolescent stage of my development because that's the last time everything was going my way. I was usually top of the class, head prefect, captain of netball, popular with boys, scholarship to uni, the works. My parents had always told me I was terrific, and of course I wanted to believe them. It seemed as if I was destined to have a dream run. And I did have a dream run, considered from the point of view of adolescence, but the therapy has helped me realise I simply wasn't prepared for the demands of real-life adulthood.

At some level, I still wanted to be seventeen – the age I was when my sister left home and I was indisputably numero uno.

But once I got to uni, I wasn't the stand-out kid anymore. And then work, and a partner and kids – I still kept thinking I had to be best at everything. That's probably why my own daughter irritated me so profoundly by being such a little angel over that woman in the super-market – and over Dad – when I knew I was being a shit.

It's painful to admit it, but I probably have been trying to be, like, head prefect all my life to prove I was better than my sister! The arro-gance was a cover for my own disappointment, my own frustration, I guess, whenever things haven't gone exactly the way I wanted them to go. Putting other people down has been a way of making me feel terrific and superior and everything. I'm embarrassed even to think about it. No wonder my colleagues stayed clear.

Anyway, we're working on the competitive thing, because the thera-pist thinks that's quite a dark aspect of my personality. She's suggesting I shouldn't deny that I have this strong competitive streak but confront it and understand where it came from and keep it in its place – balance it with all the other traits I have, some of which turn out to be quite nice, actually.

We still have some way to go with this, but there's less weeping than there was in the beginning. She always has a box of tissues on her desk, though, just in case.

~

Acknowledging that we have dark impulses and tendencies isn't the same thing as giving ourselves permission to act on them: on the contrary, it increases the likelihood that they will be harmlessly defused before they do too much damage. Kim's struggle is well explained by Rogers: 'The more [we] are able to permit these feelings to flow and to be in [us], the more they take their appropriate place in the total harmony of [our] feelings.' Yes, the 'real me' *is* dark and sometimes ugly, but the good news is that it is also light, bright, and often beautiful.

We can't choose the feelings that well up inside us, but we can choose what to do with them. Once we recognise that they are part of who we are, and why they are there at all, it's easier to decide how to handle them.

Sometimes, the best way to defuse our anger is, very simply, to admit it to the person we're angry with – 'I'm sorry, but I'm feeling really angry with you' – and then to examine how those feelings became so intense. Sometimes, the best way to allay our darkest fears is to admit to ourselves that we're scared and then see if we can convert our inhibitory response into an anticipatory one. Sometimes, the best way to discharge our malevolence – whether in the form of jealousy, rage, resentment or despair – is to take a very long, reflective walk. Denial is the real problem.

The Self is not all about Me

There's a famous extract from a sermon delivered by nineteenth-century Anglican priest the Reverend Henry Melvill (*not* Herman Melville, author of *Moby Dick*, to whom poor Henry's quote is often wrongly attributed) that captures rather beautifully the idea of human interconnectedness and interdependence: 'You cannot live only for yourselves – a thousand fibres connect you with your fellow [humans] and, along those fibres, as along sympathetic threads, run your actions as causes and return to you as effects.'

South African archbishop Desmond Tutu made a similar point when he remarked that 'we exist in a bundle of belonging'. In other words, we are herd animals who tend to become anxious or depressed – or badly behaved – when we feel cut off from the herd.

Look how our behaviour changes when we are not closely connected to each other: anonymous drivers, isolated in their automotive capsules, who behave more aggressively than they ever would if they were face to face with their fellow road-users; socially isolated people who become rude and impatient when they have to interact with others; alienated young people who behave antisocially and are vulnerable to various forms of radicalisation.

That stuff is not typical of us: it's not as if we're essentially selfish and only behave in a more civilised way because of social pressure. It's the other way around: being social creatures, our default position is to be socially integrated, cooperative and altruistic. Other forms of behaviour are aberrations. We are generally at our worst when we are socially isolated and have no sense of belonging to any social group, or of being socially accepted.

And yet it's a conundrum, isn't it? We *feel* so individual and so independent that it's sometimes difficult to acknowledge – let alone welcome – the reality of our utter interdependence. Yet we are part of each other, bound by our common humanity. We belong together. We congregate and socialise because there is no alternative for us unless, for whatever reason, we have sought refuge in the reclusive life of the hermit. (Many of us occasionally fancy the life of the hermit, but the feeling generally passes as soon as we need to buy a litre of conveniently packaged milk from a conveniently located store, staffed by those dreaded 'other people' who will probably turn out to be irritatingly friendly and attentive.)

Acknowledging our interdependency doesn't diminish the need for self-examination, self-reflection and self-discovery. But it does remind us that self-examination is not about self-indulgence or self-absorption. It's not about the joy of navel-gazing. It entails the arresting discovery that, in a cosmic sense, I am inseparable from you.

What follows from that? Simply this: when we live in ways that are true to our own sense of self, other people are also the beneficiaries. Shakespeare got it absolutely right in the advice Polonius gave to his son in *Hamlet*:

This above all – to thine own self be true,
And it must follow, as the night the day,
Thou canst not then be false to any man.

That trio again: authenticity, fidelity, integrity. When we live authentically – compassionately – we shed our pretensions and pretences and become not only more accessible to ourselves but also to others.

When we are more accepting of ourselves, we become more accepting of others. When we acknowledge our own failings and frailties, we become more tolerant of the failings and frailties of others. When we acknowledge the 'dark stuff' within us, we'll appreciate how others, too, have similar stuff to contend with.

And, in one of life's many circularities, we'll find that because compassion flows from our authentic self, exercising it puts us more closely in touch with our authentic self. It's only when we embrace that circularity that we can fully appreciate the wisdom of Mahatma Gandhi's famous remark that 'the best way to find ourselves is to lose ourselves in the service of others'.

Cogito, ergo sum . . . amo, ergo sum

Seventeenth-century French philosopher René Descartes set one of the cornerstones of Western philosophy with his famous dictum *cogito, ergo sum*: 'I think, therefore I am.'

Many twentieth-century philosophers disliked that proposition because it used the dreaded word 'I' – they would have preferred Descartes merely to have observed that 'thinking happens'. Leaving aside such philosophical argy-bargy, let's accept that thinking is a sign of consciousness, and that consciousness is a sure sign that we exist. (*Un*consciousness does not, of course, mean that we don't exist.)

But unless I'm intent on suicide, it's not my existence that I'm trying to deny when I hide from myself, is it? It's not my consciousness. No, it's something about my essence that troubles me, or frightens me, or embarrasses me, or challenges me enough to take refuge in a hiding place.

A recurring theme of this book has been that we belong to a species that requires us to treat each other well, because our very survival relies on all of us finding ways to live together in relative peace and harmony on a small planet – not just with an eye to the immediate future, but also with an eye to the future we are bequeathing to our grandchildren. And it's not just about our interactions with each other: it's also about the way we treat the other life forms who share the planet and the natural resources available to us. The alternative to compassion is chaos and, ultimately, extinction.

Each of us has a unique character, shaped by our own set of genes and experiences. Yet when we get to the absolute core of who we are, we will discover that our obligation to the groups and communities we belong to – our herds and tribes – is such an integral part of who we are, it would make no sense to attach more importance to any other aspects of ourselves than that one. Being human, I *belong* to humanity.

Too much concentration on our uniqueness can seduce us into forgetting that our species requires us to connect, to contribute . . . and to *love*. Here's how American clinical psychologist John Welwood puts it:

> If the bad news is that we can know another, and be known, only as deeply as we know ourselves – and coming to know ourselves can be a long and arduous journey – the good news is that love helps and inspires us to develop this self-knowledge. For this reason, relationships can help us face and understand ourselves more rapidly and profoundly than any other aspect of worldly life.

Amo, ergo sum – 'I love, therefore I am' – may be the best way of describing what it means to be a fully realised, fully authentic human being, since compassion is the purest expression of 'soul'. It's the compassionate self that loves unconditionally, forgives generously, listens attentively and responds sympathetically.

Cogito, ergo sum? Thinking is all very well, but, as history shows, people can think *and* lie, cheat and steal, ignore the needs of their neighbours, neglect their children, bully their colleagues and abuse their partners. People can think *and* hit each other, kill each other, plant bombs in each other's mosques and churches, go to war.

By contrast, to be a loving person is to be true to the highest ideal embedded in the human imagination. It's also the gold standard for testing any claim that we're civilised. Love, in all its manifestations, is the richest source of life's meaning and purpose, and the key to our emotional security, personal serenity and confidence. Acts motivated by love – whether in the context of our personal relationships, our work or our response to the needs of strangers – are also the most positive and the most enduring contributions we can make to a better world.

What a sad irony it would be if we let *anything* – our bruised egos, our frustrations, our fears, our inhibitions, our disappointments or even our little triumphs – distract us from the most liberating truth about us: that, simply because we are social beings, the capacity for love lies at our very core.

In *The Fire Next Time*, James Baldwin used the metaphor of the mask to describe how compassion can transform us: 'Love takes off the masks that we fear we cannot live without and know we cannot live within. I use the word "love" here not merely in a personal sense but as a state of being, or a state of grace – not in the infantile American sense of being made happy, but in the tough and universal sense of quest and daring and growth.'

As the solar systems strewn across our universe are separated from each other by dark matter but joined by light, so we are separated from each other by our individual identities but joined by our compassion. In the end, both literally and metaphorically, we are all enlivened by the same sun.

Appendix: 'We can only learn to love by loving'

Let's assume we want to find ways of more authentically expressing our true nature . . .

perhaps becoming less judgemental of others;

perhaps becoming more courageous (but also more courteous) in conversations on controversial issues;

perhaps becoming more honest (but also more sensitive) in a sexual relationship;

perhaps curbing our arrogance and embracing a new humility that better matches what we know to be true about ourselves;

perhaps becoming readier to admit to errors and faults;

perhaps becoming quicker to forgive those who have wronged or offended us;

perhaps exercising more restraint;

perhaps becoming less inclined to retreat into self-serving fantasy, denial or projection when things don't go our way.

As the British novelist and philosopher Iris Murdoch wrote, 'We can only learn to love by loving.' Relationships are the great teacher when it comes to the lesson of compassion. We learn how to do it by doing it, and relationships are our training ground (though they can sometimes feel more like a battlefield). Especially when a relationship hits a rocky patch, the determination to handle it lovingly, by showing consistent kindness and respect towards the other person – even if the relationship is disintegrating – is the best way to discover how compassion works.

It takes practice, just as any worthwhile pursuit does. No one pretends that living lovingly is easy or straightforward, or that we won't sometimes fail in the face of someone's hostility or indifference towards us. But to repeat an earlier point: because compassion flows from our essential human nature, exercising it puts us more closely in touch with our authentic self. Whatever other changes we might want to make, a shift in the direction of becoming more compassionate – always, and towards everyone – won't only be a transformative experience for us and those we encounter; it will also facilitate our *general* shift towards authenticity.

And yet for many of us, simply wanting to change, or even declaring our determination to change, doesn't seem to be enough of an incentive for us to actually *make* the change – just look at our record with New Year's resolutions. That's why some people seek the guidance and support of a counsellor or therapist to help them through the process.

Where to go for professional help

If you are fortunate enough to have a relationship with a general medical practitioner (GP) who knows you well, whose judgement you respect and who is someone you feel you can trust, then that is often the best starting point. Many GPs are well equipped to offer their patients counselling services that go well beyond specific medical issues.

If you have a personal or professional mentor, then that is the person to talk to.

If you, your GP or your mentor feel that you need more specialised psychological support or guidance, your GP will be able to refer you to a counsellor or clinical psychologist or to put you in touch with a teacher of meditation. (Meditation is always a discipline worth considering – particularly the loving-kindness technique mentioned in chapter one.) Your GP will be familiar with therapists/teachers working in your area and will be well placed to advise you on the most suitable person for you to see.

Clinical psychologists take many different approaches to therapy. Some adopt the traditional role of a counsellor, helping you to clarify the issues through discussion, and giving appropriate guidance and support. Some follow the principles of 'client-centred therapy' developed by Carl Rogers, using reflective listening to help you work things out for yourself in the context of a supportive, non-judgemental relationship.

Cognitive behavioural therapy (CBT) is a form of 'reprogramming' in which therapists teach their clients how to change unhelpful or unhealthy patterns of behaviour without being concerned about their underlying causes. (CBH is a variation that incorporates hypnosis.)

There are also various forms of analytical psychotherapy (psycho-analysis, psychodynamic psychotherapy), based on the theories of Freud and Jung, using 'depth' techniques to probe the unconscious mind in the quest for the source of the problems being experienced by the client.

In the absence of a specific recommendation, you can find the names of registered psychologists on the website of the Australian Psychological Society at www.psychology.org.au or you can call the society's national office in Melbourne on (03) 8662 3300.

Above all, remember there is nothing to be embarrassed about in seeking the services of a psychologist. This is just like going to the dentist with a toothache. Once you mention it, you'll be amazed how many people in your circle have sought this kind of help at some point in their lives – or wish they had.

As an alternative to any of those face-to-face options, there is Lifeline's free telephone counselling service, available 24/7 on 13 11 14. Contrary to popular perception, most calls to Lifeline are not from people contemplating suicide (though, of course, its service to people in crisis is invaluable), but from people simply needing to discuss a problem, or clarify an issue, who prefer to remain anonymous.

And don't forget the everyday therapies available to all of us: the simple joy of (phoneless) communion with nature, meditative walking, group singing, and the healing power of time spent with supportive friends and family members.

Finally, ponder the Gandhi quote one more time: 'The best way to find yourself is to lose yourself in the service of others.'

References

Alcaraz, Kassandra, 'Social isolation directly affects health by causing changes in the body such as inflammation', *American Journal of Epidemiology*, October 2018

Baldwin, James, *The Fire Next Time*, Dial Press, New York, 1963

Barrett, William, *Irrational Man: A study in existential philosophy*, William Heinemann, London, 1961

Batchelor, Stephen, *Flight: An existential conception of Buddhism*, Buddhist Publication Society, Kandy, Sri Lanka, 1984

Baumeister, Roy F., Kathleen D. Vohs, Jennifer L. Aaker and Emily N. Garbinsky, 'Some key differences between a happy life and a meaningful life', *Journal of Positive Psychology*, 8 (6), August 2013

Berezin, Robert A., 'On consciousness: Explaining the brain's beautiful illusion', *Medscape Medical News*, www.medscape.com, 5 April 2019

Biddulph, Steve, 'One Plus One' interview with Jane Hutcheon, ABC television, 9 June 2019

Borg, Marcus, *Reading the Bible Again for the First Time: Taking the Bible seriously but not literally*, HarperSanFrancisco, New York, 2001

Borges, Jorge Luis, 'The Life of Tadeo Isidoro Cruz' in *The Aleph and Other Stories* (translated by Norman Thomas di Giovanni), Jonathan Cape, London, 1971

Brookes, David, *The Social Animal*, Random House, New York, 2011

Burgo, Joseph, *Why Do I Do That?*, New Rise Press, Chapel Hill NC, 2012

Burnett, Thomas, 'What is Scientism?', www.aaas.org/programs/dialogue, American Association for the Advancement of Science, Washington D.C., 2019

Carey, John, *What Good Are the Arts?*, University of Oxford Press, Oxford, 2006

Caro, Jane, Antony Loewenstein, Simon Smart and Rachel Woodlock, *For God's Sake*, Macmillan, Sydney, 2013

Christakis, Nicholas A., 'How AI Will Rewire Us', *The Atlantic*, April 2019

Cox, Eva, 'Feminism has failed and needs a radical rethink', *The Conversation* (theconversation.com.au), 8 March 2016

Cupitt, Don, *The Sea of Faith: Christianity in change*, BBC, London, 1984

Didion, Joan, 'On Self-Respect', *Slouching Towards Bethlehem*, 1968, republished by Fourth Estate, London, 2017

Dostoevsky, Fyodor, *The Brothers Karamazov*, 1880, published in Penguin Classics, 2003

Eckersley, Richard, 'Redefining the Self' sidebar to 'Whatever Happened to Western Civilisation?', *The Futurist*, November–December 2012

Eliot, T.S, 'The Hollow Men' in *Poems 1909-1925*, Faber & Faber, London, 1925

Eliot, T.S., 'Choruses from The Rock' in *The Rock*, 1934, republished in *Collected Poems 1909-1962*, Faber & Faber, London, 1963

Frederickson, Barbara L., Michael A. Cohn, Kimberley A. Coffey, Jolynn Pek, Sandra M. Finkel, 'Open hearts build lives: Positive emotions, induced through loving-kindness meditation, build consequential personal resources', *Journal of Personality and Social Psychology*, 95, 2008

Freud, Sigmund, *Civilisation and its Discontents*, W.W. Norton and Co, New York, 1962

Galli, Mark, *Beyond Bells and Smells*, Paraclete Press, Brewster MA, 2008

Greenberg, Gary, 'Psychiatry's Incurable Hubris', *The Atlantic*, April 2019

Harrington, Anne, *Mind Fixers: Psychiatry's troubled search for the biology of mental illness*, Norton, New York, 2019

Hofstadter, Douglas R. and Daniel C. Dennett, *The Mind's I: Fantasies and reflections on self and soul*, Basic Books, New York, 1981

Hollis, James, *Finding Meaning in the Second Half of Life*, Gotham Books, New York, 2005

Holt-Lunstad, Julianne, 'Loneliness: A growing public health threat', Paper delivered at the 125th Annual Convention of the American Psychological Association, Washington Convention Center, Washington DC, 5 August 2017

Horne, Donald, *The Lucky Country*, Penguin Books, Camberwell, Victoria, 1964 (sixth edition, 2008)

Howard, Rachel, 'Letter of Recommendation: Lent', *New York Times Magazine*, 12 March 2009

Ignatieff, Michael, *The Needs of Strangers*, The Hogarth Press, London, 1990

Jung, C.G., H.G. Baynes, Cary F. Baynes, *Contributions to Analytical Psychology*, Harcourt Brace, New York, 1928

Jung, C.G., *Memories, Dreams, Reflections*, Collins and Routledge & Kegan Paul, London, 1963

Jung, C.G., *Jung: Selected Writings*, Selected and Introduced by Anthony Storr, Fontana, London, 1983

Kerr, Fiona and Lekki Maze, *The Art and Science of Looking Up*, The NeuroTech Institute, Adelaide, 2019

Kevles, Barbara, 'Anne Sexton, The Art of Poetry No. 15', *Paris Review*, Issue 52, 1971

Kierkegaard, Søren, *The Sickness Unto Death* (translated by Walter Lowrie), Princeton University Press, Princeton NJ, 1941

Kuper, Simon, 'How Oxford University shaped Brexit – and Britain's next prime minister', *Financial Times*, 21 June 2019

Latour, Bruno, *On the Modern Cult of the Factish Gods*, Duke University Press, North Carolina, 2011

Lewis, Ricki, 'Editing selfies linked to plastic surgery acceptance', *Medscape Medical News*, www.medscape.com, 1 July 2019

Leonard, Elmore, *Pronto*, Viking, London, 1993

Lewis, C.S., *The Four Loves*, Geoffrey Bles, London, 1960

Mackay, Hugh, *The Good Life*, Macmillan, Sydney, 2013

Mackay, Hugh, *The Art of Belonging*, Macmillan, Sydney, 2014

Mackay, Hugh, *Beyond Belief*, Macmillan, Sydney, 2016

Mackay, Hugh, *Australia Reimagined*, Macmillan, Sydney, 2018

Mackay, Hugh, *Right and Wrong* (3rd edition), Hachette, Sydney, 2019

Mackay, Hugh, *What Makes Us Tick* (3rd edition), Hachette, Sydney, 2019

Marsh, Nigel, *Fat, Forty and Fired*, Bantam, Sydney, 2005

Melvill, Rev. Henry, *Melvill's Golden Lectures for 1855*, Sermons preached at St Margaret's Church of England, Lothbury, London, 1855

Mitsubishi Corporation, *Tatemae and Honne: Distinguishing between good form and real intention in Japanese business culture*, The Free Press, New York, 1988

Murdoch, Iris, *The Sovereignty of Good*, 1970, republished by Routledge Classics, London, 2001

Murdoch, Iris, 'Metaphysics and Ethics' (1957), *Existentialists and Mystics*, Penguin Books, New York, 1999

Ortega y Gasset, José, *The Revolt of the Masses*, W.W. Norton & Company, New York, 1932

Pollan, Michael, *How to Change Your Mind*, Penguin, New York, 2018

Ricard, Matthieu, Antoine Lutz and Richard J. Davidson, 'Mind of the meditator', *Scientific American* 311(5), November 2014

Rogers, Carl, *On Becoming a Person*, Constable & Company, London, 1967

Rooney, Sally, *Conversations with Friends*, Faber & Faber, London, 2017

Saul, John Ralston, *The Doubter's Companion*, Penguin, Ringwood, Vic., 1995

REFERENCES

Seligman, Martin, *What You Can Change and What You Can't*, Random House, Sydney, 1994

Sheehy, Gail, *Passages: Predictable crises of adult life*, Bantam Books, New York, 1977

Sims, Rod, quoted in James Thompson, 'ACCC warns arrogant business sector of huge fines', *Australian Financial Review*, 6 January 2019

Skinner, B.F., *Beyond Freedom and Dignity*, Alfred A. Knopf, New York, 1971

Smee, Sebastian, *Net Loss*, Quarterly Essay 72, Black Inc., Melbourne, 2018

Sorrell, Tom, *Scientism: Philosophy and the infatuation with science*, Routledge, New York, 1991

Spufford, Francis, *Unapologetic*, Faber and Faber, London, 2012

Stark, Jill, *Happy Never After*, Scribe, Melbourne, 2018

Stephens, James, *The Crock of Gold*, Macmillan, London, 1912

Tacey, David, *The Darkening Spirit: Jung, spirituality, religion*, Routledge, London, 2013

Taylor, Charles, *Sources of the Self: The making of the modern identity*, Cambridge University Press, Cambridge UK, 1989

Terkel, Studs, *Working: People talk about what they do all day and how they feel about what they do*, 1972, republished by Ballantyne Books, New York, 1985

Thompson, Emma, quoted in Eliza Berman, 'Laughing All the Way', *Time*, 17 June 2019

Tipping, Colin C., *Radical Forgiveness*, Global 13 Publishing, Marietta GA, 1997

Walker, Campbell, quoted in Thomas Mitchell, 'Drawing crowds', *Executive Style*, Fairfax Media, Winter 2019

Welwood, John, *Love and Awakening: Discovering the sacred path of intimate relationship*, HarperPerennial, New York, 1996

Williams, Rowan, *Dostoevsky: Language, faith and fiction*, Continuum, London, 2008

Wilson, Sarah, *First, We Make the Beast Beautiful: A new story about anxiety*, Pan Macmillan, Sydney, 2017

Winnicott, Donald, *Playing and Reality*, Psychology Press, Hove, East Sussex, 2005

Wrangham, Richard, *The Goodness Paradox*, Profile Books, London, 2019

Text acknowledgements

Extracts on pages 4, 78–9 and 269 from *Flight: An Existential Conception of Buddhism*. Copyright © 1984 by Stephen Batchelor. Reprinted by permission of the author.

Extracts on pages 1, 38–9, 51 and 276 from *On Becoming a Person: A Therapist's View of Psychotherapy* by Carl R. Rogers. Copyright © 1961 by Carl R. Rogers, renewed 1989 by David E. Rogers and Natalie Rogers. Reprinted by permission of Houghton Mifflin Harcourt Publishing Company. All rights reserved.

Extract on page 41 from 'The Hollow Men', *Collected Poems 1909–1962*. Copyright © 1925 by T. S. Eliot. Reprinted by permission from Faber and Faber Ltd.

Extract on pages 103 and 171 from 'Choruses from the Rock', *Collected Poems 1909–1962*. Copyright © 1925 by T. S. Eliot. Reprinted by permission from Faber and Faber Ltd.

Acknowledgements

The shape and structure of *The Inner Self* evolved through a series of discussions with Ingrid Ohlsson, my publisher at Pan Macmillan, and I am grateful to Ingrid for her belief in the project and for her guidance and support at every stage of the writing. Ariane Durkin, the senior editor at Pan Macmillan, has been warm in her encouragement, constructive in her advice, and sympathetic in her creation of the 'architecture' of the book. Ingrid and Ariane have been ably supported by the creative editor Naomi van Groll, and editorial assistant Belinda Huang. I am grateful to Pan Macmillan's publicity manager, Clare Keighery, for organising the promotion campaign for the book.

Ali Lavau has been astute, meticulous, thoughtful and generous in her editing of my final draft, and the book is both stronger and clearer as a result of her input.

ACKNOWLEDGEMENTS

I also wish to acknowledge Alissa Dinallo's striking and original cover design.

During the writing process, I have received advice, encouragement and valuable insights from Ross Chambers, Amy Chan, Scott Cowdell, David Dale, Geoff Duncan, Ben Edwards, Geoff Gallop, Samantha Heron, Tim Mackay and Sally Renouf. Naturally, they bear no responsibility for any of my conclusions – and neither does Robert McLaughlin who, back in the 1950s, rescued me from economics and steered me in the direction of psychology and philosophy. My debt to Robert, both then and since, is immense.

My wife, Sheila, has been muse, research assistant, fearless critic and cheerleader for this project, offering support at every stage. The book is gratefully dedicated to her.

Finally, though *The Inner Self* is not a work of social analysis, I must acknowledge my enduring debt to the thousands of Australians who have illuminated and enriched my understanding of human nature by sharing their personal stories and private thoughts with me and my colleagues over the course of my long career in social research. Their willingness to talk so openly about their opinions and attitudes, hopes and fears, tragedies, triumphs, doubts and disappointments made my research possible; their frankness gave it its integrity. Some of them have reappeared in the stories I created for this book, though always in heavy disguise.

Index

INDEX

INDEX